FEDERAL ESTATE AND GIFT TAXATION

By

Stephanie J. Willbanks
Professor of Law
Vermont Law School

WEST®

A Thomson Reuters business

Mat #40889046

Sum and Substance Quick Review of Federal Estate and Gift Taxation is a publication of Thomson Reuters

© 2010 West, a Thomson business

610 Opperman Drive
St. Paul, MN 55123
1–800–313–9378

Printed in the United States of America

ISBN: 978–0–314–90798–1

To my husband, Stephen, and my children, Allison and Simon

About the Author

Stephanie J. Willbanks is a Professor of Law at Vermont Law School where she has taught Estate and Gift Tax since 1983. She has also taught Estates, Estate Planning, Income Tax, Tax Policy, and Torts. She has authored books and articles on Estates, Estate Tax, and Income Tax, including *Federal Taxation of Wealth Transfers: Cases and Problems (2d ed.), Federal Estate and Gift Taxation: An Analysis and Critique (3d ed.),* and the chapter on *Wealth Transfer Taxation* in *Wills, Trusts, and Estates* (8th ed. 2009) by Dukeminier, Sitkoff, & Lindgren. Professor Willbanks is a member of the American Law Institute, the American College of Trust and Estate Counsel and the Uniform Law Commission.

Professor Willbanks served as the Academic Dean at Vermont Law School for fourteen years and as the Director of Academic Technology for three years. She has served on committees for the American Association of Law Schools, the American Bar Association, the Vermont Supreme Court, and the Vermont Bar Association. She is also a bar review lecturer.

Preface

This book is designed as a study guide for students taking a course in Estate and Gift Tax or studying that material as part of a Wills and Trusts or Estate Planning course. It does not pretend to be a comprehensive guide to estate planning or the federal tax implications of all gratuitous transfers. There are some references to income tax issues but these references are sporadic.

This book is written in outline format to facilitate study and review. That format creates constraints and challenges. Each topic is limited to one paragraph in most cases. The result is a focus on basics. Comprehensive coverage and nuances are left to treatises and hornbooks.

Throughout most of the twentieth century, the federal estate and gift taxes have remained relatively stable. The major changes are noted in Chapter 1. In the 1990s, a small but determined group began a campaign to repeal the estate tax. Their most effective strategy was to attach the label "the death tax" to it. As a result, the estate tax became unpopular even among those who will never pay that tax.

In 2001, Congress enacted a so-called "repeal" of the estate and the generation-skipping taxes, leaving the gift tax in place to serve as a backstop to the income tax. The repeal was phased in by increasing the applicable exemption amount and lowering the top tax rate. Total repeal did not occur until January 1, 2010. Budget considerations required Congress to sunset the provisions of the 2001 Tax Act on December 31, 2010. The result is a one-year hiatus rather than an actual repeal of the estate and generation-skipping transfer taxes.

After the 2001 Tax Act, there were numerous attempts to make the repeal permanent or to increase the exemption amount and lower the top tax rate on a permanent basis. In December 2009, the House has passed yet another bill that would prevent repeal, retain a $3.5 million exemption amount, and retain a maximum tax rate of 45 percent. Much to everyone's surprise the Senate did nothing and the repeal went into effect. Despite statements that action would occur early in 2010, nothing happened. The resulting uncertainty has created serious problems for estate plans based on the existence of the estate tax and for the estates of decedents who have died in 2010.

As this book goes to press in fall 2010, it is not clear what will happen. Possibilities include: (1) a two-year extension of the 2009 exemption amount ($3.5 million) and maximum tax rate (45 percent); (2) a permanent resolution at those levels; (3) a permanent resolution at a higher exemption amount and a lower maximum rate; or even (4) a return to a $1,000,000 exemption amount and a maximum tax rate of 55 percent. Total and permanent repeal appears unlikely given current budget concerns, but it is not impossible.

I have avoided reference to a specific exemption amount or tax rate to the extent possible, but when necessary for illustration I have assumed a $3.5 million exemption amount and a maximum tax rate of 45 percent. Sample calculations in the appendices use three different models: (1) the pre–2001 Tax Act amounts and rates; (2) the 2009 amounts and rates; and (3) an exemption amount of $5 million for both the gift and estate taxes and a flat rate of 35 percent.

The 2001 Tax Act included a new carryover basis provision. § 1022. Absent Congressional action, that provision will disappear on January 1, 2011. As a result, there is no discussion of § 1022 in this book.

All references are to the Internal Revenue Code of 1986 (IRC) as amended from time to time. Reference is simply to the relevant IRC section without formal citation. Citation format of other sources has been modified to make reading of the text smoother.

The gift tax annual exclusion (discussed in chapter 5) is adjusted annually for inflation. The amount for both 2009 and 2010 is $13,000. Reference is made to this number when necessary for clarity. In future years that number may increase.

This student guide began life in a very different format, *i.e.*, Federal Estate and Gift Taxation: An Analysis and Critique. The first two editions of that book were co-authored by my former colleague, W. Leslie Peat. Without him, that book (and probably this one) would never have come to be. I thank him for his collaboration and support. I also thank my students, particularly Viktoriya Kovalenko and Michael Stanley who helped edit and proofread this edition. And, finally, I thank both Boris Bittker and Marvin Chirelstein, who inspired W. Leslie Peat and me by their example and whose work served as a constant reminder that federal taxation can be made comprehensible, and above all, that the subject need not be boring.

Professor Stephanie J. Willbanks
Vermont Law School

October 2010

TABLE OF CONTENTS

TABLE OF CONTENTS

TABLE OF CONTENTS

TABLE OF CONTENTS

TABLE OF CONTENTS

TABLE OF CONTENTS

TABLE OF CONTENTS

TABLE OF CONTENTS

TABLE OF CONTENTS

TABLE OF CONTENTS

TABLE OF CONTENTS

TABLE OF CONTENTS

TABLE OF CONTENTS

TABLE OF CONTENTS

TABLE OF CONTENTS

PART I

INTRODUCTION

CHAPTER 1

OVERVIEW

A. HISTORY

1. Estate Tax

a. Early Inheritance Taxes

In 1797, the United States imposed the first *death tax* in the form of a stamp tax. In 1862, 1864, and 1866, the government imposed an inheritance tax to fund the Civil War. In 1898, once again in a time of war, Congress imposed another inheritance tax. None of these taxes lasted very long, but they set the stage for the modern estate tax, which was adopted in 1916.

b. 1916 Estate Tax

The impetus for the 1916 estate tax was, once again, war. In addition, the populist movement had gained strength and viewed large inheritances as windfalls that increased the ability to pay taxes. That movement succeeded in passing the Sixteenth Amendment, which allowed enactment of the federal income tax. Gifts and bequests were excluded from income by § 102, and this opened the door to taxing the transfer of property at death with an estate tax.

c. 1948 Marital Deduction

When World War I ended, Congress did not repeal the estate tax. Although Congress continued to refine the estate tax, primarily in response to court decisions, it made no significant changes until 1948. In that year, Congress adopted a marital deduction that allowed a limited amount of property to pass without tax between a married couple. The primary motivation for this deduction was the desire to provide equal treatment between decedents from common law property states and those from community property states.

d. 1976 Tax Reform Act: Unification of Estate and Gift Taxes

Until 1976, the federal estate and gift taxes were separate and distinct. Each had its own rate structure and exemption amount.

3

Although courts recognized that they were *in pari materia* (of the same nature and "upon the same subject"), courts did little to reconcile them. In 1976, Congress unified the two taxes, providing one rate structure and one unified exemption amount. Congress did not, however, do a thorough overhaul of the substantive provisions governing gifts and estates. As a result, there remain some transactions that are taxed by both the gift tax and the estate tax. There is not a double tax, however, as explained in Chapter 16 and Appendix A.

e. 1981 Tax Act: Rates, Exemptions, and the Marital Deduction

In 1981, Congress continued its reform efforts. The 1976 Tax Act had converted the separate estate and gift tax exemptions into a credit equivalent to a $175,625 exemption amount, and it created a rate structure from 18 percent to 70 percent. The 1981 Tax Act increased the unified credit to an exemption equivalent of $600,000 and lowered the top marginal rate to 50 percent. It also included two significant changes to the marital deduction. First, it removed the limit on the amount of the deduction and allowed an unlimited amount to pass from one spouse to the other. Second, it enacted the *qualified terminable interest property* exception, which is explained in section F.6. of Chapter 15.

f. 2001 Tax Act: "The Death of the Death Tax"

During the 1990s, the estate tax came under attack. Critics claimed that the "death tax" (as they called it) inhibited economic growth and required the heirs of farmers and small business owners to liquidate those businesses in order to pay the tax. Although there was little, if any, evidence to support these claims, Congress succumbed to the pressure in 2001 and announced the repeal of the estate tax. The rhetoric was stronger than the reality. To meet budget goals, Congress phased in the repeal over a number of years. Those same budget goals also forced Congress to sunset the repeal of the estate tax along with a number of other tax breaks. The phase-out increased the exemption equivalent to $3,500,000 as of 2009 and lowered the top marginal rate to 45 percent.

g. The Future of the Estate Tax

The estate tax disappeared at the end of 2009, but only for one year. It is scheduled for resurrection on January 1, 2011, at the rates and exemption amount in effect prior to the 2001 Tax Act. Despite numerous attempts at permanent repeal and equally numerous attempts to keep the estate tax alive with increased exemption amounts and decreased rates, the debate still rages.

2. **Gift Tax**

   a. **Enactment**

   Congress enacted a gift tax in 1924 to prevent avoidance of the estate tax. Because the estate tax only encompassed transfers at death and those made in contemplation of death, taxpayers could make deathbed gifts and avoid the estate tax. Congress repealed the gift tax in 1926 but revived it in 1932, and it has remained in effect since that date.

   b. **Development**

   The gift tax had its own exemption amount and rate structure. It included an annual exclusion that was initially set at $5,000 but then lowered to $3,000. The 1976 Tax Act unified the gift and estate taxes with one exemption (the unified credit) and one rate schedule. The 1981 Tax Act increased the gift tax annual exclusion to $10,000 and indexed it for inflation. In 2009 and 2010, the gift tax annual exclusion was $13,000.

   c. **The Future of the Gift Tax**

   The 2001 Tax Act did not repeal the gift tax. Fearing erosion of the income tax, Congress retained the gift tax with a $1 million lifetime exemption amount and a maximum rate of 35 percent. If Congress does not act, the pre–2001 provisions will reappear. If Congress does act, it remains to be seen if the gift tax exemption amount will remain at $1 million or increase to the same amount as the estate tax exemption.

3. **Generation–Skipping Transfers**

   a. **General Principles**

   An estate tax can be avoided not only through lifetime gifts, but also by leaving property in trust and giving the next generation (or two) only a life estate and a limited (or special) power of appointment. Neither a life estate nor a limited power of appointment triggers the estate tax, so the property would pass to the next generation free of tax. The estate tax can also be minimized in families that can afford to skip alternate generations.

> **Example 1.1**
>
> Parent's will leaves her property in trust to pay the income to her children for their lives, then to pay the income to her grandchildren for their lives, and then to distribute the property to her lineal descendants. The children and grandchildren are also given the power to withdraw as much of the trust corpus as they need for their health, education, maintenance, and support. Neither a life estate nor property subject to a power that is limited by an ascertainable standard relating to health, education, maintenance, and support is included in a decedent's gross estate. §§ 2033, 2036(a)(1), 2041. Parent's estate will pay an estate tax, but the children's estates and the grandchildren's estates will not.

> **Example 1.2**
>
> Grandparent's will leaves $50 million to his children and $50 million to his grandchildren. Thereafter property is left only to grandchildren. Grandparent's estate will pay an estate tax as will estates on subsequent transfers. By splitting Grandparent's wealth, only one-half is subject to tax at each generation.

b. 1976 and 1986 Tax Acts

Congress decided to curtail such tax avoidance in 1976 by adopting a generation-skipping transfer tax. Its provisions were exceedingly complex, and Congress repealed it retroactively in 1986, refunding all taxes that had been paid under its provisions. At the same time, Congress enacted a new generation-skipping transfer tax with substantially different provisions. The underlying theory of both taxes is the same—to tax the transfer of property once at every generation.

c. The Future of the Generation–Skipping Transfer Tax

The 2001 Tax Act repealed the generation-skipping transfer tax along with the estate tax. And, like the estate tax, it is scheduled to reappear in 2011. Its future is closely connected to that of the estate tax and remains uncertain.

B. CONSTITUTIONALITY

1. Estate Tax

The United States Supreme Court has consistently upheld the constitutionality of the federal inheritance and estate taxes. The first challenge was in

Scholey v. Rew, 90 U.S. 331 (1874), where the Court held that the inheritance tax was an excise tax under Article I, section 8, not a direct tax under Article I, section 9. In *Knowlton v. Moore*, 178 U.S. 41 (1900), the Court again ruled that the 1898 inheritance tax was an excise tax not a direct tax and held that it only required geographical uniformity. Finally, in *New York Trust Co. v. Eisner*, 256 U.S. 345 (1921), the Court affirmed the constitutionality of the estate tax. Justice Oliver Wendell Holmes wrote that an estate tax had always been regarded as the antithesis of a direct tax and noted that "[u]pon this point, a page of history is worth a volume of logic." *Id.* at 349.

2. Gift Tax

Taxpayers challenged the gift tax as a direct tax in *Bromley v. McCaughn*, 280 U.S. 124 (1929), and lost. Becoming impatient with these challenges, the Court stated emphatically that: "The meaning of the phrase 'direct taxes' and the historical background of the constitutional requirements for their apportionment have been so often and exhaustively considered by this court, that no useful purpose would be served by renewing the discussion here." *Id.* at 136.

3. Exam Strategy

The federal transfer taxes—the estate tax, the gift tax, and the generation-skipping transfer tax—are excise taxes on the transfer of property and are not direct taxes. As a result, they must be "uniform throughout the United States" Article 1, section 8, and do not need to be apportioned, Article 1, section 9.

C. THEORY OF TRANSFER TAXATION

1. Rationale

a. Raise Revenue

The fundamental purpose of any tax is to raise revenue to support governmental functions. The federal estate, gift, and generation-skipping transfer taxes generate approximately 1.2 percent of net federal revenues. In 2008, they raised $28.8 billion. While the projected budget surpluses in 2001 allowed Congress the luxury of repealing the estate and generation-skipping transfer taxes, albeit only prospectively, subsequent budget deficits have prevented efforts to make the repeal permanent.

b. Redistribute Wealth

The origins of the federal estate tax in the populist movement provide another justification—redistribution of wealth. Whether or not the federal transfer taxes actually do so is a subject of much debate. An analysis of the Forbes 400 shows a decreasing number of individuals who list inheritance as a source of their wealth, and a 2006 study by the Congressional Joint Economic Committee concluded that only 8 of the 100 richest Americans trace their wealth to inheritance. JOINT ECON. COMM., 109ᵀᴴ CONG. COSTS AND CONSEQUENCES OF THE FEDERAL ESTATE TAX (COMM. STUDY 2006). One can use that data to support the argument that the transfer taxes have in fact diminished the role of inheritances and thus redistributed wealth. One can also use that data to support the argument that inheritance is such a minor factor that the transfer taxes are not necessary.

c. Multiple Tax Bases

A tax system should have more than one tax base. The federal system currently includes an income tax, a wealth tax, and various consumption taxes. A tax system with multiple components is less vulnerable to changes in the economy or individual behaviors. It also is better at taxing individuals based on their ability to pay because there are different measures of that ability.

d. Ability to Pay

One policy consideration is vertical equity, otherwise called *progressivity* or ability to pay. The transfer taxes enhance the overall progressivity by taxing only the very wealthiest, *i.e.*, the top 1.2 percent of the population.

2. Structure

a. Wealth Tax

There are a number of ways to tax wealth. One is a tax on the value of the taxpayer's property imposed on an annual or periodic basis. Local property taxes are that type of a wealth tax. Such a tax on the national level would require a constitutional amendment because the tax would be a direct tax and would need to be apportioned.

b. Transfer Tax

The federal estate, gift, and generation-skipping transfer taxes avoid the constitutional problem because they are excise taxes on the transfer of property, not a tax on the property itself. The focus of these taxes is on the value of property being transferred from a donor or the decedent to others. The donor or the decedent's estate is liable for payment of the tax.

c. Inheritance Tax

An inheritance tax focuses on the receipt of property. The recipient, *i.e.*, the beneficiary or heir, pays the inheritance tax. The early federal taxes were inheritance taxes, and a number of states have had inheritance taxes. The rate of an inheritance tax can depend on the relationship of the beneficiary to the decedent. Close family members, *e.g.,* spouses and children, may pay at a very low rate while more distant relatives or mere acquaintances may pay at a higher rate.

d. Accessions Tax

An accessions tax, like an inheritance tax, focuses on the receipt of property. Unlike an inheritance tax, an accessions tax would include the receipt of wealth from all sources, not just property transferred at death. An accessions tax would also be cumulative over time. No state has ever adopted such a tax although it would seem to be theoretically sound, undeniably constitutional, and no more or less difficult to administer than many other forms of taxation.

e. Gifts and Bequests Included in Income

Perhaps a simpler form of wealth taxation is to include gifts and bequests in income. The first national income tax, adopted by Congress in 1894, did so. That act was held unconstitutional as a direct tax in *Pollock v. Farmers' Loan and Trust Co.*, 157 U.S. 429 (1895), *rehearing*, 158 U.S. 601 (1895). The adoption of the Sixteenth Amendment overruled *Pollock*, and left the door open to taxing gifts and bequests as income. The income tax includes "all income from whatever source derived." § 61. This encompasses all "undeniable accessions to wealth, clearly realized, and over which the taxpayer has complete dominion and control." *Commissioner v. Glenshaw Glass Co.*, 348 U.S. 426, 431 (1955). Gifts and inheritances would clearly fall within that definition.

f. Taxation of Unrealized Gains at Death

Another possibility is to include unrealized gains as income in the decedent's final income tax return. Unrealized gains, *i.e.*, appreciation in the value of property, have never been taxed. To do so in the absence of a sale, exchange, or transfer of property would most likely be considered a wealth tax and unconstitutional as a direct tax. Taxing gain on the transfer of property, *e.g.*, if the taxpayer made a gift, would not be unconstitutional. Nonetheless, Congress has never considered this possibility. Instead, § 1015 requires that a recipient

9

assume the donor's basis and be taxed on any gain when the recipient disposes of the property. On the other hand, a will beneficiary or an heir receives a *stepped-up (or down) basis* equal to the date of death value of the property. § 1014. As a result, any gains not taxed before death escape the income tax. Congress repealed § 1014 and substituted a *transferred basis* rule similar to § 1015 in the 1976 Tax Reform Act, but repealed it before it became effective. Congress enacted a new transferred basis provision, § 1022, in the 2001 Tax Act. Whether or not § 1022 will survive if the estate tax repeal is rescinded is debatable.

3. Exam Strategy

The fundamental purposes of the federal estate, gift, and generation-skipping transfer taxes are to raise revenue and redistribute wealth. These taxes are excise taxes on the transfers of property.

D. POLICY CONSIDERATIONS

Whatever the form of the tax, theorists agree that a tax should be fair; that it should produce positive economic effects; and that it should be simple to administer. There are two basic principles of fairness—vertical equity and horizontal equity.

1. Vertical Equity

Vertical equity, also known as progressivity, requires that taxpayers be taxed based on their ability to pay. The greater the wealth, the greater the ability to pay. Although a flat rate of tax will require that those with greater wealth pay more, everyone would pay the same percentage. A progressive rate of tax, on the other hand, would impose increasingly higher percentages on greater wealth.

Example 1.3

Adam dies owning property valued at $10 million while Ben dies owning property valued at $50 million. Assuming a flat tax at 10 percent, Adam's estate will pay an estate tax of $1 million while Ben's estate would pay an estate tax of $5 million.

> **Example 1.4**
>
> Ann dies owning property valued at $10 million while Beth dies owning property valued at $50 million. Assume a progressive rate of tax as follows:
>
> > a 10 percent rate on the first $10 million,
> >
> > a 20 percent rate on the next $10 million,
> >
> > a 30 percent rate on the next $10 million,
> >
> > a 40 percent rate on the next $10 million,
> >
> > and a 50 percent rate thereafter.
>
> Ann's estate would still pay a tax of $1 million, but Beth's estate would pay a tax of $15 million.
>
> Until 1976, the federal estate and gift tax rates were graduated, producing progressive taxation. Since 1976, Congress has gradually reduced the top tax rates and increased the exemption amount. In 2009, the estate tax was a flat rate of tax on the amount in excess of the exemption amount.

2. Horizontal Equity

Horizontal equity requires that taxpayers who are similarly situated should be taxed the same. A taxpayer who owns $10 million of cash should be taxed the same as a taxpayer who owns $10 million of appreciated farmland. Achieving horizontal equity depends on how one defines "similarly situated" and what other policies, such as encouraging farming, Congress deems important. With the exception of these policy choices, the federal transfer taxes produce horizontal equity.

3. Economic Effects

While some would argue that a tax should be neutral, *i.e.*, not influence economic choices at all, most recognize that the mere existence of any particular tax will inevitably influence economic choices. As a result, the best that can be achieved is a positive economic effect. What is, and is not, a positive economic effect is a subject of debate. So is the question of whether or not the federal transfer taxes achieve them. Does the estate tax encourage or discourage work? Does it encourage or discourage savings?

Does it encourage or discourage consumption? Which of these does the government want to encourage or discourage? The existing studies contradict each other. Because the fundamental issue is human behavior, there will never be a definitive answer.

The federal transfer taxes are not good vehicles for directing economic activity. The gift tax is essentially voluntary, as taxpayers can choose whether or not to make taxable gifts. The estate tax only occurs once for each taxpayer, and there is no way to forecast how many taxpayers will die in any year owning enough property to trigger the tax. Congress has not tried to regulate taxpayer behavior by adjusting the transfer taxes. Instead, it has used the income tax to achieve desired economic effects.

4. Feasibility

Any tax should be easy to administer. It should not impose significant costs for planning, compliance, or enforcement. It is difficult to assess the feasibility of the federal transfer taxes as much of the cost of planning the transmission of wealth will be incurred even if there is not a tax. Again, whether or not these taxes impose costs out of proportion with the revenues they generate is a matter of debate.

E. OVERVIEW OF THE TRANSFER TAXES

1. The Gift Tax

a. Nature of the Tax

The gift tax is an excise tax imposed on the transfer of property without receipt of consideration. § 2501. Gratuitous services and transfers to political organizations, § 2501(a)(4), are excluded from the gift tax. So are *qualified transfers*, *i.e.*, transfers to educational organizations for tuition and transfers to providers for medical care and insurance. § 2503(e).

b. Definition of a Gift

A gift is a transfer of property without consideration in money or money's worth. § 2512(b). The gift tax is only imposed when the gift is complete, *i.e.*, when the donor has given up dominion and control. Regulation § 25.2511–2(b).

c. Exclusions and Deductions

Section 2503(b) excludes a certain amount of gifts each year to each donee. (The amount of the gift tax annual exclusion increases periodically with inflation and was $13,000 in 2009 and 2010.) To qualify, the gift must be one of a present, not a future, interest. Transfers to charitable organizations and to spouses are also excluded. §§ 2522, 2523.

d. Exemption Amount

Section 2505 provides a credit against the gift tax that allows a taxpayer to transfer a specific amount ("the exemption amount") during life before paying any gift tax. The exemption amount is currently $1 million and the credit amount is $345,800. This exemption is in addition to the gift tax annual exclusion, transfers to spouses, charities, and political organizations, and transfers for tuition and medical expenses. As a result, few, if any, taxpayers ever pay a gift tax. The exemption amount is coordinated with the § 2010 unified credit in the estate tax so that the total amount transferred free of estate or gift tax cannot exceed the estate tax exemption amount.

2. The Estate Tax

a. The Gross Estate

(1) General Principles

The gross estate includes all property owned outright or in substance by the decedent and that transfers from the decedent to others as a result of her death. Unlike the income tax, there is no one, broad, all-encompassing provision that brings all such property into the gross estate. Instead, a series of provisions accomplishes that result. Also, unlike the income tax, case law often defines the parameters of the estate tax.

(2) Section 2033

Section 2033 includes the value of all property interests owned by the decedent at the time of her death and that transfer from the decedent to others as a result of death. This section primarily includes probate property, *i.e.*, property that is subject to creditors' claims. Property owned by the decedent alone or as a tenant in common is included by this section.

(3) Section 2034

Section 2034 provides that the value of the gross estate is not diminished by spousal rights. It does not bring any property interests into the gross estate.

(4) Section 2035

Section 2035(a) includes in the gross estate a limited number of transfers that occur within the three years before death. Life insurance and certain interests retained by the decedent are the only transfers brought back into the gross estate if the transfer occurs within three years of death. Section 2035(b) includes the gift tax paid on all transfers within three years of death. § 2035(b).

(5) Section 2036

Section 2036(a)(1) includes any property interest in which the decedent has retained the possession or enjoyment of property or the right to income from the property for his life or for a period which does not in fact end before his death. Section 2036(a)(2) includes any property interest in which the decedent has retained the right to designate the persons who will possess or enjoy the property or the income from it for his life or for a period which does not in fact end before his death.

(6) Section 2037

Section 2037 includes a reversion retained by the decedent if it exceeds five percent of the value of the property immediately before death and if possession or enjoyment of the property can only be obtained by surviving the decedent.

(7) Section 2038

Section 2038 includes any property over which the decedent has the power, at the moment of death, to alter, amend, terminate, or revoke.

(8) Section 2039

Section 2039 includes an annuity or other payment that is receivable by any beneficiary by reason of surviving the decedent if the decedent had a right to payment or was in fact receiving payments under the same contract.

(9) Section 2040

Section 2040 includes the value of property owned as joint tenants with the right of survivorship or as tenants by the entirety.

(10) Section 2041

Section 2041 includes property over which the decedent had a general power of appointment, *i.e.*, the right to appoint the property to himself, his creditors, his estate, or the creditors of his estate.

(11) Section 2042

Section 2042 includes the amount receivable as life insurance proceeds on the life of the decedent either (1) by the estate or (2) by any beneficiary if the decedent owned an incident of ownership in the policy.

(12) Section 2044

Section 2044 includes qualified terminable interest property, *i.e.*, property that qualified for the marital deduction pursuant to § 2056(b)(7).

b. Deductions

(1) General Principles

Deductions reduce the amount that is subject to tax. If the marginal tax rate is 45 percent, a $100 deduction will save the estate $45. Although deductions generally favor those in higher tax brackets more than those in lower brackets, the estate tax is now a flat tax. As a result, a deduction benefits all taxpayers the same. Credits, on the other hand, reduce the amount of tax and, therefore, usually provide a greater benefit.

(2) Section 2053

Section 2053 allows a deduction for funeral expenses, expenses of administration, and claims against the estate. Claims must have been incurred in a bona fide transaction for adequate and full consideration in money or money's worth. Certain taxes are allowed as claims against the estate.

(3) Section 2054

Section 2054 allows a deduction for losses attributable to fires, storms, shipwrecks, or other casualties or from theft.

(4) Section 2055

Section 2055 allows a deduction for transfers to qualified charitable organizations. There are no monetary limits but split interests and gifts in trust must meet strict requirements.

(5) Section 2056

Section 2056 allows an unlimited deduction for transfers to a surviving spouse as long as the property interest is not a non-deductible terminable interest. There are exceptions to the terminable interest rule for (1) life estates with powers of appointment (2) qualified terminable interest property, and (3) estate trusts.

(6) Section 2058

Section 2058 allows a deduction for state death taxes. This replaces the § 2011 credit for state death taxes, which was repealed in 2001. It will disappear when, and if, the § 2011 credit is reinstated.

c. Credits

(1) General Principles

A credit is subtracted from the tentative amount of tax and reduces tax liability dollar for dollar. As a result, credits are restricted to very limited circumstances and often limited in amount or percentage.

(2) Section 2010

Section 2010 provides a credit for the amount of tax on the "applicable exemption amount." This is the amount that the decedent can pass free of tax. In 2009, the exemption amount was $3.5 million. The § 2010 credit is coordinated with the § 2505 gift tax credit so that a decedent cannot transfer more than the applicable exemption amount whether during life or at death.

(3) Section 2011

Section 2011 provides a credit for the amount of any state estate, inheritance, succession, or accessions tax. It was repealed in 2001, but is scheduled to return in 2011.

(4) Section 2013

Section 2013 provides a credit for estate taxes paid with respect to the transfer of property to the decedent within 10 years before or 2 years after his death.

(5) Sections 2012 and 2014

These sections allow a credit for certain gift taxes and death taxes.

3. The Generation–Skipping Transfer Tax

a. Taxable Transfers

The generation-skipping transfer tax is imposed on (1) direct skips, (2) taxable distributions, and (3) taxable terminations. § 2611(a). A **direct skip** is a gift or bequest to an individual who is two or more generations below the transferor. § 2612(c). The creation of a trust where all the interests are held by individuals two or more generations below the transferor is a direct skip. § 2613(a)(2). A **taxable distribution** is a distribution from a trust to a person who is two or more generations below the transferor. § 2612(b). A **taxable termination** is the termination by death, lapse of time, or otherwise of an interest in trust property if only individuals two or more generations below the transferor have interests in the trust immediately after the event. § 2612(a).

b. Exemptions and Exclusions

Outright transfers that qualify for the gift tax annual exclusion are excluded from the generation-skipping transfer tax. § 2642(c). Transfers in trust must meet special rules. § 2642(c)(2). The exemption amount is the same as for the estate tax (in 2009 it was $3.5 million). § 2631.

F. RELATIONSHIP BETWEEN THE GIFT, THE ESTATE, AND THE INCOME TAXES

1. The Gift Tax and the Estate Tax

The gift tax serves to prevent avoidance of the estate tax. Both are transfer taxes. Courts interpret similar language in a similar manner. If a transfer of property is not a completed gift, that property will be included in the gross estate. In most cases, if a transfer of property is a completed gift, that property will not be included in the gross estate. There are, however, some exceptions.

2. The Income Tax

a. General Principles

The purpose and function of the income tax differ from that of the transfer taxes. There has been little attempt to coordinate the income tax with either the gift tax or the estate tax. The exception is § 2511(c), which was enacted in 2001. That section provides that a gift is not complete if the donor is taxed as the grantor under the grantor trust rules in subchapter J, *i.e.*, §§ 671–679. Section 2511(c) became effective on January 1, 2010, but its future is uncertain because the repeal of the estate tax lasts only until January 1, 2011.

b. Definition of Gift

The gift tax defines a gift as a transfer of property without adequate and full consideration in money or money's worth. § 2512(b). Love, affection, and the release of marital rights are not consideration in money or money's worth. Regulation § 25.2512–8. The income tax excludes gifts from gross income (§ 102) and defines a gift as a transfer that proceeds from detached and disinterested generosity or out of affection, respect, admiration, charity or like impulses. *Commissioner v. Duberstein*, 363 U.S. 278, 285 (1960). As a result, the same transfer could be a gift for purposes of the gift tax and not a gift for purposes of the income tax, subjecting the transferor to both the gift tax and the income tax.

Example 1.5

Henry plans to marry Wendy and agrees to transfer $3 million worth of stock, in which he has a basis of $100,000, to her if she will release her marital rights. Wendy agrees. Henry transfers the stock to Wendy before they are married and, in fact, before Henry's divorce from his prior spouse, Sally, has been finalized. The transfer to Wendy is a gift for gift tax purposes. It is not a gift for income tax purposes. *Farid–Es–Sultaneh v. Commissioner*, 160 F.2d 812 (2d Cir. 1947). A careful planner will avoid this trap by making marriage part of the consideration for the agreement and by making sure that the transfer does not occur until the marriage. Such planning should ensure that the gift tax marital deduction will shield the transfer from the gift tax and that § 1041 will apply to prevent recognition of gain on the transfer.

---

c. Transfers with Retained Interests

The income, gift, and estate taxes all apply where a taxpayer makes a transfer, usually into a trust, and retains the right to income from the property or the ability to designate who will possess or enjoy the trust property or the income from it. In some cases the taxpayer will continue to be taxed on the income from the property even though it is a completed gift. In some cases the transfer will be a completed gift but the property will be included in the gross estate.

d. Basis

(1) General Principles

Basis is an income tax concept, and it represents the taxpayer's investment in the property. § 1011. Basis is usually the cost of the property. § 1012.

(2) Basis of Property Received by Gift: § 1015

When a donor makes a gift, she does not recognize any gain or loss for purposes of the income tax. The receipt of the property is not taxable to the recipient, *i.e.*, he does not need to report that property as income. § 102. Section 1015 provides that a recipient acquires the taxpayer's basis when a taxpayer makes a gift of appreciated property. As a result, the recipient rather than the donor will pay any income tax on that gain, but only when the recipient sells the property.

Example 1.6

Dan buys 10 shares of stock for $10 per share ($100). Some years later the stock appreciates in value to $50 per share ($500), and Dan gives the stock to Carl. Carl acquires Dan's basis ($100). If Carl sells the stock, he realizes and recognizes a gain of $400, *i.e.*, the difference between his amount realized of $500 and his basis of $100.

---

(3) Basis of Property Received by Bequest: § 1014

One would think that the same rule applied at death, but that is not the case. Instead, § 1014 provides that a beneficiary receives a *stepped-up basis* in the property; that is, the beneficiary's basis is the fair market value of the property on the date of death. This allows a decedent to transfer property at death, and any appreciation in the value of the property is never taxed as income.

> **Example 1.7**
>
> Dan buys 10 shares of stock for $10 per share ($100). Instead of giving the stock to Carl, Dan dies when the stock has a value of $50 per share ($500). Dan bequeaths the stock to Carl. Carl's basis is the date of death value ($500). If Carl then sells the stock, he does not realize or recognize any gain.

G. ROLE OF STATE LAW

1. State Law Creates Property Interests

The gift, estate, and generation-skipping transfer taxes are federal taxes. Federal law does not create property interests. State law creates the property interest. Federal law dictates how those property interests will be taxed.

2. Federal Courts Must Give "Proper Regard" to Decisions of Lower State Courts

In determining whether, or how, to impose a federal transfer tax, a federal court will often need to interpret state law. In *Commissioner v. Estate of Bosch*, 387 U.S. 456 (1967), the Court held that it was bound only by a decision of a state's highest court in determining the nature and scope of that state's property law. The Court did rule that it would give "proper regard" to the relevant rulings of other courts of the state. *Id.* at 465.

3. Exam Strategy

First, determine the nature and scope of the property interest in question. Look to state law for that determination. Second, analyze which court is making the decision. A federal court will interpret the IRC, which is after all a federal statute, but it must apply those provisions to state created property rights. It will only give proper regard to, and not be bound by, the decisions of state courts that are not the highest courts of that state.

CHAPTER 2

VALUATION

A. GENERAL PRINCIPLES

Valuation is a question of fact—what is this particular piece of property worth at this particular time in this market? While there are basic legal principles that govern this issue, the final decision on value will depend on all the facts and circumstances. Valuation is a frequently litigated issue and one that often involves differing expert opinions. The court is not bound to accept the opinion of any expert and must make its own determination of value.

1. Willing Buyer/Willing Seller Test

The transfer taxes are imposed on the fair market value of the transferred property. **Fair market value** is the price that a willing buyer would pay a willing seller, neither being under any compulsion to buy or sell and both having reasonable knowledge of relevant facts. Regulations §§ 2031–1(b), 25.2512–1. Fair market value is not determined by a forced sale, and it is not determined by the value of an item to a particular individual. It is the price that two strangers would negotiate when dealing at arm's length.

2. The Market

Fair market value must be determined by the market in which the item is commonly bought and sold. Most items are bought and sold in the general marketplace and that is the market that determines their value. Regulation § 20.2031–1(b). For example, the fair market value of a used automobile is what a member of the general public would pay for a vehicle of the same description, make, model, age, and condition and in the locality in which the donor or the decedent lived. It is not the price that would be paid by an automobile dealer or at a used automobile auction. *Id.* In some cases, such as works of art, there is a specialized market that must be considered. In *Estate of O'Keeffe v. Commissioner*, 63 T.C.M. (CCH) 2699 (1992), for example, the court noted that "it is necessary to examine the history of the market for [Georgia] O'Keeffe works, the prospects for the market for O'Keeffe works as of the date of death, the types of works to be valued, and the art market in the United States." *Id.* at 2700.

3. Methods of Valuation

Different methods of valuation may be used depending on the nature of the property to be valued. The three most commonly used valuation methods are: (1) the market approach, (2) the capitalization of income approach, and (3) the cost approach.

a. The Market Approach

The market approach looks at what the market is actually paying for this type of property. This approach may rely on actual sales of the particular property in issue, but only if the sale is reasonably close in time to the actual valuation date. In most cases, the market approach relies on the sale of comparable properties. The properties must be similar in nature, size, and scope to the property to be valued. The sales must also be in the same or a nearby market and must be reasonably close in time to the actual valuation date. Sales occurring after the valuation date may be considered, but not if they are influenced by facts that were not known on the actual valuation date.

b. The Capitalization of Income Approach

Business assets or those held for investment may be valued using the capitalization of income approach. The first step is to determine the income produced by the particular property at issue. Then an appropriate rate of return must be selected. This rate of return is then applied to the projected stream of income to produce the fair market value. This method is most commonly used for business interests and commercial real estate for which there are no readily available market values.

c. The Cost Approach

The cost approach estimates the price of replacing or reproducing the particular asset. This approach considers all the facts and circumstances surrounding the particular asset, including the original cost, depreciation, and capital improvements. This method is most commonly used for specific business assets and life insurance policies.

4. Burden of Proof

The transferor—the donor or the decedent's estate—has the burden of proof on the issue of valuation. The burden is the same whether the transferor refuses to pay the tax and is being sued by the government, or whether the transferor pays the tax and is suing the government for a refund. In other words, it does not matter whether the transferor is the plaintiff or the defendant; the transferor still has the burden of proof. The burden of proof may shift to the government, but only if the taxpayer has complied with all the statutory substantiation and record-keeping requirements and cooperates with all reasonable requests for witnesses, information, documentation, meetings, and interviews. § 7491(a). *See, e.g., Estate of Jelke v. Commissioner*, 89 T.C.M. (CCH) 1397, 1400 (2005).

5. Intra–Family Transactions

Transactions between family members are subject to special scrutiny. There is a presumption that transfers between family members are grounded in donative intent. "[T]he family relationship often makes it possible for one to shift tax incidence by surface changes of ownership without disturbing in the least his dominion and control over the subject of the gift or the purposes for which the income from the property is used." *Commissioner v. Culbertson*, 337 U.S. 733, 746 (1949). Courts will carefully scrutinize such transfers to determine that they are both bona fide and at arm's length.

a. Bona Fide Transactions

A bona fide transaction is one that is in reality what it purports to be on paper. Sales and loans are closely examined to determine if the promissory notes are intended to be valid debt instruments.

Illustrative Case

In *Estate of Berkman v. Commissioner,* 38 T.C.M. (CCH) 183 (1979), the decedent lent money to his daughter, his son-in-law, and their wholly owned corporation. The court found that the promissory notes were indeed bona fide, stating "[e]xamination of the notes reveals that they were executed in proper legal form and signed by the obligors. Moreover, the transferees carried out their obligations under the notes; they paid the interest due every month without exception. Finally, there is no evidence to support the respondent's contention that at the time of the transfers the decedent did not intend to collect the notes." *Id.* at 186.

Illustrative Case

In *Estate of Kelley v. Commissioner*, 63 T.C. 321 (1974), taxpayer and his wife sold property to their three children and reserved life estates for themselves. The court held that the promissory notes constituted valuable consideration. Although taxpayer and his wife forgave each payment as it became due, the vendors' liens remained in effect. The court noted that "[a]t any time prior to the forgiveness of the final note relating to a particular transfer, petitioners could have demanded payment of the amounts falling due and, in case of default, could have foreclosed the vendor's lien on the property to satisfy the obligations. . . . [The notes were also] subject to sale or assignment by [the taxpayer and his spouse] at any time, and a purchaser or assignee could have enforced the liens." *Id.* at 323–324.

Illustrative Case

In Revenue Ruling 77–299, 1977–2 C.B. 343, on the other hand, the IRS found that the transfer was merely a disguised gift and not a bona fide sale. In this situation, Grandfather, who had made gifts equal to the gift tax annual exclusion each year to his grandchildren, decided to give them unimproved real property. Grandfather's attorney advised a sale with forgiveness of each installment payment as it came due. Without consulting the grandchildren, Grandfather structured the deal as his attorney advised. The grandchildren signed non-interest bearing notes that were non-negotiable. The IRS found that this was a prearranged plan with no intent to collect on the notes, noting that "[a] finding of an intent to forgive the notes relates [not to donative intent, which is irrelevant] but to whether valuable consideration was received and, thus, to whether the transaction was in reality a bona fide sale or a disguised gift." The IRS concluded that the transaction was "merely a disguised gift rather than a bona fide sale."

Illustrative Case

In *Estate of Maxwell v. Commissioner*, 3 F.3d 591 (2d Cir. 1993), the decedent transferred her residence to her son and his wife when she was 82 years old and suffering from cancer. The appellate court affirmed the trial court's holding that this was not a bona fide sale even though the parties had stipulated to the fair market value of the property on the date of the transaction. The court noted, "There is no question that the mortgage note here is a fully secured, legally enforceable obligation on its face. The question is whether it is actually what it purports to be, *i.e.*, a bona fide instrument of indebtedness, or whether it is a facade." *Id.* at 595. Because the court found an implied agreement that the decedent would never demand payment, the promissory notes had "no value at all." *Id.*

(1) Exclusion for Retained Interests

Transactions that are bona fide sales for adequate and full consideration are excluded from the gross estate under §§ 2036, 2037, and 2038. The issue of what is, or is not, a bona fide transaction has taken on a special meaning in the context of transfers to family limited partnerships. See discussion at sections E.3. and H of chapter 8.

b. Arm's Length Transactions

Intrafamily transactions are also scrutinized to determine if the terms and conditions are the same as would be negotiated by strangers, *i.e.*, at arm's length.

Illustrative Case

In *Estate of Berkman v. Commissioner*, 38 T.C.M. (CCH) 183 (1979), the court looked at a number of factors to determine that some of the promissory notes were not negotiated at arm's length. Although conceding that the decedent had a profit motive in making the loans and that the interest rate was higher than he was otherwise earning, the court considered: (1) the decedent's age; (2) the length of the notes; (3) the fact that no principal was due until maturity; (4) the lack of a security interest; and (5) the identity of the debtors—family members who were the natural objects of his bounty. Based on all these factors, the court concluded that the transfers were not at arm's length or free from donative intent.

Illustrative Case

In *Cobb v. Commissioner*, 49 T.C.M. (CCH) 1364 (1985), decedent owned a horse training center which she leased to Cobb. When decedent wanted a more predictable source of income and less management responsibility, she renegotiated the lease with Cobb; made him the manager of the farm property; and gave him an option to purchase the farm. Decedent died owning the property so Cobb never had the opportunity to exercise his option. After determining that the option was in fact a property interest capable of being transferred, the court held that the option was an arm's length business transaction and not a gift. The court noted that: (1) the option and the lease were interdependent parts of one transaction; (2) both sides benefitted—Cobb received a longer lease and an option while decedent retained a tenant that she trusted, with an assured rent for a longer period of time; (3) there was a long-standing relationship between the parties that was friendly but always business-like; (4) there was a series of negotiations between the parties; (5) there were formalized written documents binding both parties that were prepared by counsel; and (6) Cobb was not the natural object of decedent's bounty. The court concluded that there was no gift because the option "was part of an arm's-length business transaction, entered into between parties who were competent and for valid business purposes, with no element of donative intent on decedent's part." *Id.* at 1372.

Illustrative Case

In *Estate of Higgins v. Commissioner*, 61 T.C.M. (CCH) 1789 (1991), decedent transferred 10,269 shares of stock in Dominion Bankshares Corporation to Higgins Oil Company. Decedent was the controlling shareholder of Higgins Oil Company and a member of its board of directors. With one exception, all other shareholders were members of decedent's family. At the time of the transfer, Higgins Oil Company was in arrears on payment of a note to Grayson National Bank. Higgins Oil Company sold the stock a month after decedent's transfer and used the proceeds to pay the note, to pay taxes, and to purchase inventory items. The court concluded that the decedent's transfer of stock in Dominion Bankshares to Higgins Oil was a gift to the other shareholders of

Higgins Oil and not a business transaction conducted at arm's length. "We do not believe that a third party bargaining at arm's length would have transferred an asset valued at over $143,000 without any type of consideration." *Id.* at 1797.

(1) Buy–Sell Agreements and § 2703

In determining whether a buy-sell agreement will establish the value of property, § 2703(b)(3) requires that the terms of that requirement be "comparable to similar arrangements entered into by persons in an arm's length transaction."

Illustrative Case

In *Estate of True v. Commissioner*, 390 F.3d 1210 (10th Cir. 2004), the court applied the arm's-length-transaction standard to determine whether or not the buy-sell agreement was a testamentary substitute. It relied on the following factors: (1) the decedent's age and health at the time of entering into the agreement; (2) the lack of enforcement of the agreement; (3) the exclusion of significant assets from the agreement; (4) the lack of negotiation between the parties; (5) the arbitrary manner in which the price term was selected; (6) whether the agreement allowed adjustments or revaluation of price terms; and (7) whether the parties were equally bound by the terms of the agreement. Reviewing all these factors, the court held that the buy-sell agreement in this case did not control the estate or gift tax value of decedent's business interests.

6. Exam Strategy

Valuation is intensely factual so it is unlikely that you will be asked to value a specific piece of property. You may, however, be asked to state general rules. If, as is usually the case, the transfer is from one family member to another, you should begin with the general rule that such transactions are subject to special or close scrutiny. Then use the facts to determine if the transfer is (1) bona fide, (2) at arm's length, and (3) free from donative intent. A transaction is bona fide if it is, in reality, what it purports to be. It is at arm's length if the terms are similar to what strangers would negotiate. It is free from donative intent if the price at which the property is changing hands is, in essence, the fair market value.

B. VALUATION DATE

1. Gift Tax

A gift occurs only when the transfer is complete. A transfer is complete when the donor has given up dominion and control over the property so that he no longer has any "power to change its disposition whether for his own benefit or the benefit of another." Regulation § 25.2511–2(b). The date that the transfer is complete is the valuation date for purposes of the gift tax.

2. Estate Tax

a. General Rule

Property subject to the estate tax is valued on the date of the decedent's death. § 2031. In most cases, this does not present a problem. In some cases, death itself can affect the valuation of property.

Illustrative Case

In *Goodman v. Granger*, 243 F.2d 264 (3d Cir. 1957), *cert. denied*, 355 U.S. 835 (1957), decedent contracted with his employer for deferred compensation that was subject to a covenant not to compete. Decedent died while still employed, and his estate argued that the deferred compensation agreement had no value even though payments would be made to decedent's estate. The Third Circuit held that the payments were to be valued "as of the time of [decedent's] death when the limiting factor of the contingencies would no longer be considered. Death ripened the interest in the deferred payments into an absolute one, and death permitted the imposition of the tax measured by the value of that absolute interest in property." *Id.* at 269.

---

b. Immediately Before Death

Some property interests are included in the gross estate if their value exceeds a specified amount "immediately before death." Section 2037 provides one example. The question then becomes whether or not to consider the decedent's actual health immediately before death or only the standard mortality tables. If the decedent's health were to be considered, the property interest would have a very low value unless the decedent died unexpectedly or in an accident.

Illustrative Case

In *Estate of Roy v. Commissioner*, 54 T.C. 1317 (1970), the court held that property interests subject to § 2037 must be valued by reference to the mortality tables rather than the decedent's actual life expectancy. To hold otherwise, the court reasoned, would be to ignore the language of § 2037 and the intent of Congress.

---

(1) Use of Mortality Tables and Terminal Illness

The regulations now provide that the tables must be used unless the individual who is the measuring life is terminally ill on the valuation date. Terminal illness is defined as "an incurable illness or other deteriorating physical condition . . . if there is at least a 50 percent probability that the individual will die within 1 year. However, if the individual survives for eighteen months or longer . . . that individual shall be presumed to have not been terminally ill on [the valuation date] unless the contrary is established by clear and convincing evidence." Regulation §§ 20.7520–3(b)(3), 25.7520–3(b)(3).

3. Alternate Valuation Date

a. General Principles

The estate tax return is due nine months after decedent dies. § 6075(a). The value of assets may change dramatically in that time period or before distribution to the beneficiaries. Recognizing this, Congress enacted § 2032 that allows for the executor to choose the alternate valuation date, which is six months after the decedent's death. The executor may not choose the alternate valuation date unless both the value of the gross estate and the estate tax due will be decreased by the election. § 2032(c).

b. Property That is Sold During the Six Months Immediately Following the Date of Death

Property that is sold, exchanged, distributed, or otherwise disposed of before the alternate valuation date is valued as of the date of disposition. § 2032(a)(1).

29

c. Property Interests Affected by the Lapse of Time

Any property interests that are affected by the mere lapse in time are valued as of the date of death. § 2032(a)(3) Examples are life estates, terms certain, and remainders.

Example 2.1

Greg died on February 1. On that date his property had the following values:

Blackacre	$ 250,000
Greenacre	$ 400,000
Whiteacre	$ 500,000
ABC, Inc. stock	$1,000,000
XYZ, Inc. stock	$2,000,000

Greg also was the remainder beneficiary of a trust created by his father that had a value of $750,000 on February 1. Greg's estate sold Whiteacre for $450,000 on May 1. It sold Greenacre on June 1 for $350,000. On August 1, the remaining properties had the following values:

Blackacre	$ 200,000
ABC, Inc. stock	$ 800,000
XYZ, Inc. stock	$1,800,000

The remainder interest had a value of $760,000; neither the trust property value nor the interest rate had changed. The value of Greg's estate on February 1 was $4,900,000. If his estate elects the alternate valuation date, August 1, Whiteacre will be valued at $450,000 and Greenacre at $350,000 because they were sold before August 1. The trust remainder would be valued at $750,000, the date of death value, because the change in value was attributable solely to the lapse of time. The remaining assets would be valued as of August 1. So Greg's estate would have a value of $4,350,000. Because both the value of his gross estate and the estate tax decreased (§ 2032(c)), his estate can elect the alternate valuation date of August 1.

---

d. Proposed Regulations to Limit Reductions in Value to Market Conditions

The IRS has issued proposed regulations to clarify that § 2032 is available only to reduce the value of assets due to market conditions. This would prevent actions of the executor, a trustee, a closely-held business, or other individual or entity from decreasing the value of the asset. The proposed regulations would be consistent with the general rule, discussed immediately below, that post-death events are ignored in valuing decedent's assets.

Illustrative Case

In *Flanders v. United States*, 347 F.Supp. 95 (N.D. Cal. 1972), the trustee of a trust owning decedent's interest in real property entered into a land conservation agreement that reduced the assessed value of the land. The court refused to take that agreement into account for purposes of the alternate valuation date even though it decreased the value of the land. The proposed regulations would not alter this result.

Illustrative Case

In *Kohler v. Commissioner*, 92 T.C.M. (CCH) 48 (2006), the decedent owned stock in a company that was reorganized two months after his death. At the time of the reorganization, restrictions were placed on the stock that decreased its value. The court held that those restrictions and the post-death reorganization should be taken into account when the estate elected to use the alternate valuation date. The proposed regulations would alter the result in this case.

---

4. Post–Death Events

a. General Principles

Section 2031(a) includes in the gross estate "the value *at the time of his death* of all [decedent's] property. . . . " (Emphasis added.) The "time of death" means "the date of death." Unless the executor elects the alternate valuation date, events occurring after decedent's death are not usually considered in valuing assets. Under the market approach, discussed above, sales occurring after decedent's death may be used to establish the value of decedent's assets only if those sales are not affected by decedent's death and are close in time to decedent's death.

Illustrative Case

In *Estate of Curry v. Commissioner*, 74 T.C. 540 (1980), decedent was an attorney specializing in Indian land claims. He contracted with another attorney and was entitled to receive a stated percentage of attorneys' fees awarded in a list of cases that were docketed before his death. The Commissioner valued this contractual right in part on the actual recovery by decedent's estate in two cases four months after death. The court rejected that approach stating, "[a]lthough appealing because of the simplicity, we must reject respondent's methodology . . . [the Commissioner] must distinguish between a contractual right to receive future income and the actual receipt of the income subsequent to death." *Id.* at 548. After consideration of all the facts and circumstances, the court valued the right to recovery in those two cases at $95,000 rather than the actual $100,544 received by the estate.

Illustrative Case

In *Estate of Andrews v. United States*, 850 F.Supp. 1279 (E.D. Va. 1944), the author V.C. Andrews died while under contract to write two books. The publisher hired a ghostwriter to complete those two books and later to write six additional books. There were three publishing contracts with the ghostwriter. In valuing V.C. Andrews' name as an asset of her estate, the court relied on the first, but not the second or third contracts. The court noted the risky and speculative nature of the ghostwriting venture and that had the first ghostwritten book failed, there would have been no further contracts.

---

b. **Future Tax Liability, *e.g.*, Built–In Capital Gains**

Courts have considered potential tax liability in some cases (usually built-in capital gains), but not in others (on retirement accounts). *Compare Dallas v. Commissioner*, 92 T.C.M. (CCH) 313 (2006) *and Estate of Jelke v. Commissioner*, 89 T.C.M. (CCH) 1397 (2005) *with Estate of Kahn v. Commissioner*, 125 T.C. 227 (2005) *and Estate of Smith v. United States*, 300 F. Supp. 2d 474 (S.D. Tex. 2004).

c. **Claims Against Decedent's Estate**

The IRS not only allows, but in fact requires, consideration of post-death events in determining the valuation of claims to be deducted in calculating the decedent's taxable estate under § 2053. See section B.4.b. of Chapter 13.

5. **Generation–Skipping Transfer Tax**

Property subject to the generation-skipping transfer tax is also valued on the date of the transfer, whether it is a direct skip, a taxable distribution, or a taxable termination.

6. **Exam Strategy**

Assets are valued as of a specific date. In analyzing a valuation issue, look for specific dates. Gifts are only taxed if they are completed transfers. Completion occurs when the donor has given up the power to change the beneficial ownership of the property. Gifts must be valued at that date. Generation-skipping transfers are also valued as of the date of the transfer. Property in the gross estate is valued as of the date of death or the alternate valuation date. Post-death events are usually not considered in valuing property. Always refer explicitly to the facts that you rely on.

C. SPECIFIC ASSETS

1. **General Principles**

All assets are valued at their fair market value, *i.e.*, at what a willing buyer would pay a willing seller neither being under a compulsion to buy or sell and both having reasonable knowledge of relevant facts. Regulations §§ 20.2031–1(b), 25.2512–1. Because the particular asset being valued was not in fact sold in an arm's length transaction on the valuation date, the donor or the decedent's estate must make reasonable approximations and assumptions. For example, the donor's or decedent's actual life expectancy is rarely used to value assets such as life estates and remainders. Instead, standardized valuation tables that incorporate a generalized mortality component are used. § 7520.

2. **Real Estate**

Real estate is valued at its highest and best use unless the real estate qualifies for special use valuation pursuant to § 2032A. See section F.2. In most cases, the market approach is used to value real estate. In some situations the capitalization of income approach is used. In all cases, the estate will employ qualified real estate appraisers to value the real property.

3. Automobiles

Automobiles are valued at what the particular market in which the donor or decedent lived would pay for a vehicle of the same or approximately the same description, make, model, age, condition, and the like. It is not what a dealer in used automobiles would pay; rather, it is what a member of the public would pay on that day for that automobile. Regulations §§ 20.2031–1(b), 25.2512–1.

4. Stocks and Bonds

a. Selling Price

If there is an established market for the stocks or bonds, the fair market value is the mean between the highest and lowest quoted selling prices on the valuation date. Regulations §§ 20.2031–2(b)(1), 25.2512–2(b)(1). If there were no sales on the valuation date, sales within a reasonable period before and after the valuation date will be used by taking a weighted average of the means on the nearest date before and the nearest date after the valuation date. *Id.* Thus, if decedent dies on a Saturday when the markets are closed, the means between the highest and lowest quoted selling prices on the Friday before and the Monday after her death will be used and greater weight will be given to the Friday mean than the Monday mean.

b. No Selling Price Available

If there are no selling prices, bid and asked prices may be used. Regulations §§ 20.2031–2(c), 25.2512–2(c). If the corporation is closely held, there might not be any bid and asked prices or even any market for the stock. In that case, all the facts and circumstances will be considered including the corporation's net worth, prospective earning power, and dividend-paying capacity, among others. Regulations §§ 20.2031–2(f), 25.2512–2(f). *See also* Regulations §§ 20.2031–3, 25.2512–3.

5. Promissory Notes

There is a presumption that the fair market value of notes, whether secured or unsecured, is the amount of unpaid principal plus interested accrued to the date of death or the date of the gift. Regulations §§ 20.2031–4, 25.2512–4. The estate or the donor has the burden of proving that a note is worth less than its face amount or that it is worthless. *Id.*

6. Bank Accounts

The amount on deposit in the bank on the date of decedent's death is the fair market value. Regulation § 20.2031–5. If checks are outstanding on the date of death and if they are subsequently honored by the bank, the balance remaining in the account may be reported but only if the checks were given for adequate and full consideration in money or money's worth. *Id.* This is simply a rule of convenience because those checks represent valid claims against the estate that would be deductible under § 2053.

7. Household Goods and Personal Effects

In reporting the value of household goods and personal effects, a room by room itemization is desirable. Regulation § 20.2031–6. Items in the same room, none of which have a value greater than $100 may be grouped together. *Id.* The executor must submit appraisals by qualified appraisers for any item worth more than $3,000 or any collection worth more than $10,000. Instructions to Form 706.

8. Life Insurance

a. Estate Tax Value of Policies on Decedent's Life

Life insurance is valued differently for estate tax purposes than for gift tax purposes. The gross estate includes *the amount receivable* by the executor or other beneficiary as life insurance on the life of the decedent. § 2042. It is, therefore, unnecessary to value life insurance policies on the decedent's life as the executor needs to report what was actually received. The amount received could exceed the face amount of the policy if the decedent had allowed dividends and interests to accumulate in the policy.

b. Estate Tax Value of Policies on the Life of Another

A decedent may own a life insurance policy on the life of another. This happens when the insured attempts to avoid including the insurance proceeds in his gross estate by transferring the policy to another. If the owner then dies before the insured, the fair market value of that policy is included in the owner's gross estate under § 2033. The value of life insurance policy in this situation is normally established by sales of comparable policies by that company. Regulation § 20.2031–8. Usually the value of a term insurance policy is the proportionate part of the gross premium paid before decedent's death or the date of the gift. *Id.* The value of a cash value or whole life policy is the interpolated terminal reserve (essentially the cash surrender value) plus the proportionate part of the gross premium paid before decedent's death or the date of the gift. *Id.* In most cases, that value can be established simply by contacting the insurance company.

c. **Gift Tax Value**

The value of a life insurance policy that is given away during life is established in the same way as life insurance policies on the life of another, *i.e.*, through comparable sales. Regulation § 25.2512–6. Again, in most cases the value is established by contacting the insurance company.

9. **Exam Strategy**

Valuation depends on all the facts and circumstances and is essentially a question of fact. As a result, it is unlikely that you will be required to determine the fair market value of a particular asset in an examination. The regulations set out the basic rules for the assets described in this section. Regulations §§ 20.2031 and 25.2512–1. Remember, though, that the fair market value of an asset is important in determining if a transaction is indeed a sale or a part sale/part gift or entirely a gift.

D. DISCOUNTS AND PREMIUMS

1. **General Principles**

Because assets are not in fact sold on the valuation date, it is difficult to establish value unless the asset is one that is commonly sold in a public marketplace. Valuing assets sold in the public marketplace can present challenges because factors such as transfer restrictions or the size of the property interest will also affect valuation. The law will allow a discount or require a premium in the valuation of such assets.

2. **Lack of Marketability**

Regulation § 20.2031–1(b) states that fair market value is established in the market in which the item is most commonly sold to the public, taking into account the location of the item. *See also* Regulation § 25.2512–1. If the market is restricted to a limited group, *e.g.*, the donor's or decedent's immediate family members, the value of the asset will undoubtedly be less than if there were no such restriction. Transfer restrictions are now governed by §§ 2703 and 2704. See section F.5.

3. **Blockage**

The size or amount of property that is the subject of a gift or in the decedent's estate can affect its value. Assume that the decedent owns 10,000 shares of stock in a corporation. If all of those shares were offered for sale at one time, the price would decrease because the supply would exceed the demand. The regulations acknowledge this and note that in such a case the price might be that which an underwriter could obtain rather than a sale on the open market. Regulations §§ 20.2031–2(e), 25.2512–2(e).

Illustrative Case

When Georgia O'Keeffe died at the age of 98, she owned approximately 400 works or groups of work of her own art. *Estate of O'Keeffe v. Commissioner*, 63 T.C.M. (CCH) 2699 (1992). The estimated fair market value of these individual works on the date of her death was $72,759,000. *Id.* at 2700. The court noted that if all or a substantial portion of those works were offered for sale at one time, it would depress the market price for each item. It held that, "[t]he fair market value of the aggregate of the works in the estate, therefore, as of the date of death, was substantially less than the total of the fair market value of each individual work." *Id.* After reviewing "the history of the market for O'Keeffe's works, the prospects for the market for O'Keeffe's works as of the date of [her] death, the types of works to be valued, and the art market in the United States," the court concluded that one-half the value of the art would be discounted by 75 percent and the other half by 25 percent. *Id.* at 2700, 2707.

Example 2.2

Assume that one acre of land in a particular location is selling for $10,000 per acre. Dad owns 500 acres of land in that location. Does that mean that Dad's land is worth $5,000,000? Not necessarily. Even if each acre of land in that location was identical, it is highly unlikely that Buyer would pay that amount for Dad's 500 acres. The price would undoubtedly be something less, reflecting the fact that if 500 separate parcels, each one acre in size, were offered for sale on the same day, the supply would exceed the demand and depress the price.

---

4. **Control**

A large block of stock or other ownership interest might, on the other hand, command a higher price because it represents a controlling interest in that business. Regulations §§ 20.2031–2(e), 25.2512–2(e).

Example 2.3

Assume that shares of stock in XYZ, Inc. are selling on an established market for $10 a share. Sam owns 60 percent of the stock in XYZ, Inc. Bert, a potential buyer, might be willing to pay more than $10 a share because that block of stock represents a controlling interest in the corporation.

Illustrative Case

In *Estate of Salsbury v. Commissioner*, 34 T.C.M. (CCH) 1441 (1975), the decedent owned 51.8 percent of the stock of Salsbury Laboratories. The court noted that the decedent could elect the entire board of directors, or remove a director and thereby control the business affairs of the corporation, including the declaration of dividends and even the issuance of additional stock. After reviewing all the evidence, the court applied a 38.1 percent control premium in the valuation of decedent's stock in his estate.

Illustrative Case

In *Estate of Chenoweth v. Commissioner*, 88 T.C. 1577 (1987), the decedent owned all of the stock of a corporation. He left 51 percent of the stock to his surviving spouse and 49 percent to his daughter. The issue was what control premium, if any, could be applied in computing the marital deduction. The court noted that:

> While we would tend to agree that the sum of the parts cannot equal more than the whole—that is, the majority block together with the control premium, when added to the minority block of the company's stock with an appropriate discount for minority interest, should not equal more than the total 100 percent interest of the decedent . . . it might well turn out that the sum of the parts can equal less than the whole—that is, that the control premium which is added to the majority block passing to decedent's surviving spouse might be less than the property minority discount attributed to the shares passing to decedent's daughter Kelli.

Id. at 1589–1590. The court denied the government's motion for summary judgment and remanded the case for a determination of value.

5. Minority Interests

a. General Principles

Few people own controlling interests in businesses. Far more people own minority interests. In fact, taxpayers may try to create minority interests in order to obtain a discounted value. The value of a minority interest is arguably less than its proportionate share of the value of the asset. Assume, for example, that a shareholder owns a five percent interest in a $100 million corporation. The value of that five percent interest may be far less than $5 million. Discounts for minority interests are well recognized by the courts, and they can be substantial in amount. A major impetus for the creation of family limited partnerships and similar entities is the ability to decrease the value of the property held by these entities through application of minority discounts.

b. Minority Interest as Swing Vote

Of course, what appears to be a minority interest might represent a *swing vote* within the corporation, *i.e.*, one that can influence the decision because the other interests are equally divided, or in some cases because it is larger than any other ownership interest. If so, the value of that minority interest might include a control premium rather than a minority discount.

Example 2.4

Assume that shares of stock in MNO, Inc. sell for $20 per share. Don owns a five percent interest in MNO, Inc. Because his interest is so low, he cannot affect the election of members of the board of directors or the operation of the business. A buyer would probably pay him less than $20 a share for the stock. If MNO, Inc. were a publicly traded company with a very large number of shares, a five percent interest might represent a controlling interest and, thus, have a premium attached to it rather than a discount. As is true for all valuation issues, the final determination will depend on all the facts and circumstances.

---

c. Publicly Traded Stock

If the interest is traded on an established market, that market will set the value. Discounts and premiums are rarely applied in valuing publicly traded stocks and bonds. Where the stock, or other owner-ship interest, is not publicly traded, there is always an issue regarding the value of the business before application of a minority discount. Both the underlying value and the appropriate discount factor are questions of fact, and experts rarely agree.

6. Exam Strategy

Valuation is a question of fact and depends on all the facts and circumstances. Learn what the rules are and when to apply them, but do not worry about whether the discount would be 20 percent or 40 percent. Do not focus solely on the numbers; what appears to be a minority interest because it is less than 50 percent, might be a controlling interest or the swing vote. Instead, focus on the general principles. Always use the facts.

E. INTERESTS THAT CHANGE WITH THE PASSAGE OF TIME

1. General Principles

Interests in property, not just the underlying property itself, must often be valued. Valuation of such interests may be affected by the passage of time. A life estate decreases in value as the life tenant ages even if the value of the underlying property stays exactly the same. Conversely, a remainder increases in value with the passage of time. The valuation of such property interests depends not only on the underlying value of the property, but also on the expected rate of return and the age of the life tenant or the term of years.

2. Remainders and Reversions

a. Definitions

A remainder is a future interest in a person other than the transferor and represents the right to receive the property at some date in the future. A reversion is a future interest in the transferor and also represents the right to receive the property at some date in the future. Remainders and reversions may be vested or contingent. This discussion of valuation focuses on vested interests; the valuation of contingent interests is often speculative depending on the nature of the contingency.

b. Time Value of Money

To understand how remainders and reversions are valued, it is critical to understand the time value of money.

Example 2.5

Don creates an irrevocable trust with Friendly National Bank as the trustee to pay the income to Henry for five years and the remainder to Ruth. Don transfers $100,000 into the trust. The value of Ruth's remainder is not $100,000 because Ruth must wait for five years to acquire the possession or enjoyment of the trust property. The value of Ruth's remainder is the present value of the right to receive the $100,000 at the end of five years. If Don had provided that income was to be paid to Henry for his life, then the value of Ruth's remainder would be the present value of the right to receive the $100,000 at the end of Henry's life. How does one determine that value?

---

c. **Present Value**

Consider a simple question: which has greater value, a dollar in hand today, or the promise of a dollar a year from now? The answer is, of course, the dollar today—not because you could spend it (though that isn't necessarily a bad reason), and not because the donor might go bankrupt (we will define away that possibility), but because you could earn interest on it over the next year. By the end of the year, you would have $1.05 (assuming you could earn interest at five percent). Thus, the promise of the dollar deferred is worth something less than $1.00. Just how much is it worth? A little over 95 cents. To ask the question in a slightly different way, what amount, invested at five percent, will yield enough so that the original value plus interest will equal $1.00? The answer is the same—just over 95 cents.

Now suppose that the receipt of the dollar is to be postponed for two years. Then the question becomes more complicated: what amount, invested at five percent, will yield enough so that the original value, plus interest in year one, plus interest in year two on the original value *and* on the first year's interest, will equal $1.00? There is nothing terribly complicated about this; we have simply introduced the familiar notion of compound interest, and the answer is about 91 cents. And so on and so forth, until we determine the present value of a dollar to be paid five years from now. Fortunately, there is no need to make the calculations each time we are faced with the problem. Instead, we can simply look to the tables for terms of years and remainders for the appropriate factor.

d. Actuarial Tables

The IRS publishes tables that incorporate the interest rate and the length of the term. In the case of a remainder following a life estate, the tables include a mortality component. At one time, the IRS set an interest rate and published those tables in the regulations. In 1988, Congress enacted § 7520 that requires the IRS to set the interest rate on a monthly basis, and the IRS has published tables accordingly. IRS Publications 1457 and 1458. Those tables are updated every ten years to take into account the most recent mortality data available.

If we look at Table B, which governs terms of years, we discover that the value of the remainder after a term of two years at a five percent interest rate is .907029, and after a five-year term, .783526.

Example 2.5 Revisited

Don created an irrevocable trust to pay the income to Henry for five years and the remainder to Ruth. Donor transferred $100,000 to the trust when the applicable federal interest rate was five percent. The value of Ruth's remainder interest is $100,000 multiplied by .783526 or $78,352.60.

If Don had left the property to Henry for life and the remainder to Ruth, we would need to consult Table S. Assuming an interest rate of 5 percent and that Henry is 60 at the time of the transfer is, we discover that the appropriate factor is .39261. So the value of Ruth's remainder in this situation is $39,261.

---

e. Reversions

Reversions are valued in the same way because a reversion is simply a retained future interest in the donor. In Example 2.5, Don's reversion would be $78,352.60 if the trust were income to Henry for five years and then the property returned to Don.

f. Actual Values versus Actuarial Table Values

All this sounds fine, all very mathematical and precise, but what has it got to do with the real world? Interest rates will change, the asset may not earn the presumed rate of return, and the income beneficiary may walk in front of a speeding bus tomorrow. The answer is that, on one level, the actuarial value has nothing to do with the real world, and on another, it has everything to do with it. Of course, the income beneficiary may walk in front of the bus; on the other hand, he may live far beyond his actuarial life expectancy. In either case the actual values of the life estate and remainder will be vastly different from what the tables would have predicted. But if we consider a very large number of people who make gifts of remainders, presumably everything will average out. Thus, from the point of view of the government, which deals with very large numbers of donors, the tables presumably *do* reflect the real world.

g.   Actual Income Earned versus Assumed Rates of Return

As for the objections that the rate of return selected may not be realistic, and that the value of the asset may change, we are reminded of the old riddle, "What's green, hangs on the wall, and whistles?" The answer is "a red herring." It isn't green? You could paint it green. It doesn't hang on the wall? What's to stop you from hanging it on the wall? It doesn't whistle? So it doesn't whistle. The point is that *some* assumption must be made about the rate of return or no present value calculation is possible. As for future changes in the asset value, any system which attempted to factor this in would become very complicated, and we would have the same problem selecting an appropriate rate of change as we have in selecting a rate of return. The interest rate assumptions will change as rapidly as one could wish, but will still be unreliable as predictors of actual rates of return. That the system is not perfect is something that we simply have to live with, content in the knowledge that, arbitrary or not, the system allows us to determine values, pay whatever taxes may be due as a result, and get on to other matters.

h.   Values Dependent on Joint Lives or Other Factors

One final problem is what to do if the remainder (or the donor's reversion) depends on the joint lives of two or more people, or on someone dying before she marries, or on someone dying before age 50 without children. The tables in publication 1458 provides factors for remainders following two lives as well as for one life and a term of years. In other cases, the IRS will provide the appropriate factor after consultation with its actuaries. If the donor retains an interest that is too difficult to value, the IRS presumes that such an interest has no value.

Illustrative Case

In *Smith v. Shaughnessy*, 318 U.S. 176 (1943), the decedent, who was then 72 years old, created a trust to pay the income to his 44–year-old wife for her life, and to return the property to the decedent if he was living at her death, otherwise to whomever his wife appointed in her will. In rejecting the taxpayer's argument that there was no completed gift, the Court stated: "We cannot accept any suggestion that the complexity of the property interest created by a trust can serve to defeat a tax." *Id.* at 180.

Illustrative Case

In the companion case of *Robinette v. Helvering*, 318 U.S. 184 (1943), a 30–year-old woman, contemplating marriage, created a trust reserving a life estate in herself and creating a secondary life estate in her mother and her stepfather if she should predecease them. The remainder was to go to her issue at age 21 with a further provision for the distribution of property by the last surviving life tenant if no issue existed. The mother and stepfather created similar trusts. The Court held that the transfer was subject to the gift tax and refused to deduct the value of the donor's reversion, stating:

> In this case, however, the reversionary interest of the grantor depends not alone upon the possibility of survivorship but also upon the death of the daughter without issue who should reach the age of 21 years. The petitioner does not refer us to any recognized method by which it would be possible to determine the value of such a contingent reversionary remainder. . . . But before one who gives this property away by this method is entitled to deduction from his gift tax on the basis that he had retained some of these complex strands it is necessary that he at least establish the possibility of approximating what value he holds. Factors to be considered in fixing the value of this contingent reservation as of the date of the gift would have included consideration of whether or not the daughter would marry; whether she would have children; whether they would reach the age of 21; etc.

> Actuarial science may have made great strides in appraising the value of that which seems to be unappraisable, but we have no reason to believe from this record that even the actuarial art could do more than guess at the value here in question.
>
> *Id.* at 188.

3. Life Estates and Terms of Years

A life estate is the right to receive the income from property for a period of time, measured by the life expectancy of the life tenant. A term of years is simply the right to receive the income from property for a specified number of years. The value of these interests, like the value of remainders and reversions, depends on the age of the life tenant or the specified number of years as well as the projected rate of return and the value of the property. In the case of one life tenant or a term of years, the value of the income interest is simply the value of the property minus the value of the remainder interest.

Example 2.5 Revisited Again

Don created an irrevocable trust to pay the income to Henry for five years and the remainder to Ruth. Don transferred $100,000 to the trust when the applicable federal interest rate was five percent. The value of Ruth's remainder interest is $100,000 multiplied by .783526 or $78,352.60. The value of Henry's term of years is then $21,647.40, which is the difference between the value of the property transferred ($100,000) and the value of the remainder ($78,352.60).

Example 2.6

Debra creates an irrevocable trust to pay the income to herself for her life and the remainder to Sam, her son. Debra is 50 years old at the time of the transfer. Assume that the applicable federal interest rate is three percent and that Debra transfers $1 million into the trust. Consulting Table S, we discover that the remainder factor is .43883. This means that the value of Sam's remainder is $438,830 and the value of Debra's retained life estate is $561,170. Notice that the total of the two values—the values of the remainder plus the value of the life estate—equals the amount transferred into the trust, *i.e.*, $1,000,000.

4. **Special Valuation Rule for Applicable Retained Interests: § 2702**

a. **The Problem**

The essence of a gift is the shift of beneficial interest from the donor to the recipient that diminishes the donor's estate. Taxpayers will often try to use valuation principles to avoid transfer taxation. One technique involves the use of retained income interests. If a taxpayer retains the right to income for her life, the property will be in her gross estate pursuant to § 2036(a)(1). The same is true if she retains the right to income for a term of years and dies within that term. *Id.* If the taxpayer retains the right to income for a term of years and outlives the term, nothing is in her gross estate. In that case, the property is transferred to the remainderman at the gift tax value, which might well be substantially less than its estate tax value.

Example 2.7

Debra creates an irrevocable inter vivos trust with Friendly National Bank as the trustee to pay Debra the income for 15 years and then to transfer the trust property to Debra's daughter, Helen. Debra is 70 years old and the applicable federal interest rate is five percent when she transfers $1,000,000 to the trust. The value of the remainder is $481,017. Assume that Debra's life expectancy is 15 years, but she lives for 17 years. At this time the trust has a fair market value of $3,000,000. Nothing is in Debra's gross estate and she was able to transfer that $3,000,000 to Helen at a significantly reduced tax cost.

If Debra was the trustee and had discretion to distribute the trust income to herself or to accumulate it, she could shift even greater economic benefit to Helen. The gift tax value would be the same.

---

b. **The Solution**

Congress limited the ability to shift value in this manner when it enacted § 2702. This section applies to any transfer of an interest in trust (1) to a member of the transferor's family if (2) the transferor or an applicable family member (3) retains an interest in the trust. If these conditions are met, the value of the retained interest is zero ($0) unless the interest is a qualified interest, which is one that prevents taxpayers from shifting economic benefits without paying a gift tax.

(1) **Qualified Interests**

Qualified interests are: (1) grantor retained annuity trust interests (GRATs); (2) grantor retained unitrust interests (GRUTs); and

(3) any non-contingent remainder interest if all of the other interests in the trust are GRATs and/or GRUTs.

(2) Grantor Retained Annuity Trust Interest (GRAT)

A grantor retained annuity trust interest is the right to receive a fixed amount payable not less frequently than annually. Regulation § 25.2702–3(b). The fixed amount must be a stated dollar amount or a fixed fraction or percentage of the initial fair market value of the property transferred to the trust. The fixed amount must be paid periodically, but not less frequently than annually. *Id.* The right to receive $75,000 per year payable annually would be a grantor retained annuity trust interest.

(3) Grantor Retained UniTrust Interest (GRUT)

A grantor retained unitrust interest is the right to receive a fixed percentage of the fair market value of the trust property determined annually. Regulation § 25.2702–3(c). The fixed amount must be paid periodically, but not less frequently than annually. *Id.* The right to receive six percent of the trust assets valued annually would be a grantor retained unitrust interest.

5. Annuities

a. General Principles

Annuities are valued in much the same way. An annuity is a contractual right to a specified payment for a term of years or for life. Here the question is: assuming a rate of return of x percent, how much money must be set aside today so that, using some of the principal and the income on a declining principal balance, the beneficiary will receive $1.00 a year and wind up with a zero balance at the end of the term (or upon the death of the beneficiary, as the case may be). Once again, the IRS tables in publication 1457 provide the answer.

b. Annuity for a Term of Years

Again, the example of a term of years is the simplest to understand. Let us assume that X contracts to pay Y $1.00 a year for five years. Clearly, X doesn't have to set aside the whole $5.00 because X can earn interest at, say, six percent. A six percent annuity table would tell us that in fact about $4.21 should do the trick, and the table would be correct:

Year	Interest Earned on Balance	Principal to Make up Difference	Principal Balance at Year End
0	.00	.00	4.21
1	.25	.75	3.46
2	.21	.79	2.67
3	.16	.84	1.83
4	.11	.89	.94
5	.06	.94	.00

c. **Annuity for Life**

If you needed to know how much must be set aside to pay an annuity of $1.00 a year for a beneficiary's life, you would look to a life table to find the answer. Assuming, for example, an annuitant aged 50 and a six percent interest rate, the table would tell us that about $12.95 would have to be set aside to make the $1.00 annual payments for life.

d. **Actual Lives versus Actuarial Lives**

So, you may ask: what happens when an annuitant lives beyond her life expectancy? The balance is now zero, so what happens to the payments? Well, like the batteries promoted by a drum-beating rabbit in a long-running series of television commercials, they keep going and going and going. . . . Where does the money come from to make the payments to the super-annuated annuitant? From the purchase of annuities for people who walk in front of buses. If, as in the usual case, the issuer of the annuity is in the business of selling annuities, it will be selling enough of them so that things will average out. Does an annuity begin to sound like the flip side of life insurance? It should, and you should therefore not be surprised to learn that most commercial annuities are sold by life insurance companies.

e. **Frequency of Payment**

One other issue can arise. Table S in publication 1457 provides the annuity factor only for an annuity that is paid once a year. How do you value an annuity that is paid every quarter or every month? Table K, also in publication 1457, provides an adjustment factor for these situations.

Example 2.8

Mary transfers property to Nancy in exchange for Nancy's promise to pay Mary $25,000 each quarter for the rest of Mary's life. Assume that Mary is 70 years old at the time of the exchange and that the applicable federal interest rate is four percent. The value of Mary's annuity is determined first under Table S. The annuity factor for age 70 at four percent is 10.0589. So the first step is to multiply the $25,000 payment by this factor, which produces $251,473. Because the payments are made quarterly, the tentative value of $251,473 must be multiplied by the factor from Table K for quarterly payments at four percent, which is 1.0149. This produces a final value of $255,219. If the property that Mary transferred to Nancy had a fair market value of $250,000 at the time of the transfer, there would be no gift from Mary to Nancy. Because the value of the annuity is higher than the value of the property transferred, Nancy might be considered as having made a gift of that difference to Mary. As we will see in section C.2. of chapter 3, if the annuity was negotiated at arm's length, was bona fide, and was free from donative intent, there would be no gift.

---

f.   **Lottery Payments: A Special Situation**

Assume that David wins the state lottery jackpot and is entitled to receive 25 annual payments of $100,000. David dies after receiving 10 payments; there are 15 payments remaining. How should the right to receive 15 annual payments of $100,000 be valued? The stream of lottery payments would seem to be an annuity, and courts have so held. The question is whether to value these payments under the actuarial tables if there are substantial restrictions on the owner's ability to sell, assign, or otherwise transfer the right to these payments. The regulations provide that the tables do not apply if the annuity is subject to an "other restriction." Regulation § 20.7520–3(b).

The court in *Donovan v. United States*, 2005–1 U.S.T.C. ¶ 50,322 (D. Mass. 2005) rejected the estate's argument that lottery payments subject to transfer restrictions were subject to an "other restriction" that produced an "unrealistic and unreasonable result" under the tables. The Sixth Circuit, *Negron v. United States*, 553 F.3d 1013 (6th Cir. 2009) and the Fifth Circuit, *Cook v. Commissioner*, 349 F.3d 850 (5th Cir. 2003) concurred. The Second Circuit, *Estate of Gribauskas v. Commissioner*, 342 F.3d 85 (2d Cir. 2003) and the Ninth Circuit, *Shackleford v. United States*, 262 F.3d 1028 (9th Cir. 2001) disagreed.

6. **Actuarial Valuation Tables**

    a. **General Principles**

    As we have seen, Congress has chosen to rely on presumed actuarial values for annuities, life estates, terms of years, remainders, and reversions. Because economic conditions change quickly, Congress has delegated authority to the IRS to issue a general set of tables and monthly interest rates. § 7520. The tables are updated every ten years to take into account changed mortality figures.

    b. **Exception for Certain Restrictions**

    The actuarial tables will apply to the valuation of annuities, life estates, remainders, and reversions unless that interest is "subject to any contingency, power or other restriction." Regulations §§ 20.7520–3(b)(ii), 25.7520–3(b)(ii). Restraints on transferability that do not alter the fundamental nature of the asset were ignored by the Fifth and Sixth Circuit in the lottery cases noted above. The Second and the Ninth Circuit disagreed. It is not yet clear what types of restrictions will be sufficient to require individualized valuation rather than reliance on the tables.

    c. **Exception for Terminal Illness**

    The tables will not apply "to determine the present value of an annuity, income interest, remainder interest, or reversionary interest if an individual who is a measuring life dies or is terminally ill" at the time of valuation. Regulations §§ 20.7520–3(b)(3), 25.7520–3(b)(3). An individual is considered terminally ill if there is at least a 50 percent probability that the individual will die within one year. *Id.* If the individual survives eighteen months, the presumption is that the individual was not terminally ill although this presumption can be overcome. *Id.*

7. **Exam Strategy**

When asked to value a particular asset or property interest, the first step is to determine the nature of that asset or property interest. The next step is to identify the relevant measuring life, if any. For example, assume that Donna creates an irrevocable inter vivos trust to pay the income to Joan for her life and then to distribute the trust property to Kevin. If the relevant interest is Kevin's remainder, then the measuring life is Joan. Kevin will receive the property only after Joan's death. The third step is to determine the relevant interest rate. These are published monthly and would most likely be provided in the facts of the exam question. The next step is to decide which table applies. Table B is for interests based on a term of years; Table S is for interests based on life expectancies. Finally, determine the applicable factor and multiply that factor by the value of the property interest. Because this requires access to the tables and mathematical computation, it is an unlikely question for an in-class exam.

F. BUSINESS INTERESTS

1. General Principles

Some business interests, such as stocks and bonds, are easy to value because there is an established market for these business interests. The regulations provide rules, discussed above, for their valuation. The valuation of an interest in a closely-held business is more difficult because the market approach does not usually provide an easy answer. The capitalization of income approach provides some evidence of value.

There are a number of factors that will be considered in valuing business interests that are not sold on an established market:

the company's net worth;

the tangible and intangible assets, including goodwill;

the demonstrated earning capacity of the business;

the economic outlook in general and in the particular industry;

the company's position in the industry and its management; and

the value of similar businesses.

Regulations §§ 20.2031–2(f)(2) and 3, 25.2512–2(f)(2) and (3). *See also* Revenue Ruling 59–60, 1959–1 C.B. 237.

2. Special Use Valuation

a. General Principles

Congress has provided a special valuation rule for real property used in a trade or business or farming under certain conditions. § 2032A. The policy is to protect heirs and beneficiaries who continue operating the trade or business or farm from being forced to sell that asset to pay the estate tax.

b. Location and Use of the Real Property

The real property must be located in the United States, and it must be used in trade or business or for farming. The property must have been owned by a decedent who was either a citizen or resident of the United States for five of eight years immediately before the date of decedent's death. The property must also be used in a trade or business or for farming in which the decedent or a member of the decedent's family materially participated for the same time period.

c. Qualified Heir

The property must pass to a member of the decedent's family who uses the property in trade or business or farming for ten years after decedent's death. If the heir sells the property or fails to continue the business or farming, the heir is liable for tax benefit provided by special use valuation in decedent's estate.

d. Share of the Gross Estate

At least 50 percent of the gross estate must consist of real and personal property used in the trade or business or for farming. In addition, at least 25 percent of the gross estate must consist of real property used in the trade or business or for farming.

e. Limitation on Reduction in Value

The difference in value between the highest and best use of the real property and the use in the trade or business or farming cannot exceed $1,000,000 (2009 amount as adjusted for inflation).

3. Family Limited Partnerships and Limited Liability Companies

Taxpayers often try to avoid taxation by limiting the value of the asset subject to taxation. One method is to divide the property into shares, each of which represents a minority interest in the property. If successful, each interest will be valued at a substantial discount. A popular vehicle for achieving this goal is the family limited partnership. The gift and estate tax consequences of the creation and transfer of interests in family limited partnerships is at section E.3 of chapter 8. At this point, it is only important to recognize that the family limited partnership or family limited liability company is often created only to achieve the tax savings associated with minority and lack of marketability discounts. To avoid inclusion of the underlying assets in the taxpayer's estate at death, rather than the discounted value of the partnership or limited liability company interests, there must be a *substantial nontax business purpose* for creation of the partnership or limited liability company.

4. Transfers of Business Interests: § 2701

a. General Principles

Owners of closely held business may also attempt to freeze the value of that asset during life by transferring the right to future appreciation in the business to other family members. Assume that Parent owns all of the common stock in Corporation and wants to transfer Corporation to Child but retain a flow of income from, and other rights in, Corporation. Parent can recapitalize (at no income tax cost) the Corporation so that there are now two types of stock: (1) common stock that carries with it the risks of failure and the benefits of success and (2) preferred stock that will produce a flow of income and a preference upon liquidation. Parent structures the preferred stock so that almost all the existing value of Corporation is in the preferred stock, thereby "freezing" the value of this asset in his estate. Parent then transfers the common stock to Child at no gift tax cost.

b. Applicability of § 2701

After a number of failed attempts in regulating these types of transactions, Congress finally enacted the special valuation rules in chapter 14, including § 2701. Section 2701 provides valuation rules for the transfer of interests in partnerships and corporations where the transferor retains an applicable interest. An **applicable retained interest** is a distribution right (*i.e.*, a right to a dividend) if the transferor and applicable family members own 50 percent of the value or voting control of the stock of the corporation (or 50 percent of the capital or profits interest in a partnership) immediately before the transfer. Liquidation rights, puts, calls, and conversion rights are also applicable retained interests.

c. Valuation of the Retained Interest and Junior Equity Interests

If the distribution right is not a dividend payable at a fixed rate on a periodic basis on cumulative preferred stock, its value is zero. § 2701(a)(3). The junior equity (common stock) must have a value of at least ten percent of the equity interests plus the amount of debt owed to the transferor and applicable family members. § 2701(a)(4). If dividends are not paid, the taxable gifts or the taxable estate of the transferor is increased by an amount equal to what the transferor would have received from the qualified payment plus an amount equal to what the transferor would have received had he reinvested those deemed dividends at the same rate of return. § 2701(d).

5. Buy–Sell Restrictions Disregarded: § 2703

a. General Principles

Congress also provided that any restriction on the right to sell or use property as well as any option, agreement, or right to acquire or use property at less than its fair market value will be disregarded in valuing business interests. § 2703(a). This prevents taxpayers from manipulating the value of these interests through buy-sell agreements and similar devices.

b. Exception for Bona Fide Business Arrangements

The § 2703(a) rule will not apply if: (1) the restriction is a bona fide business arrangement; (2) the restriction is not a device to transfer property to family members for less than full and adequate consideration in money or money's worth; and (3) the terms are comparable to similar arrangements between persons in an arm's length transaction. § 2703(b). Prior to the adoption of § 2703, the courts had held that buy-sell agreements would establish the value of the stock subject to that agreement only if: (1) the price was determinable from the agreement; (2) the terms of the agreement were binding both during life and at death; (3) the agreement was legally binding and enforceable; and (4) the agreement was established for bona fide business reasons and not as a testamentary substitute. *Estate of True v. Commissioner*, 390 F.3d 1210 (10th Cir. 2004). In *Estate of Amlie v. Commissioner*, 91 T.C.M. (CCH) 1017 (2006), the Tax Court held that § 2703 supplemented and did not replace the judicially created rules.

Illustrative Case

In *Estate of Amlie v. Commissioner*, 91 T.C.M. (CCH) 1017 (2006), the decedent owned stock subject to a buy-sell agreement at the time of her death. The Tax Court held that the estate had met its burden of satisfying the § 2703(b) factors as supplemented by

---

case law and, therefore, the value of the stock was determined pursuant to the buy-sell agreement. The court found that the agreement was an arm's length transaction in light of the many acrimonious disputes between decedent's children over the management of her assets. It also found a business purpose for the agreement because it guaranteed both a price and a buyer for the decedent's minority interest in bank stock. The court relied on the testimony of an attorney with extensive experience in the purchase and sale of closely held business interests who testified that this transaction was comparable to similar arrangements in other cases.

Illustrative Case

In *Estate of Blount v. Commissioner*, 428 F.3d 1338 (11th Cir. 2005), the court found that the buy-sell agreement was not binding during life because the decedent owned approximately 83 percent of the corporation, was the only person on the board of directors, and was president of the company. As the court put it, "The only parties to the contract who were needed to change it were Blount and BBC, an entity that he completely controlled." *Id.* at 1344. As a result, the buy-sell agreement did not establish the value of the stock for estate tax purposes.

Illustrative Case

In *Holman v. Commissioner*, 601 F.3d 763 (8th Cir. 2010), the court held that the § 2703(b) exception did not apply because the transfer restrictions on the partnership interests were created as a disincentive to the donor's children so that they would not sell or transfer the stock. The court found no business purpose for the restrictions.

6. **Treatment of Certain Lapsing Rights and Restrictions: § 2704**

Section 2704 provides that the lapse of voting or liquidation rights where the individual holding that right and his family control the business entity will be treated as the transfer by gift or a transfer includible in the gross estate. This prevents the taxpayer from shifting economic benefits to other family members by allowing certain rights and restrictions to lapse.

7. **Exam Strategy**

Create a flow chart. Step one is to determine which tax applies. Section 2032A special use valuation only applies to the estate tax while § 2701 only applies to the gift tax. Some principles apply to both. Step two is to determine the nature of the asset. Again some rules only apply to certain types of assets, for example, special use valuation only applies to real property and § 2701 only to interests in partnerships and corporations. Step three is to list the factors for each category. Recognize that certain principles—bona fide transaction and arm's length agreement—cut across the categories. Use analogous doctrines and always, always use the facts.

PART II

THE GIFT TAX

CHAPTER 3

DEFINITION OF A GIFT

A. DEFINITION OF A GIFT

1. Common Law

At common law, a gift occurs when the donor actually or constructively delivers property to the donee with intent to make a gift, *i.e.*, *donative intent*. This definition is far too vague and subjective to serve the purposes of the gift tax, but both prongs of the common law definition are present in the gift tax. Delivery is equivalent to the requirement of completion discussed in chapter 4. Donative intent is simply another way of determining whether or not the donor received adequate and full consideration in money or money's worth.

2. Gift Tax Definition

a. Statutory Provisions

Section 2501 imposes a tax on "the transfer of property by gift" but never defines the term "gift." The only statutory definition is provided by § 2512(b) which states: "Where property is transferred for less than an adequate and full consideration in money or money's worth, then the amount by which the value of the property exceeded the value of the consideration shall be deemed a gift." This definition has two parts. The consideration must be (1) adequate and full, and it must also be (2) in money or money's worth.

b. Purpose of the Gift Tax

The primary purpose of the gift tax is to prevent avoidance of the estate tax. Without a gift tax, taxpayers could give away their property while on their death bed and avoid the estate tax. As a result, the essence of a gift, at least for purposes of the gift tax, is a diminution of the donor's estate. As the Court in *Commissioner v. Wemyss* said, "[the gift tax is designed] to reach those transfers that are withdrawn from the donor's estate." 324 U.S. 303, 307 (1945).

A secondary purpose is to prevent avoidance of the income tax. This is why Congress did not repeal the gift tax in 2001 when it repealed the estate and generation-skipping transfer taxes.

c. Comparison of Values

To determine if a transfer is a gift, compare the value of the property transferred with the value of the consideration received. This is easier said than done when the value of the property transferred is in dispute, as it often is. Regulation § 25.2512–8 creates a safe harbor that excludes transaction *in the ordinary course of business.* See section C.

3. Income Tax Definition

a. Definition

The income tax excludes gifts and bequests from gross income. § 102. Once again, the IRC provides no definition. That task was left to the Supreme Court in *Commissioner v. Duberstein*, 363 U.S. 278 (1960), where it held that, for purposes of the income tax, a gift proceeds from "detached and disinterested generosity" or from "affection, respect, admiration, charity or like impulses." *Id.* at 285. The focus, therefore, in the income tax is on the donor and the donor's motivation.

b. Coordination with the Gift Tax

As stated in section F.2. of chapter 1, there has been little, if any, attempt to coordinate the income tax and the gift tax. The differing definitions make it possible for a transaction to be a gift for the purposes of one tax and not the other.

Illustrative Case

In *Farid–Es–Sultaneh v. Commissioner*, 160 F.2d 812 (2d Cir. 1947), the issue was the taxpayer's basis in stock. She had received the stock from her fiancé prior to their marriage to protect her in the event that they did not marry. She also released all of her marital rights, which are not consideration in money or money's worth. The court noted that the income tax was not *in pari materia*

> (upon the same subject matter) with the gift tax and held that the taxpayer's release of her rights was sufficient consideration for the contract. As a result, she had purchased her stock and was entitled to a cost basis in it rather than the donor's basis, which would have carried over to her had the transaction been a gift. § 1015.
>
> The release of marital rights is not consideration in money or money's worth for purposes of the gift tax. *Merrill v. Fahs*, 324 U.S. 308 (1945); Regulation § 25.512–8. As a result, S.S. Kresge, the fiancé in *Farid–Es–Sultaneh*, would have been liable for the gift tax. The transfer in the case, however, occurred in 1923 before enactment of the gift tax.

4.   Exam Strategy

If the question involves the gift tax, be sure to use the correct definition: a (1) transfer of (2) property (3) without adequate and full consideration (4) in money or money's worth. Focus on the value of what the transferor is giving away and the amount of the consideration that the donor receives. The consideration must be in money or its equivalent. Remember that fair market value is what a willing buyer would pay a willing seller both having reasonable knowledge of the facts and neither being under a compulsion to buy or sell.

B.   TRANSFERS OF PROPERTY

1.   General Principles

Section 2501 requires that there be (1) a transfer (2) of property. Both are required. In most situations, there is no question that the donor has made a transfer and that what the donor transferred was property. Transfers are not effective until they are complete. See chapter 4.

a.   Indirect Transfers

Transfers may be direct or they may be indirect.

> **Example 3.1**
>
> Zelda sends her nephew, Ned, $10,000. This is a direct transfer. If Ned has given Zelda nothing in return, it is a gift.

Example 3.2

Zoe transfers Blackacre to her daughter, Donna, on condition that Donna allow her brother, Bert, to live on Blackacre for his life. Zoe has made a direct gift to Donna and an indirect gift to Bert. Regulation § 25.2511–1(h)(2). Any time a transfer to one person is conditioned on performance of services for another or a transfer of property from the recipient to another there will be an indirect transfer from the original transferor to the ultimate recipient.

Example 3.3

Zach agrees to transfer Greenacre to his son, Silas, if Silas (who is an attorney) will handle his cousin's (Claire's) divorce for her. Zach has made a direct gift to Silas and an indirect gift to Claire. Regulation § 25.2511–1(h)(3).

Example 3.4

Zephyr transfers Whiteacre to Corporation and receives nothing in return. Zephyr has made a gift to the shareholders of Corporation because she has increased the value of their stock in Corporation. Regulation § 25.2511–1(h)(1).

---

b.   **Focus is on the Donor not the Recipient**

The gift tax is imposed on the act of transferring property away from the donor; it is not imposed on the receipt of the property by the donee. The gift tax is the primary and personal liability of the donor; it is an excise upon his act of making the transfer; and it is measured by the value of the property passing from the donor, not what is received by the donee. The identity of the recipient need not be known or even ascertainable at the time of the gift. Regulation § 25.2511–2(a).

Example 3.5

Mia creates an inter vivos trust and transfers $500,000 to Friendly National Bank as trustee for the benefit of her children and their

---

issue. Mia reserves no power to revoke or alter the trust. Even if Mia does not have any children at the time she creates the trust, the transfer will be considered a gift.

c. Role of State Law

State law creates property interests. Federal law taxes those interests. Whether or not a shift in economic benefit from one to another is a gift will depend on state property law.

Illustrative Case

In *Autin v. Commissioner*, 109 F.3d 231 (5th Cir. 1997), a successful business executive with an excellent reputation helped his son start a business in 1974 by incorporating the business with him. Father received 51 percent of the stock and son received 49 percent. At the same time, father signed a "counter letter and agreement to convey" that stated that father had no interest in the stock held in his name and that he would transfer those shares to his son whenever his son requested. *Id.* at 233. The purpose of the transaction was to launch the son in the marine industry in which the son had no reputation but the father did. In June 1988, when the business was well established, father transferred the stock to his son. The Fifth Circuit held that the counter letter conveyed legal rights under Louisiana law. Any gift, therefore, occurred in 1974 upon incorporation and not when the father transferred the stock to his son in 1988. The statute of limitations most likely barred any inquiry into the nature of the 1974 dealings between the father and the son. As a result, it was not clear who provided the money and other property transferred into the corporation and, thus, impossible to determine if the father had actually made a gift to the son at that time.

---

2. Transfers to Political Organizations

Section 2501(a)(4) provides that transfer of money or other property to political organizations are not transfers of property by gift. The transfer must be to an organization as defined in § 527(e)(1) of the IRC, *i.e.*, "a party, committee, association, fund, or other organization." A contribution to an individual would be a gift unless the transferor could establish that he received adequate and full consideration in money or money's worth.

See Dupont v. United States, 97 F.Supp. 944 (D. Del. 1951), where the court held that contributions to the National Economic Council were gifts. *But see Stern v. United States*, 436 F.2d 1327, 1330 (5th Cir. 1971), where the court held that political contributions were so "permeated with commercial and economic factors" that they were not gifts.

3. Qualified Transfers

Transfers directly to educational institutions for tuition and to a medical care provider or insurer are excluded from the definition of a transfer of property by gift. § 2503(e). These transfers are discussed in section G below.

4. Exam Strategy

To determine if there is a gift, first look for the transfer. There may be more than one. Some transfers will be direct; others will be indirect. The gift tax covers both. § 2511. Once you identify the actual transfer, then determine the nature of the property that is transferred. The gift tax encompasses transfers of all property, real and personal, tangible and intangible. *Id.* The donor does not need to relinquish all of her interest in the property. She can transfer a joint tenancy interest, or an interest as a tenant in common, or a life estate, or a remainder. Finally, identify the recipient. Although the gift tax is not focused on the receipt of the property, transfers to some recipients are excluded. These are political organizations, educational organizations if for tuition, and medical care and medical insurance providers. It is also important to identify the recipient for purposes of the gift tax annual exclusion, which is discussed in chapter 5.

C. BUSINESS TRANSACTIONS

1. Fair Market Value

A gift occurs when the transferor receives less than adequate and full consideration. To determine if there is adequate and full consideration, one must know the fair market value of the property transferred. Remember that fair market value is what a willing buyer would pay a willing seller both having knowledge of the relevant facts and neither being under a compulsion to buy or sell. Regulation § 25.2512–1(b). Fair market value can be established by the transaction in question, but only if the transaction is a genuine business transaction. The regulations provide that "a sale, exchange, or other transfer of property made in the ordinary course of business" is not a gift. Regulation § 25.2512–8. **A business transaction** is one that is (1) bona fide, (2) at arm's length, and (3) free from donative intent. *Id.*

2. The Ordinary Course of Business

a. Inventory Transactions

A taxpayer who sells property at a discount as part of her business does not make a gift. This is particularly true of inventory transactions, where the seller is in the business of selling this type of property.

Example 3.6

Max Merchant advertises "Televisions for $100 While Supply Lasts." Max Merchant has 50 televisions that he will sell for $100 each. Max sells Amy a television set for $100. Even though it cost Merchant $125 and he sold the television at a loss, he has not made a gift to Amy. This is a transaction in the ordinary course of Merchant's business.

The same result occurs even if Amy happens to be Max's daughter. Max was willing to sell the television set to anyone for that price. The fact that Amy is a natural object of Max's bounty is irrelevant.

Example 3.7

Dan Dealer advertises an "End of the Year Clearance Sale" on automobiles. The list price of the car is $25,000, and Dan sells the car to Ned for $21,000. If that price was the result of an arm's length negotiation, then there is no gift. This is true even though Oliver bought the same car the day before for $21,500 and Joan bought the same car the next day for $20,500. Given the nature of retail sales of automobiles, there will often be differing prices depending on who the sales person is and how strong the incentive for selling the vehicle is.

Now assume that Ned is Dan Dealer's nephew and that Dan sells the car to Ned for $17,000. He sold the same car to Oliver for $21,500 and to Joan for $20,500. In this situation, the sale to Ned at the lower price appears to be motivated by donative intent. If Dan only made that deal because of his relationship with Ned, the transaction would be in part a sale and in part a gift. See section D.1.

---

b. Other Business Transactions

The transaction does not need to be an inventory type transaction. Any transfer that is in the ordinary course of business qualifies. Regulation § 25.2512–8. This does not mean that the donor must actually be carrying on a trade or business.

Illustrative Case

In *Estate of Anderson v. Commissioner*, 8 T.C. 706 (1947), senior executives transferred common stock in the corporation to junior executives pursuant to a long-established plan. The purpose of the plan was for stock ownership to reflect management responsibility. The corporation was involved in the cotton merchandising business. The court assumed for purposes of its analysis that the stock was worth more than the junior executives had paid for it. Despite this, the court held that there was no gift. The court noted that profit-sharing plans, like the one in question in this case, were common both in the cotton merchandising business and in businesses in general. The court held that the transferor did not need to be engaged in carrying on a trade or business for the business transaction exception in regulation § 25.2512–8 to apply. The court in *Estate of Anderson v. Commissioner*, said: "Bad bargains, sales for less than market, sales for less than adequate consideration in money or money's worth are made every day in the business world, for one reason or another; but no one would think for a moment that any gift is involved, even [a gift] in the broadest sense of the term." *Id.* at 720.

---

c. Requirements

Any individual can seek refuge in the safe harbor of regulation § 25.2512–8. The transfer must be (1) bona fide, (2) at arm's length, and (3) free from donative intent.

(1) Bona Fide

A transaction is bona fide if it is, in reality, what it purports to be on paper. If there is a deed, did the recipient record it? Was title to stock transferred on the books of the corporation? Did the transferor charge interest on the promissory note? Did the transferor intend to collect on the debt? These are but a few of the questions that will be asked. See chapter 2, section A.5.a. for cases illustrating this requirement.

(2) Arm's Length

A transaction is at arm's length if the terms are similar to those that strangers to each other would negotiate. See chapter 2, section A.5.b. for cases illustrating this requirement.

(3) Free from Donative Intent

Whether or not a transfer is free from donative intent will depend on all the facts and circumstances. One of the most critical factors is the parties' relationship to each other. Another is the value of the property transferred. Asking whether or not a transfer is free from donative intent is, in essence, asking whether or not the transferor received full and adequate consideration. The issue arises most often when there is no clear fair market value established independent of the transaction under question.

Example 3.8

Olivia Owner puts her house on the market and does not use a real estate broker. Olivia has looked at the advertisements in her local newspaper, has learned what others in her area have received when they sold their houses, and has considered what she paid for the house, both originally and in improvements. She lists the house for $325,000. Bob and Betsy are the first potential buyers to view the house. They immediately offer Olivia $325,000, and she accepts. Olivia receives 20 more calls about the house, and it is possible that she could have sold the house for more than $325,000. As long as there is no donative intent involved in the transaction, there will not be a gift. Olivia was a willing seller, and Bob and Betsy are willing buyers. It is irrelevant that Olivia could have made a better deal with someone else.

---

3. Intra Family Sales

Transactions between family members are common. The presumption is that such transactions are motivated by donative intent. If Bob in example 3.8 was Olivia Owner's son, the $325,000 price would not necessarily be the fair market value. Or, to put it in other terms, the $325,000 would not necessarily be adequate and full consideration in money or money's worth.

That is not to say that intra family transfers are always gifts. Parents can sell property to children, siblings can sell property to each other, and aunts can sell property to nephews all in the ordinary course of business. The transfers are, however, subject to special scrutiny and the transferor will have the burden of establishing that the transfer is (1) bona fide, (2) at arms' length, and (3) free from donative intent.

4. Exam Strategy

If a transferor receives consideration, compare the consideration to the value of the property transferred. If the consideration does not appear to equal the value of the property transferred, consider whether the transaction falls within the business transaction exception. Examine each factor separately. Use the facts to determine if the transaction is what it purports to be (bona fide); if it was negotiated (arm's length); and if it was on terms that strangers would have made (arm's length and free from donative intent). Give intra family transactions special scrutiny; presume that these transactions are gifts. This presumption can be rebutted, but the donor has the burden of proof.

D. ADEQUATE AND FULL CONSIDERATION

Suppose Amanda owns Skyacre that has a fair market value of $100,000, and she wants to transfer Skyacre to her son, Simon. Amanda, having spent a year in law school, is aware of the gift tax and wants to avoid it. She considers herself clever and decides to sell Skyacre to Sam in a *bargain sale* for $100. She claims that she did not have *donative intent*. No gift, no tax! Amanda forgot that the law does not like manipulative schemes like this. Thus, § 25212(b) is couched in terms of consideration received by the donor not in terms of the donor's intent, donative or otherwise.

1. Part–Sale/Part–Gift

If the transferor receives no consideration at all, the transfer is a gift. § 2512(b). If the transferor receives fair market value, *i.e.*, adequate and full consideration, the transfer is not a gift. But if the transferor receives some consideration, but it is not adequate and full, the transfer is considered partly a sale and partly a gift.

Example 3.9

Ted sells Wildacre to Ken for $100,000. Is this a gift? You cannot answer that question without knowing the facts: the fair market value of Wildacre; Ted's relationship with Ken; whether or not Ted owes Ken money; and the like. Assume that the fair market value of Wildacre is

---

> $250,000 and that Ted's basis, *i.e.*, his investment, in Wildacre is $40,000. The transaction is, in part, a sale. Ted realized $100,000; his gain on the transfer is $60,000, which he must report on his income tax return. In addition, Ted has made a gift of $150,000, *i.e.*, the difference between the fair market value of the property transferred ($250,000) and the consideration received ($100,000). § 2512(b).

2. Net Gifts

a. The Transaction

Having learned that a *bargain sale* will not avoid the gift tax, Amanda decides to transfer Skyacre to her son, Simon, on condition that he pay the resulting gift tax that will be due. What Amanda did not realize is that the gift tax is a tax on the transfer of property, so she, the donor, is primarily liable for payment of the tax. Regulation § 25.2511–2(a). The payment of that obligation by someone else, in this case her son, Simon, enriches her.

b. The "Two Separate Transfers" Theory Discredited

Amanda claims that the transaction is two separate transfers, *i.e.*, a transfer of Skyacre by her to Simon followed by a second transfer by Simon to the IRS, *i.e.*, the payment of the tax. This, however, ignores the reality of the transaction. The donor transferred the property *on condition that* the recipient pay the tax. Once again, Amanda's cleverness has not allowed her to escape the gift tax.

c. Only a "Net Gift" Theory Discredited

Having lost the "it-is-two-separate-and-distinct-transfers" argument, Amanda claims that the transaction is simply one gift equal to the difference between the value of the property transferred (Skyacre) and the gift tax paid by Simon. Assume the gift tax due is $40,000. Acknowledging the detriment to Simon in paying this tax, Amanda argues that the transaction is a gift of $60,000, the difference between the fair market value of the property ($100,000) and the gift tax paid ($40,000). This again ignores the reality of the transaction. There were in fact two transfers. The transfer of Skyacre worth $100,000 from Amanda to Simon, and the transfer of $40,000 from Simon to the IRS on behalf of Amanda.

d. Part–Sale/Part–Gift

Amanda's transfer of Skyacre to Simon is really a sale in part and a gift in part. That is precisely how the Supreme Court in *Diedrich v.*

Commissioner, 457 U.S. 191 (1982), characterized a so-called "net gift" for purposes of the income tax. In that case the donor realized and recognized income equal to the difference between the amount paid to the IRS on his behalf and his basis in the property. The same characterization will apply for purposes of the gift tax.

e. Calculation of the Amount of the Gift

In example 3.9, you know both the fair market value of the property and the amount the recipient paid for it. But how do you determine the amount of the gift when the amount of the gift determines the amount of the tax and the amount of the tax determines the amount of the gift?

Example 3.10

Frank owns stock in MNO, Inc. and transfers it to his niece, Nancy, on condition that she pay the gift tax. Assume that the stock had a value of $1,000,000 and the gift tax on that amount would be $400,000. Frank has made a net gift to Nancy. The value of the gift is not $1,000,000. If the gift tax on a $1,000,000 gift was $400,000, then the net gift would only be $600,000. But if the gift is only $600,000, then the tax would not be $400,000.

This appears to be a never-ending spiral. It is broken, however, by a simply algebraic formula that says that the gift tax due is equal to the tentative tax (computed on the full fair market value of the property transferred) divided by 1 plus the rate of tax. Revenue Ruling 75–72, 1975–1 C.B. 310. Assume a flat rate of tax of 40 percent. The gift tax on the full fair market value would be $400,000. To determine the actual tax, this is divided by one plus the rate of tax, *i.e.*, 1.40 and the answer is $285,714. So the gift would be $714,286.

---

3. Exam Strategy

Identify the components of the transaction and separate them into steps. Measure the consideration flowing in each direction. The consideration paid by the recipient must flow to the donor or his benefit. Remember that the essence of a gift for purposes of the gift tax is the diminution in the donor's estate.

E. IN MONEY OR MONEY'S WORTH

Consideration must be in money or money's worth. That means that some contracts, while legally enforceable, are also gifts.

Example 3.11

Dad promises to give Son $500,000 if Son graduates from law school and passes the bar. Son, who had wanted to open his own restaurant, attends law school and passes the bar. Could Son sue Dad if Dad failed to pay? Yes, because there is a contract. Son performed his part of the bargain. He gave up his plans to open a restaurant, attended law school, and passed the bar. Is this a gift? Yes, at least for purposes of the gift tax. The consideration that Dad received is not reducible to money or money's worth. Dad's estate is diminished by the transfer of $500,000 to Son. Whether or not it is a gift for purposes of the income tax is a different question. To be excluded from Son's income by § 102, Dad's transfer must have been motivated by detached and disinterested generosity.

---

1. Love and Affection

Neither love nor affection is consideration in money or money's worth. Regulation § 25.2512–8.

Example 3.12

Mother promises to give Greenacre to Daughter if Daughter calls once a week and visits Mother once a month. Daughter does so. Mother transfers Greenacre to Daughter after five years. Is Daughter's promise to call and visit consideration? Maybe so, at least in the law of contracts. Daughter might well be able to recover if Mother failed to transfer Greenacre. But the consideration for the contract, *i.e.*, calling and visiting, cannot be reduced to money or money's worth. If the rule were otherwise, there would be wholesale avoidance of the gift and estate taxes. Every transfer would be predicated on such consideration.

---

2. Marital Rights

For the same reason, the release of marital rights is not consideration in money or money's worth. Regulation § 25.2512–8. It does not matter that those rights can be valued, transferred, or sold.

Illustrative Case

In *Commissioner v. Wemyss*, 324 U.S. 303 (1945), the taxpayer proposed marriage to Mrs. More, a widow who was receiving income from two trusts established by her prior husband. If she remarried, Mrs. More would lose that income. So the taxpayer agreed to transfer stock to her to induce her to marry him. There was a contract, but there was also a gift. The Court stated that "money consideration must benefit the donor to relieve a transfer by him from being a gift . . . [the gift tax] aims to reach those transfers which are withdrawn from the donor's estate." *Id.* at 307.

Illustrative Case

In the companion case of *Merrill v. Fahs*, 324 U.S. 308 (1945), the taxpayer agreed to set up a trust for his fiancée in exchange for her marital rights. In rejecting the argument that the fiancée paid consideration in money or money's worth, the Court relied on the change in language in the estate tax from "fair consideration" (which had been interpreted to include marital rights) to "adequate and full consideration in money or money's worth" (which had been adopted to ensure that marital rights would not be sufficient consideration for the estate tax). The Court then held that the gift tax had to be interpreted the same as the estate tax because the language was the same and the purpose of the two taxes was the same.

a. Rationale

The rationale is plain. The opposite rule would produce wholesale avoidance of the estate tax. Imagine the estate tax without a marital deduction. Alex and Beth agree that Alex will leave all of his property to Beth if she agrees to give up her marital rights. When Alex dies, Beth presents her claim in probate. It is a valid, bargained-for claim. As a result, Beth would be treated like a creditor. Because claims against the estate are subtracted to reach the taxable estate, Alex would have a zero balance in his taxable estate.

b. Marital Deduction

Of course, this concern has been eliminated by the enactment of the marital deduction, which did not exist at the time that *Commissioner v. Wemyss* and *Merrill v. Fahs* were decided. Today, a couple intending to marry should make marriage part of the consideration for the contract. That is, Alex agrees to marry Beth and transfer property to her while Beth agrees to marry Alex and release all her rights to share in his property at death or divorce. Because marriage is part of the consideration, the contract is not enforceable until the parties marry. As we will see in chapter 4, gifts are not taxed until they are complete, and gifts are not complete until the donor has given up control. In this context, that occurs when the contract is enforceable, *i.e.*, when one party could sue the other party for enforcement. Because that does not occur until marriage, the transfer is then between spouses and the marital deduction will prevent the transfer from being counted as a taxable gift. § 2523.

3.   Exam Strategy

Analyze each step in the transaction. Does any benefit flow to the donor? That benefit must be in money or property. Remember that the essence of a gift is the diminution of the donor's estate. Any consideration that does not replenish the donor's estate will not be in money or money's worth.

F.   THE LEGAL OBLIGATION OF SUPPORT

1.   Discharge of the Obligation of Support

a.   General Principles

The right to support, as opposed to the right to share in property upon death or divorce, is consideration in money or money's worth. Revenue Ruling 68–379, 1968–2 C.B. 414. A parent has a legal duty to support her child, and spouses have a legal duty to support each other. So transfers in discharge of this duty are not gifts.

b.   Same–Sex Couples

The laws of some states now allow same-sex marriage, civil unions, or domestic partnerships. It is not clear if the IRS or courts would follow state law that recognizes a duty to support in these relationships. *See* 1 U.S.C. § 7 (the Defense of Marriage Act). The usual rule that state law creates property rights and federal law taxes those rights might not apply in this situation. If so, any payment for the benefit of the other person would be a gift.

c.   Extent of Duty to Support a Spouse

Are all transfers to spouses and minor children exempt from the gift tax? Obviously not. Exactly what is encompassed in the obligation of support is a question of state law and depends on all the facts and circumstances.

> **Example 3.13**
>
> Wanda buys a $50,000 automobile and gives it to her husband, Henry, for his birthday. Is this a gift? Or is it simply the discharge of her legal obligation to support her spouse? While an automobile might well be part of the legal obligation of support, particularly if Henry is employed, it is unlikely that a $50,000 automobile is required. Because there is now an unlimited deduction for gifts between spouses (§ 2523), there is no need to determine the reach of the duty of spousal support.

d. Extent of Duty to Support Children

While the marital deduction resolves the issue of transfers between spouses, it does not apply to transfers to minor children. The gift tax annual exclusion, discussed in chapter 5, prevents litigation of the exact boundaries of the legal obligation of support. That exclusion, however, is limited in amount and does not prevent large transfers to minor children from being classified as taxable gifts.

> **Example 3.14**
>
> Pat buys a $20,000 automobile for her child, Chris, who is 17 years old. Is this a gift? Or is it part of the obligation of support? State law will determine the scope of the duty to support. If the purchase of a car is not part of that duty, it is a gift which exceeds the amount of gift tax annual exclusion.

> **Example 3.15**
>
> Paul transfers stock worth $200,000 to a trust to pay the income to his child, Carl (who is 5) until Carl is 30 years old at which time the trustee is to distribute the trust principal and any accumulated income to Carl. If Carl dies before reaching age 30, the trust property will be distributed to his estate. Paul is not the trustee. This is obviously a gift unless the trustee is required to distribute income for Carl's support.

2. Divorce

The legal obligation to support a spouse terminates upon divorce. Divorce also requires the couple to split their property. If release of marital rights is not consideration for a prenuptial agreement, is it consideration at divorce? Surely, the same principles would apply.

Illustrative Case

In *Harris v. Commissioner*, 340 U.S. 106 (1950), the Court noted that a court determination of property rights would not result in a gift tax because the obligation was a legal one imposed by the court. If the parties had, however, voluntarily agreed to separate their property without any recourse to the court, then an unequal exchange would have resulted in a gift. Of course, the parties in this case had an agreement and their agreement was submitted to the state court for approval. The parties also provided that their agreement would survive any decree. As a result, there were two grounds for enforcement—the decree and the agreement. The Court held that the divorce decree in this case determined the resolution of the property interests and, as a result, there were no gift tax consequences.

---

a.   **Section 2516**

Congress has resolved this issue for all taxpayers who follow the rules of § 2516. That section provides that a settlement of marital or property rights as well as payment of support for minor children will be excluded from the gift tax. Section 2516 requires (1) a written agreement and (2) divorce within one year before the agreement is signed or within two years after it is signed. Careful planning should ensure that divorcing couples satisfy the requirements of this section. Section 2516 does not, however, shield all transfers from the gift tax.

Illustrative Case

In *Spruance v. Commissioner*, 60 T.C. 141 (1973), the taxpayer created a trust for the benefit of his ex-wife and their children. The trust was to pay income to the ex-wife and the children. On the death of the taxpayer and his ex-spouse, the trust property would be distributed to the children. The IRS determined that there was a gift to the children equal to the difference between the value of the property transferred to the trust and value of the income interests transferred to the ex-wife and the minor children. The Tax Court affirmed, holding that there was insufficient evidence to

---

> support the argument that the ex-wife had bargained away some of her rights in exchange for the ultimate transfer to the children. (That argument did prevail in *Leopold* as we will see in section E.4. of chapter 13.)

3. Exam Strategy

Identify the parties to the transfer and determine their relationship. Does state law impose a duty to support? What is the extent of that duty? In a divorce, apply § 2516. Remember that § 2516 does not shield all transfers in the divorce context from the gift tax; it only applies to spousal maintenance, child support, and the division of property pursuant to the agreement.

G. QUALIFIED TRANSFERS

Section 2503(e) excludes qualified transfers from the statutory definition of a gift. **Qualified transfers** are (1) transfers to educational organizations for tuition and (2) transfers to medical care providers and to insurance companies for medical insurance. Only transfers paid directly to providers qualify. If the transferor reimburses an individual for such expenses, that transfer will be a gift.

1. Tuition Paid to an Educational Organization

Section 2503(e) only excludes tuition paid directly to an educational organization. This does not include amounts paid for room and board, books, supplies, or expenses that are not direct tuition costs. Regulation § 25.2503–6(b)(2). The educational organization must be one that maintains a regular faculty and curriculum and that has a regularly enrolled group of students in attendance at the place where the educational activities are regularly carried on. *Id.*

2. Medical Expenses and Insurance Premiums

Section 2503(e) also excludes payments for medical care, as defined and limited by § 213(d). This includes payments for the diagnosis, cure, mitigation, treatment, or prevention of disease, or for the purpose of affecting any structure or function of the body. Regulation § 25.2503–6(b)(3). It also includes medical insurance premiums. *Id.* The exclusion does not apply to amounts paid for by insurance or amounts that are sent to the individual to reimburse him for such expenditures.

3. Transfers for Support

All other transfers for support, *i.e.,* food, clothing, shelter, and the like, are gifts as long as the donor does not have a legally enforceable obligation to support the recipient. While the gift tax annual exclusion might shelter some of these payments, often the total of such payments exceeds the limit of that exclusion.

Example 3.16

Jane's daughter, Chloe, recently graduated from college and moved to Big City. Jane pays Chloe's rent ($1,500 per month), utilities ($200 per month), and food ($500 per month) for one year. The rent alone, $18,000 per year, exceeds the amount of the gift tax annual exclusion in 2009. Because Jane does not have a legal obligation to support Chloe, any excess over the amount of the gift tax annual exclusion is a taxable gift.

Illustrative Case

In *Estate of Cavett v. Commissioner*, 79 T.C.M. (CCH) 1662 (2000), decedent and his companion resided and traveled together. They had a loving relationship but never married. While decedent paid all the bills, the companion managed the household, made all travel arrangements, and arranged entertainment. The court held that the transactions were gifts, not compensation for services because it found that the relationship "resembled that of a successful marriage and not an employment relationship" and that the companion's services were motived "from love and affection and not from any expectation of profit." *Id.* at 1667. Although this was a gift tax case, the parties agreed that the test was whether or not the transfer proceeded from "detached and disinterested generosity" and "out of affection, respect, admiration, charity or like impulses." *Id.* at 1667 (citing *Commissioner v. Duberstein*, 363 U.S. 278, 285 (1960)). That, of course, is the income tax definition of a gift, not the gift tax definition.

Whether or not the result in *Estate of Cavett* would have been different had the court applied the gift tax definition is not clear. To exclude the transfers, the court would have had to find that they were, in essence, business transactions. There was no bargained for exchange in the case, and it was clear that many of the transfers resulted from donative intent. So the result would probably have been the same.

H. BELOW–MARKET LOANS

1. General Principles

One way to provide an economic benefit is to allow someone to use property without paying for that use. In Example 3.16, assume that Jane owned a condominium in Big City and she allowed Chloe to stay there without paying rent. Jane can provide the same benefit to Chloe through the rent-free use of property as she can by paying her rent.

Example 3.17

Jason lends his son, Cyril, $10,000,000 and does not charge any interest. Cyril invests the money and earns a 5 percent rate of return. Cyril has $500,000 of income. Jason has shifted that benefit to Cyril.

Illustrative Case

When the interest-free loan was a demand loan, *i.e.*, one that the lender could recall at any time, courts initially refused to find a gift. In *Dickman v. Commissioner*, 465 U.S. 330 (1984), however, the Supreme Court acknowledged that the transfer was not of the property itself but of an interest in property, *i.e.*, the right to use that property. The Court analogized the interest-free loan to the rent-free use of real property and held that the right to use the money without paying interest was, in fact, a gift.

---

2. Section 7872

Congress responded to the *Dickman* case by enacting § 7872. This section applies to gift loans, to loans from employers to employees, to loans from a corporation to a shareholder, and to any loan that is motivated by tax avoidance. It treats all gift loans as if they were demand loans, and it imputes two transfers equal to the amount of forgone interest. The amount of foregone interest is determined by the applicable federal interest rate. The first transfer is a gift from the Lender to the Borrower. The second transfer is an imputed payment of interest from the Borrower to the Lender. The transfers are deemed to occur on the last day of the calendar year in which the loan is outstanding. Loans between individuals that do not exceed $10,000 are excluded.

> **Example 3.17 Revisited**
>
> Same facts as example 3.17. In this situation § 7872 would impute a transfer from Jason to Cyril equal to the amount of the forgone interest. Forgone interest is computed based on the applicable federal rate compounded semiannually. This first transfer is a gift from Jason to Cyril. Section 7872 also imputes a transfer from Cyril to Jason of the same amount. This would be interest income to Jason.

3.   Exam Strategy

If the transaction is a loan of money, apply § 7872 to impute transfers from the borrower to the lender and vice versa. If the transaction is the loan of other property or the rent-free use of property, apply the general principles of *Dickman*. The lender or the owner of the property would be the donor.

I.   SHIFTING ECONOMIC BENEFITS

It is possible to shift economic benefits through a variety of techniques. *Dickman* and § 7872 have closed one loophole. The valuation rules in §§ 2701 to 2702 have closed others. See sections E.4. and F.4. of chapter 2. Other possibilities remain.

1.   Waiver of Fees or Commissions

An executor or a trustee is entitled to payment for services rendered. The failure to collect that payment would be a gift to the residuary estate or the trust beneficiaries. If, however, the executor or trustee waives the right to fees before, or within a reasonable time after beginning to serve, that waiver does not result in a gift. Revenue Ruling 70–237, 1970–1 C.B. 13; Revenue Ruling 66–167, 1966–1 C.B. 20. One does not need to charge for one's services, and the performance of gratuitous services is not a gift. See section J.

2.   Allowing the Statute of Limitations to Run on a Loan

A creditor has the right to the return of principal as well as interest. If the debtor has the resources to repay the loan and the creditor allows the statute of limitations to run without suing for payment, the creditor has made a gift to the debtor. *Estate of Lang v. Commissioner*, 613 F.2d 770 (9th Cir. 1980); Revenue Ruling 81–264, 1981–2 C.B. 185.

3.   Failure of Closely–Held Corporation to Pay Dividends

If a closely-held (family) corporation has more than one class of stock, the failure to pay dividends can shift economic benefits from one group of stockholders (usually shareholders of preferred stock) to another (usually shareholders of common stock). The courts have refused to second guess the business judgment of boards of directors when dividends are not paid on preferred stock. *Daniels v. Commissioner*, 68 T.C.M. (CCH) 1310 (1994); *Hutchens Non–Marital Trust v. Commissioner*, 66 T.C.M. (CCH) 1599 (1993). As a result, the failure to pay dividends is not a gift. Sections 2701 and 2704 might apply however.

4. Failure to Redeem or Convert Stock

A shareholder might have the right to convert preferred stock to common stock or the right to require the corporation to redeem her stock. The shareholder's failure to assert such rights can shift economic benefits to other shareholders. In *Snyder v. Commission*, 93 T.C. 529 (1980), the court held that the failure to convert preferred stock with a noncumulative dividend to preferred stock with a cumulative dividend resulted in a gift to the common shareholders.

5. Exam Strategy

Analyze the transaction to determine if there is a possible shift of economic benefit. Does someone benefit if the donor acts or refrains from acting? If there is a business purpose to the donor's actions, or failure to act, then there will most likely not be a gift. Apply the three-part business transactions test: (1) bona fide; (2) arm's length; and (3) free from donative intent.

J. GRATUITOUS SERVICES

Section 2501 applies the tax only to the transfer *of property*. Performing services without a charge is, therefore, not a gift.

Illustrative Case

In *Commissioner v. Hogle*, 165 F.2d 352 (10th Cir. 1947), the taxpayer was a stockbroker who established trusts for the benefit of his children. The taxpayer bought and sold stocks for the benefit of the trust. The court held that the taxpayer had not made gifts to the trusts of the value of his services even though his activities were such that any income generated by his activities was taxed to him rather than the trust.

---

1. Shifting Economic Benefits

The failure to tax gratuitous services allows taxpayers to shift economic benefits and opportunities to their children and other natural objects of their bounty. Dad consults with Daughter about her business. Mother drafts an estate plan for Son. Uncle paints Niece's house. Aunt represents Nephew in his divorce. In some cases, the benefit can be significant. Taxing these events, however, raises very difficult issues of valuation and, at the bottom line, a judgment of what the taxpayer should have charged for their services.

2.   What Is Property?

The line between property and services is not always clear. Assume that Mom has an idea for a novel that she tells her Son. He writes the novel; it is published; and it is made into a movie. Son receives significant royalties. Has Mom transferred property to Son? Dad operates a successful cosmetics company and has an idea of a new line of cosmetics. Dad tells Daughter, and Daughter creates a separate company to develop the new line of cosmetics. Has Dad transferred property to Daughter?

A patent or a copyright is a property right. A trade secret is also protected by the law and would most likely be treated as property. It is not clear, however, when an idea becomes sufficiently definite to merit legal protection. As a result, there will be many opportunities to shift economic benefits without paying a gift tax.

3.   Exam Strategy

A donor can shift economic benefits, free from the gift tax, by performing gratuitous services. Contracts create property rights and may, therefore, create gift tax consequences. Drawing the line between property and services is difficult so reason by analogy if necessary.

K. DISCLAIMERS

1.   In General

Taxpayers can also shift economic benefits by refusing to accept an interest in property. Mom bequeaths her property to Son. Son does not need the property and knows that if he disclaims that property will pass to his Child. Even though Son's disclaimer ensures that Child receives Mom's property, Son is not the transferor for purposes of the gift tax if the requirements of § 2518 are met.

2.   Section 2518 Requirements

Section 2518 requires that:

(a)   the disclaimer must be an irrevocable and unqualified refusal to accept an interest in property;

(b) the disclaimer must be written;

(c) the disclaimer must be received by the transferor, the transferor's legal representative, or the person who holds title to the property within nine months of (1) the transfer or (2) age 21.

(d) the disclaimant not accept any interest in or benefit from the property; and

(e) the property pass without direction by the disclaimant.

3. Post–Mortem Planning

Disclaimers are often used for post-mortem estate planning, particularly to save estate taxes. A disclaimer may, however, create a generation-skipping transfer. See section D.5.a. of chapter 17.

Illustrative Case

In *Estate of Monroe v. Commissioner*, 124 F.3d 699 (5th Cir. 1997), Louisa Monroe died at age 91 survived by her husband, Edgar, but no children. She had a multimillion dollar estate that was left in part to her husband and in part to 31 family members, employees and friends. Edgar was concerned about the impact of the federal estate and generation-skipping transfer taxes on the estate and the beneficiaries. At Edgar's behest, his nephew, Robert, suggested to 29 of the beneficiaries that they disclaim their interests and they did so. Robert was very careful to inform each beneficiary that their renunciation had to be voluntary and without consideration. Nonetheless, many of the beneficiaries testified at trial that they expected Edgar to "take care of" them.

The Tax Court held that 28 of the disclaimers were not unqualified because the beneficiaries were induced or coerced into executing the disclaimers for consideration, *i.e.*, an implied promise that they would be better off if they did so. The Fifth Circuit reversed and remanded because the Tax Court had misinterpreted the meaning of the term "unqualified" in § 2518. The court noted that "a primary purpose of the law authorizing qualified disclaimers is to facilitate post-mortem estate tax planning and to increase family wealth on the 'expectation' that there will thus remain more wealth to pass on to disclaimants in the future." *Id.* at 709. The court held that a disclaimer was qualified only if the disclaimant had received actual bargained-for consideration and that the expectation of a future benefit was not such consideration.

---

4. Partial Interests

An individual can disclaim an undivided portion of an interest in property. § 2518(c). The undivided portion must be either a specific pecuniary amount or a fraction or percentage of the property.

Example 3.18

Tom bequeathed $500,000 to Melvin and 600 shares of stock in X, Inc. to Ned. Melvin disclaims $200,000 and Ned disclaims 400 shares of stock. If all the other requirements of § 2518 are met, Melvin's and Ned's disclaimers are valid. Regulation § 25.2518–3(c), –3(d) (Ex. 1).

Example 3.19

Tom bequeathed Blackacre to Faith and Greenacre to Hope. Faith disclaimed 100 of the 500 acres in Blackacre and Hope disclaimed a one-half interest in Greenacre. If all the other requirements of § 2518 are met, Faith's and Hope's disclaimers are valid. Regulation § 25.2518–3(b), –3(d) (Ex. 3 and Ex. 4).

---

5. Life Estates and Remainders

An individual may disclaim a life estate or a remainder interest if that is the only interest the individual receives. If an individual is given a fee interest in property, the disclaimer of a life estate is not a qualified disclaimer because the individual still owns the remainder interest. Regulation § 25.2518–3(d) (Ex. 3). The reverse is also true. If an individual is given a fee interest in property, the disclaimer of a remainder interest is not a qualified disclaimer because the individual still owns a life estate in the property. Regulation § 25.2518–3(b).

6. Joint Tenancy Interests

An individual may disclaim a survivorship interest in property held in joint tenancy.

Example 3.20

Roger and Evan own Skyacre as joint tenants with the right of survivorship. Either may sever the joint tenancy unilaterally under state

---

law. Roger dies on May 1. On September 1, Evan sends a letter to the executor of Roger's estate disclaiming the one-half interest from Roger. Assuming the other requirements of 2518 are met, the disclaimer is valid. Regulation § 25.2518–2(c)(6).

7. Exam Strategy

The intended recipient does not need to accept property or even a power to appoint. If § 2518 applies, the disclaimant will not be the transferor. If the relevant document (will, trust, etc.) does not designate where the property goes, state law will do so. A disclaimer could create generation-skipping transfer tax consequences. See chapter 17.

CHAPTER 4

COMPLETION

A. GENERAL PRINCIPLES

1. The Rule

A gift occurs when the donor delivers the property—actually, constructively, or symbolically—to the recipient with the intention of making a gift. This is the common law definition of a gift. The gift tax incorporates the concept of delivery in the requirement of completion.

A gift is not taxed until it is complete. A gift is complete when the donor has "so parted with dominion and control as to leave in him no power to change the disposition, whether for his own benefit or the benefit of another." Regulation § 25.2511–2(b). A gift is incomplete not only when the donor can revoke it, but also whenever the donor can change the beneficial interest among beneficiaries even if he cannot benefit himself.

2. The Rationale

The gift tax is imposed on the transfer of property. The donor is primarily liable. If the donor does not pay the gift tax, the beneficiary must do so. It would be unfair to make a beneficiary pay the gift tax if the donor could then turn around and give the property to someone else.

3. Federal Law Is Controlling

Federal law controls whether or not a gift is complete even though state law creates the property interests that are taxed and even though state property law requires delivery. *See Wells Fargo Bank New Mexico, N.A. v. United States*, 319 F.3d 1222 (10th Cir. 2003). The rules governing when a gift is complete are not found in the Internal Revenue Code but rather in the regulations at § 25.2511–2(b) through 2(j) and in case law.

4. Coordination With the Estate Tax and the Income Tax

a. Estate Tax

The primary purpose of the gift tax is to prevent evasion of the estate tax. Both tax the gratuitous transfer of property. Although the gift tax and the estate tax are *in pari materia* (about the same subject matter), there is not complete symmetry.

85

(1) Incomplete Transfers

If a transfer is incomplete, the property interest will be included in the gross estate. There is symmetry between the gift tax (there is none) and the estate tax (it is imposed) in these situations.

Example 4.1

Don creates a revocable trust with Friendly National Bank as Trustee to pay the income to Angela for her life and the remainder to Fanny. The transfer of property into the trust is not a completed gift because Don can change the beneficial ownership and even get the property back. *Burnet v. Guggenheim*, 288 U.S. 280 (1933); Regulation § 25.2511–2(b). If Don does not revoke, the trust property will be in his gross estate. § 2038.

---

(2) Completed Transfers

The opposite is not necessarily true; some completed gifts are brought back into the gross estate.

Example 4.2

Dora buys Wildacre, taking title as joint tenants with the right of survivorship with her daughter, Kera. Dora pays the entire purchase price; Kera provides none of the consideration. There is a completed gift of an undivided one-half interest in Wildacre. When Dora dies, however, the entire date-of-death value of Wildacre will be in her gross estate because she provided all of the consideration. § 2040(a). There is not a double tax because the calculation of the estate tax gives full credit for the prior completed gift. § 2001(b); see chapter 16 and Appendix A.

---

b. Income Tax

Although the gift tax also prevents evasion of the income tax, there has been no significant attempt to coordinate these two taxes.[1] The

---

1. Section 2511(c), adopted in 2001, is the exception. When Congress repealed the estate tax, it realized the potential for income tax avoidance. So it retained the gift tax. It also provided that the grantor trust rules, §§ 671–679, would then determine if a gift was complete for purposes of the gift tax. The future of § 2511(c) is uncertain.

rules in §§ 671–691 dictate when an individual will be taxed as the owner of the income generated by a trust. In some situations, the transfer of property does not relieve the donor of income tax liability and the gift is an incomplete gift. The revocable trust example, above, is one such situation. Don will be taxed on the income from the trust (§ 676), even if it is distributed to someone else. That distribution, of course, will be treated as a completed gift because Don has no power to change the disposition once that income has been paid to another beneficiary. In other situations, the transferor is treated as the income owner even though the transfer is complete.

Example 4.3

Greg creates an irrevocable, inter vivos trust with Friendly National Bank as Trustee to pay the income to Ralph for his life. At Ralph's death, the trust property will be distributed to Greg. Because Greg has no control over the return of the property (it will happen only when Ralph dies), Greg has made a completed gift of the income interest. If his reversion exceeds five percent of the value of trust, the income will be taxed to Greg. § 673.

B. SPECIFIC CASES

1. Outright Gifts

A gift of cash or property is complete whenever the donor gives up the right to have the property returned. Regulation § 25.2511–2(b). Usually, this is when the donor has actually delivered the property to the recipient.

2. Real Property

A gift of real property is not complete until title passes to the recipient. State law determines whether this happens when the deed is delivered or when the deed is recorded. *See, e.g., Estate of Stewart v. Commissioner*, 92 T.C.M. (CCH) 357 (2006) (gift completed under New York law when deed was delivered, not when recorded); *Estate of McRae v. Commissioner*, 30 B.T.A. 1087 (1934) (gift completed under California law when deed was delivered to recipient even though recipient did not record deed for 10 years); *Estate of Whitt v. Commissioner*, 751 F.2d 1548 (11th Cir. 1985) (under Alabama law, gift was not completed until deed was recorded). Signing a deed without delivery, however, does not transfer title. As a result, there is not a completed gift. *Estate of Mortimer v. Commissioner*, 17 T.C. 579 (1951).

3. Joint Tenancies and Tenancies in Common

The creation of a joint tenancy is a completed gift when title passes. If the property is real property, state law determines whether the gift is complete upon delivery of the deed or upon recording. The creation of a joint tenancy in personal property will depend both on the nature of the personal property and on state law. The same rules apply to the creation of tenancies in common. Even though the creation of a joint tenancy is a completed gift, some or all of the value of the property will be included in the gross estate of the donor under § 2040. See chapter 7. The gross estate will, however, only include the value of the decedent's interest in property held as tenants in common under § 2033. See chapter 6.

4. Joint Bank Accounts

The creation of a joint bank account is a revocable transfer because either joint owner can withdraw the entire amount on deposit. As a result, the creation of a joint bank account is not a completed gift until the funds are withdrawn. Regulation § 25.2511–1(h)(4).

Example 4.4

Jim deposits $50,000 into a joint bank account with Ellen on December 1. Ellen withdraws $20,000 on January 15. Jim has made a gift to Ellen because she has not paid any consideration. The gift is complete on January 15 because Jim can no longer change the beneficial ownership. Before that date, he could legally withdraw all the funds on deposit without liability to Ellen.

---

5. Prenuptial Agreements

a. General Principles

Because marital rights are not consideration in money or money's worth, the transfer of property pursuant to a prenuptial agreement is a gift. When that gift is completed depends on the terms of the agreement as well as state law. In most cases, prenuptial agreements are either explicitly made contingent on marriage (*i.e.*, mutual promises to marry) or are enforceable only on marriage (because release of marital rights is the consideration). Any gift, therefore, becomes complete on the date of marriage.

Example 4.5

Brad agrees to transfer $250,000 of stock to Mona, and Mona agrees to release all of her rights to share in Brad's property on death or divorce. They sign the agreement on November 15 and marry on January 2. Assume that the agreement is only valid upon marriage. Because the release of marital rights is not consideration in money or money's worth, Brad has made a gift to Mona. Regulation § 25.2512–5; *Merrill v. Fahs*, 324 U.S. 308 (1945). Even if Brad does not transfer the stock until two years after their marriage, the gift is still complete at the time they marry. *Estate of Copley v. Commissioner*, 15 T.C. 17 (1950); Rev. Rul. 69–347, 1969–1 C.B. 227. The prenupital agreement is enforceable once they marry. Once Brad's legal obligations are fixed, the gift is complete.

---

b. Marital Deduction

If the gift occurs once the parties are married, it qualifies for the gift tax marital deduction. § 2523. In rare cases, an agreement might be enforceable prior to marriage. In such cases, the gift would not qualify for the marital deduction because the parties are not married at that time. § 2523(a).

C. PROMISES

1. In General

A mere promise does not create a gift or a contract.

Example 4.6

On September 25, Peter tells Margery that he will send her $20,000. Peter never does so. He has not made a completed gift because he has not parted with dominion and control over the money. Margery cannot sue Peter and recover because there is no contract.

Assume that Peter makes the promise on September 25 but does not give her the money until the following February 1. The gift is completed on February 1 when Peter actually gives Margery the money. At that time he has given up control over the money.

Illustrative Case

In *Bradford v. Commissioner*, 34 T.C. 1059 (1960), J.C. and Eleanor were married. J.C. worked in investment banking and securities and his partnership was a member of the New York Stock Exchange. J.C. owed American National Bank $305,000. When the New York Stock Exchange adopted a rule requiring all members to disclose their indebtedness, the bank agreed to substitute a promissory note signed by Eleanor for $205,000 of the debt. At the time Eleanor signed the promissory note, her net worth was only $15,780, of which $12,000 consisted of equity in the family home. She was not employed and her only source of income or wealth was her husband. The bank was aware of Eleanor's financial situation and, in fact, continued to look to J.C. to repay the debt. The Tax Court, emphasizing the practical nature of the tax, held that Eleanor did not make a completed gift to J.C. at the time she signed the promissory note. Her act was simply a promise to pay in the future if the bank demanded payment from her.

---

2. Contracts

A promise can become a contract. Consideration for the contract need not be in money or money's worth. As a result, some contracts can result in gifts. A transfer of property, *i.e.*, a gift, in this situation is complete when the contract becomes legally enforceable.

Example 4.7

When Son is 15, Dad promises to pay Son $25,000 if Son does not smoke before age 21. Son performs his part of the bargain and does not smoke. When Son turns 21, Dad transfers the $25,000 to him. The gift is complete at this time. Revenue Ruling 79–384, 1979–2 C.B. 344.

Assume that Dad did not pay Son until Son turned 23. The gift was complete when Son turned 21. He could have sued Dad to enforce the contract. Even though the actual transfer did not occur until Son was 23, the gift was complete when he turned 21.

---

3. Employee Death Benefit

Employers often provide benefits to the family of an employee who dies. The estate tax consequences are discussed at section C of chapter 9. If carefully structured, this benefit can avoid the estate tax. If it is not included in the employee's gross estate, will the benefit be subject to the gift tax? In other words, has the employee made a transfer of property, *i.e.*, the death benefit, to his spouse? If an employee had his employer send one-half his paycheck each month to the employee's mother, there would be no question that the employee has made a gift to his mother unless he is repaying a loan, paying for the purchase of property, or has received adequate and full consideration in money or money's worth from his mother.

Illustrative Case

In *Estate of DiMarco v. Commissioner*, 87 T.C. 653 (1986), the decedent began working at IBM in 1950. He married in 1953. He was still employed by IBM at his death in 1979. IBM adopted a plan in 1934 that provided group term life insurance and an uninsured and unfunded survivor's income benefit. With the exception of the top 30 executives, all IBM employees, including decedent, were automatically covered by the plan. Employees could not designate the recipient of the survivor's income benefit; only spouses, dependent children, and dependent parents would receive this benefit. Decedent died while still working for IBM, and IBM paid his spouse the survivor's income benefit that was equal to three times his annual compensation. The Tax Court held that decedent did not make a gift of this benefit to his spouse. Until he died, there was no certainty that the benefit would be paid. And death, as the court held, does not make the gift complete. The court relied on regulation § 25.2511–2(f) which provides: "The relinquishment or termination of a power to change the beneficiaries of transferred property, occurring otherwise than by the death of the donor (the statute being confined to transfers by living donors) [is a completed gift]."

D. PROMISSORY NOTES

A promise to make a gift in the future does not necessarily become enforceable when written. If a promissory note is merely a promise to pay in the future, it is not a completed gift when signed. Revenue Ruling 67–396, 1967–2 C.B. 351. The promissory note does become a completed gift when it is paid or negotiated for value. *Id.* If the promissory note is legally binding, *i.e.*, it was given in exchange for property or services, there is a completed gift when that note is gratuitously transferred to another. Revenue Ruling 84–25, 1984–1 C.B. 191.

Illustrative Case

In *Bradford v. Commissioner*, 34 T.C. 1059 (1960), J.C. and Eleanor were married. J.C. worked in investment banking and securities and his partnership was a member of the New York Stock Exchange. J.C. owed American National Bank $305,000. When the New York Stock Exchange adopted a rule requiring all members to disclose their indebtedness, the bank agreed to substitute a promissory note signed by Eleanor for $205,000 of the debt. Even though Eleanor has signed a promissory note, the court held that there was no completed gift. Under the specific facts of that case, the bank did not expect her to pay on the note and, instead, looked to J.C. and the security he had originally given the bank for payment.

E. CHECKS

1. The Rule

A gift by check is not completed until the check is paid, certified, accepted by the drawee bank, or negotiated for value to a third person. Revenue Ruling 67–396, 1967–2 C.B. 351. Until that happens, the payor can stop payment on the check and thus control whether or not the recipient will in fact receive the funds.

Example 4.8

Aunt sends Niece a check on December 23. Niece receives the check on December 27 and deposits it in her bank on December 30. The check clears Aunt's bank on January 3. Because Aunt could have stopped payment on the check up until January 3, the gift would not be complete until that date.

Donors usually expect that those gifts are complete when the check is sent not when it clears their bank. This rule presents problems for donors who make gifts by check at the end of the calendar year and expect those gifts to qualify for that year's gift tax annual exclusion.

2. The Relation–Back Doctrine

a. General Principles

The relation-back doctrine allows a donor to treat a gift by check as made when sent, not when it clears the bank, but only if certain conditions are met. This doctrine first appeared in the context of the income tax deduction for charitable donations. *Estate of Spiegel v. Commissioner*, 12 T.C. 524 (1949). The doctrine was extended to the estate tax where checks were given for charitable donations. *Estate of Belcher v. Commissioner*, 83 T.C. 227 (1984). In both situations, the donor or his estate would have been entitled to a charitable deduction.

b.   Application to the Gift Tax

Historically, no deduction was allowed if a donor made gifts to family members at the end of the year and the gift checks did not clear the donor's bank until the new year. Nonetheless, the court in *Metzger v. Commissioner*, 38 F.3d 118 (4th Cir. 1994), applied the relation back doctrine to gifts to family members. The IRS has acquiesced. Revenue Ruling 96–56, 1996–2 C.B. 161.

c.   Requirements

The relation-back doctrine will apply to gifts by check to non-charitable recipients if the following conditions are met:

1.   The check was deposited, cashed, or presented in the calendar year for which completion is sought and within a reasonable time of issuance;

2.   The donor intended to make a gift;

3.   The delivery of the check was unconditional;

4.   The donor was alive when the check was paid by the drawee bank; and

5.   The check was paid by the drawee bank when it was first presented for payment.

Revenue Ruling 96–56, 1996–2 C.B. 161.

F.   REVOCABLE TRUSTS

1.   The Rule

The transfer of property to a revocable trust is not a completed gift because the donor has not given up dominion and control over the property. *Burnet v. Guggenheim*, 288 U.S. 280 (1933); Regulation

§ 25.2511–2(b). The trust document will usually specify whether or not it is revocable. If not, state law will control. Some states presume that a trust is revocable unless it specifically indicates otherwise; in other states the presumption is the opposite.

The date-of-death value of property in a revocable trust will be included in the decedent's gross estate. § 2038.

2. Transfers From Revocable Trusts to Others

Transfers from revocable trusts to individuals other than the donor will be completed gifts. Once the trustee has made the distribution, the donor cannot retract it.

Example 4.9

Barry transfers $500,000 to Friendly National Bank as Trustee to pay the income to Cheryl for 10 years and then to distribute the trust property (principal) to Norman. Barry reserves the right to revoke the trust at any time. Because of this reserved right, Barry has not made any completed gifts when he transfers the money to the trustee.

When Friendly National Bank as trustee distributes $6,500 to Cheryl on March 1, Barry has made a completed gift at that time to Cheryl. That gift will qualify for the gift tax annual exclusion. See chapter 5.

---

3. Release of Right to Revoke

The release of the right to revoke will make the gift complete. Once Barry has given up the right to revoke, he can no longer change the beneficial ownership. Regulation § 25.2511–2(f).

G. RETAINED INTERESTS

1. Powers Held by the Donor

A gift is incomplete, not just when the donor can revoke it, but any time that the donor can change the beneficial ownership. Regulation § 25.2511–2(b). "A gift is also incomplete if and to the extent that a reserved power gives the donor the power to name new beneficiaries or to change the interests of the beneficiaries as between themselves." Regulation § 25.2511–2(c). Each interest in a trust must be reviewed separately because one interest might be a completed gift while another might not.

Example 4.10

John created an inter vivos, irrevocable trust and transferred $1 million to Friendly National Bank as trustee to pay the income to Linda for her life. At Linda's death, the trustee is to distribute the trust property (principal) to Linda's children. John reserved the power to add or delete remainder beneficiaries other than himself, but he could not change the income beneficiary. The gift of the income interest to Linda is a completed gift. John has given up all dominion and control over that property interest. The trust is irrevocable, and John has not reserved any power over the income. The remainder, however, is not a completed gift. Although the trust is irrevocable and John could not become a remainder beneficiary, he still has control over the trust property. He can determine who will receive that property. As a result, the gift of the remainder is incomplete.

Example 4.11

Jane created an inter vivos, irrevocable trust and transferred $1 million to Friendly National Bank as trustee to pay the income to Melvin for his life and the remainder to Luke. Jane retained the power to terminate the trust. At termination, the trust property will be distributed to Luke. The gift of the income interest is incomplete. Jane can change the beneficial enjoyment of that interest by terminating the trust. Regulation § 25.2511–2(c). The gift of the remainder interest, however, is complete. Jane cannot change Luke's interest. If she terminates the trust, the property will be distributed outright to Luke. His remainder interest will become a fee simple interest. The ability to alter the time or manner of enjoyment of the property does not make the gift incomplete. Regulation § 25.2511–2(d).

2. Ascertainable Standards

a. Donor as Trustee

If the donor is serving as the trustee, the donor has all the powers of the trustee. Fiduciary obligations do not insulate the donor from the gift tax.

> **Example 4.12**
>
> Damon creates an inter vivos, irrevocable trust and transfers $5 million to the trust. The trustee has sole and absolute discretion to distribute trust income to Damon's three children in whatever amount the trustee decides; any income not distributed will be accumulated. At the death of the last of the three children to die, the trustee is to distribute the trust property to Damon's surviving descendants in equal shares. Damon is serving as trustee, and his discretion is limited only by the duty to act in good faith. As a result, he has control over the trust income and the gift of the income is an incomplete gift. The remainder is a completed gift because Damon cannot change the beneficial ownership of it.

b. Definition

If the donor is serving as the trustee and her power is limited by an ascertainable standard, the gift is complete. Regulation § 25.2511–2(g). An **ascertainable standard** is one that is clearly measurable and one under which the holder is legally accountable. Regulation § 25.2511–1(g)(2). An ascertainable standard is one relating to health, education, support, or maintenance or to maintain the beneficiary in her accustomed standard of living. *Id.* The rationale is that the donor has given up control over the trust property because the beneficiary can sue for distribution of trust property, and the court will enforce the standard.

> **Example 4.13**
>
> Damon creates an inter vivos, irrevocable trust and transfers $5 million to the trust. The trustee must distribute trust income equally to Damon's three children. The trustee also has discretion to distribute trust property (principal) to any of Damon's children for their health, education, or support. Damon is serving as the trustee. The gift of the income interest is complete because payments of income are mandatory and in equal shares. The gift of the remainder is also complete because Damon's power is limited by an ascertainable or fixed standard. Regulation § 25.2511–2(g)(2).

c. Other Examples

The power to distribute trust property to meet an emergency is an ascertainable standard. Regulation § 25.2511–2(g)(2). The power to distribute trust property for the beneficiary's comfort, happiness, or welfare is not an ascertainable standard. *Id.* But a power to distribute trust property for the reasonable support and comfort of the beneficiary is an ascertainable standard. *Id.* (Other ascertainable standards are described with reference to §§ 2036(a)(2) and 2038 in chapter 8, section C.2. and with reference to § 2041 in chapter 10, section B.)

d. Exam Strategy

It is easy to remember the four statutory ascertainable standards; just remember the mnemonic **hems**, which stands for health, education, maintenance, and support. Refer to the regulations and case law for other examples.

3. Powers Exercisable Only in Conjunction With Others

If the donor has the power to change beneficial ownership but only in conjunction with another person, the gift might be complete or it might be incomplete. It all depends on whether or not the other person has an interest that is substantially adverse to the exercise of the power. Regulation § 25.2511–2(e).

Example 4.14

Thelma creates an irrevocable, inter vivos trust and transfers $1 million to Friendly National Bank as trustee to pay the income to her sister, Sue, for life and the remainder to her niece, Nell. Thelma reserves the right to add new income beneficiaries with the consent of Sue. Because Sue has an interest in the trust and that interest is both substantial and adverse to the exercise of Thelma's power, the gift of the income interest is complete. The rationale is that Thelma is no longer in control because she must obtain Sue's consent. The remainder interest is, of course, complete because there is no power to change the beneficiaries.

Example 4.15

Thelma creates an irrevocable, inter vivos trust and transfers $1 million to Friendly National Bank as trustee to pay the income to her sister, Sue, for life and the remainder to her niece, Nell. Instead of the power to add income beneficiaries, Thelma reserves the right to add new remainder beneficiaries again only with the consent of Sue. In this situation, the income interest is complete because Thelma has reserved no power to

---

change its disposition. The remainder is not a completed gift, because Sue does not have any interest in the remainder, let alone one that is substantial and adverse to the exercise of the power to change beneficiaries. As a result, Thelma has control over the remainder and it is not a completed gift.

4. **Powers Held by Others**

a. **Power to Replace the Trustee**

If the donor has the power to replace the trustee at any time for any reason and appoint herself trustee, she will be deemed to have the trustee's powers. If the trustee has any discretion over distributions that is not limited by an ascertainable standard, the donor will be deemed to have those powers. This is true even if the donor has not exercised her power to replace the trustee. Regulation § 20.2038–1(a)(3); *Estate of Wall v. Commissioner*, 101 T.C. 300 (1993). If the donor's power is limited to replacing one corporate trustee with another corporate trustee or to appointing only a trustee that is neither related nor subordinate to the donor, then the trustee's powers will not be imputed to the donor. Revenue Ruling 95–58, 1995–2 C.B. 191.

Example 4.16

Jamal creates an inter vivos, irrevocable trust with Friendly National Bank as trustee. The trustee has sole and absolute discretion to distribute trust property among Jamal's children or to accumulate it. The trustee also has discretion to distribute trust property (principal) to any of Jamal's children for their comfort and happiness. If Jamal retains the power to replace Friendly National Bank as trustee and to become trustee himself, the gifts of the income and the remainder will be both incomplete. Even though Jamal is not serving as the trustee, the trustee's powers will be imputed to him.

Instead, assume that Jamal can replace Friendly National Bank only with another corporate trustee. As long as any new trustee is neither related nor subordinate to Jamal, the gifts will be complete. Jamal's power to replace the trustee will not be sufficient to put him in control over the trust property.

b. **Power to Benefit the Donor**

A donor may create a trust for her own benefit.

Example 4.17

Jenny creates an inter vivos, irrevocable trust with Friendly National Bank as trustee. The trustee has sole discretion whether to distribute trust income to Jenny or to accumulate it. At Jenny's death, the trust property will be distributed to Jenny's issue in whatever shares the trustee deems equitable taking into account all the facts and circumstances. As long as Jenny cannot replace the trustee with herself or a related or subordinate party, the transfer will be complete because Jenny has given up all dominion and control over the property. Of course, the income interest is not a gift because it is for Jenny's own benefit.

If the trustee's power to distribute income was limited by an ascertainable standard, then the gift would be incomplete. Regulation § 25.2511–2(b). The donor could force the trustee to distribute pursuant to the standard; as a result, the donor would be able to control who received the property.

H. LOANS AND FORGIVENESS OF DEBT

1. **No Gift on Loan**

If a donor lends someone money, the debtor has a legal obligation to repay and so the donor has not made a gift. The debtor will usually sign a promissory note agreeing to repay. It is presumed that the fair market value of the note equals the amount lent. Intra-family transfers, however, are subject to special scrutiny to determine (1) if the promissory note is bona fide, (2) the transaction is at arm's length, and (3) the transaction is free from donative intent. *Estate of Berkman v. Commissioner*, 38 T.C.M. (CCH) 183 (1979), discussed below.

2. **Interest–Free Loans**

If the donor fails to charge interest, the amount of the forgone interest is a gift. § 7872. This section imputes a transfer between the lender and the borrower on the last day of the calendar year. § 7872(a). Thus, the gift is complete on December 31.

3. **Forgiveness of Debt**

a. **General Principles**

Assume Parent lends Child money and charges interest at the applicable federal rate. Parent forgives each payment as it comes due.

Is there a gift at the time of the original loan or only when each payment is due? Why would Parent care? Parent needs to know when the gift is complete in order to file a gift tax return. Gift tax returns are due on April 15 of the year following the gift. More importantly, as you will see in chapter 5, each donor is entitled to transfer a specified amount—the amount of the gift tax annual exclusion—to each recipient each year without having to report that gift as a taxable gift. § 2503(b). The gift tax annual exclusion is adjusted annually for inflation; in 2010, it is $13,000.

Example 4.18

Parent lends Child $100,000 and charges interest at the applicable federal rate. Each annual payment of principal and interest is $13,000. Parent forgives each payment as it becomes due. Has Parent made a gift to Child of $100,000 at the time of the loan? If this is true, Parent must file a gift tax return and report the gift. Or has Parent only made gifts to Child each year? If this is true, Parent does not need to file a gift tax return and report the gift if the total forgiven plus other gifts to Child in the year do not exceed the amount of the gift tax annual exclusion. The answer is not entirely clear. Much will depend on the particular facts and circumstances of each case.

Illustrative Case

In *Estate of Kelley v. Commissioner*, 63 T.C. 321 (1974), taxpayers sold remainder interests in farmland to their children. Each child executed vendor's lien notes securing the debt. Each payment was forgiven as it came due. The Tax Court found that the children's notes were valuable consideration for the exchange because they were valid, enforceable obligations. The court noted that the taxpayers could have enforced the vendor's liens at any time even though they did not do so. The court reached the same conclusion in *Estate of Haygood v. Commissioner*, 42 T.C. 936 (1964).

Illustrative Case

In *Estate of Berkman v. Commissioner*, 38 T.C.M. (CCH) 183 (1979), the taxpayer made loans to his daughter and son-in-law. Even though the court found that a number of the loans were not

---

made at arm's length, it held that all were bona fide transactions. In this case, no principal payments were due until maturity. The promissory notes were in proper legal form and signed by the debtors, and the debtors paid the interest due every month.

Illustrative Case

In Revenue Ruling 77–299, 1977–2 C.B. 343, the taxpayer had made annual gifts to his grandchildren equal to the amount of the gift tax annual exclusion. When he decided to give each of them real property, his attorney suggested a sale on the installment basis with the annual payments equal to the amount of the gift tax annual exclusion. The taxpayer did so and the grandchildren signed non-interest bearing promissory notes that were non-negotiable. The IRS determined that there was a gift on the transfer of the real property because the notes executed by the grandchildren were not consideration. This prearranged plan was merely a disguised gift according to the IRS.

Illustrative Case

In *Miller v. Commissioner*, 71 T.C.M. (CCH) 1674 (1996), taxpayer lent money to her two sons. Although the sons signed promissory notes, the court found that there was no security for the loan, no discussion of the terms of the note, and no demand for repayment by the mother. The notes were, therefore, not adequate and full consideration. As a result, the taxpayer had made gifts to her sons.

b. **Factors**

Whether or not a particular transaction will be a gift only each year that payments are forgiven or a gift at the time of the loan, will depend on all the facts and circumstances. Important factors include:

- the transferor's expressed intent not to collect on the loan;

- whether there are negotiations or even discussion of the terms of the deal between the parties;

- whether or not interest is charged and at what rate;

101

- whether or not promissory notes are signed;

- whether or not there are actual payments made;

- whether the lender has a security interest;

- whether the debtor has the ability to pay;

- the lender's (seller's) health and expectation of repayment;

- what records, if any, are kept by the lender.

I. EXAM STRATEGY

Completion depends on the donor's control, not her ability to regain possession of the property. Examine each interest separately. A transfer may be partially complete and partially incomplete.

CHAPTER 5

THE ANNUAL EXCLUSION

A. GENERAL PRINCIPLES

1. Purpose

Congress enacted § 2503(b), known as the gift tax annual exclusion, to obviate the need for keeping records and accounting for small and routine gifts. A tax system needs some type of de minimis exception to prevent overloading the IRS and to ensure taxpayer compliance. The exclusion, however, has become much more than a device to eliminate the burden of keeping track of each and every routine gift. It is now a significant component of most estate plans.

2. Amount

The exclusion as originally enacted in 1932 was $5,000. Concerned with the possibility that wealthy taxpayers were avoiding tax by transfers at this level, Congress decreased the exclusion to $4,000 and later $3,000. The exclusion remained at this level until 1981 when Congress raised it to $10,000 and indexed it for inflation. The amount of the exclusion in 2010 is $13,000.

3. Exclusion is Per Donee

The exclusion applies per donee. That means that a donor can transfer the amount of the gift tax annual exclusion to as many recipients as she wants without filing a gift tax return. A donor could transfer an amount equal to the gift tax annual exclusion to 10 or 20 or even 100 different recipients and so decrease her estate.

4. Indirect Gifts

A taxpayer cannot avoid the gift tax through indirect transfers.

Example 5.1

Mother owns stock that she wants to transfer to Daughter. The stock has a value greatly in excess of the gift tax annual exclusion. So Mother transfers shares to Daughter and shares to 23 other relatives. Within one month of Mother's transfers, these 23 other relatives transfer their shares to Daughter. These transfers will be treated as indirect gifts from Mother to Daughter.

Illustrative Case

In *Heyen v. United States*, 945 F.2d 359 (10th Cir. 1991), the court held that substance prevailed over form on the facts in Example 5.1. As a result, there was only one gift from Mother to Daughter. Mother's failure to file a gift tax return reporting this gift was found to be fraudulent and justified the imposition of penalties.

---

5. **Reciprocal Gifts**

A taxpayer cannot increase the amount of the gift tax annual exclusion through reciprocal gifts.

Example 5.2

Blake and Crystal are siblings and each has two children. Each year Blake makes gifts to his children and to Crystal's two children equal to the gift tax annual exclusion. Crystal does the same. These will be treated as indirect gifts made by Blake to his children and Crystal to her children. *Schultz v. United States*, 493 F.2d 1225 (4th Cir. 1974); *Furst v. Commissioner*, 21 T.C.M. (CCH) 1169 (1962). Because the amount of the gifts from Blake to his children and from Crystal to her children exceeds the amount of the gift tax annual exclusion, Blake and Crystal are required to file gift tax returns. They will not owe any gift tax, however, until their taxable gifts, *i.e.*, those in excess of the amount of the gift tax annual exclusion, exceed the exemption amount in § 2505.

The reciprocal gift rule applies both to outright gifts and to gifts in trust.

Illustrative Case

In *Sather v. Commissioner*, 251 F.3d 1168 (8th Cir. 2001), brothers and their wives made gifts of stock to trusts for their own children and for each others' children. The court applied the two-pronged test of *United States v. Estate of Grace*, 395 U.S. 316 (1969), *i.e.*, (1) the transfers must be interrelated and (2) the transfers must leave the transferors in approximately the same economic position as if they had made the transfers themselves. The court held that where the transfers to the children were made on the same day and in the same amount, the transfers were interrelated. The court also held that the benefit to the children was sufficient to satisfy the second prong of the test.

---

6. **Annual Forgiveness of Debt**

Taxpayers who own property with significant value face obstacles if they want to transfer that property to their children at no gift tax cost. They could make the children co-owners and transfer a percentage of the ownership to the children each year. The transaction costs may be significant, and annual appreciation may require too many years of annual gifts. Another solution is to sell the property to the children and forgive each payment as it comes due. As noted in section H.3. of chapter 4, the danger with this scheme is the possibility that the form of the transaction will be ignored and the transaction will be taxed as one gift at the time of the initial transfer.

7. **Exam Strategy**

The gift tax annual exclusion is a *per donee per year* exclusion. That is, each donor can transfer an amount equal to the gift tax annual exclusion to an unlimited number of recipients each year. The gifts must be ones of present, not future, interests. If one donor is making gifts to a large number of individuals who are not obviously the natural object of the donor's bounty, determine if there are subsequent transfers by these recipients to family members of the donor. The donor cannot use indirect gifts to increase the amount of the exclusion. Remember that the amount in 2010 is $13,000 and that this amount is adjusted periodically for inflation.

B. SPLIT GIFTS

1. **Separate Gifts by Spouses**

A husband and a wife are separate taxpayers. Each can transfer the amount of the gift tax annual exclusion to their children, their grandchildren, and others every year. If one spouse owns most, or all, of the property, this richer spouse can transfer property to the poorer spouse to enable the poorer spouse to make such gifts. Any prearranged plan or agreement to do so, however, might result in a determination that only one spouse has made the gifts, directly and indirectly, to the children, the grandchildren, and others.

2.   Joint or Split Gifts

In some situations, a donor wants to benefit a family member and a spouse does not. In others, the recipients are stepchildren. In these cases, the couple can utilize the split gift provision in § 2513 to maximize the tax-free transfers by the richer spouse.

3.   Section 2513

Section 2513 treats gifts as if made one-half by each spouse if:

- both spouses are citizens or residents of the United States at the time of the gift;

- they consent to have all gifts made by either of them during the year treated as made one-half by each other;

- if they divorce or one dies, they do not remarry during the year; and

- they signify their consent on a gift tax return.

Section 2513 does not double the total benefit of the gift tax annual exclusion. Together the couple can give one donee only twice the amount of the gift tax annual exclusion; in 2010 this would be $26,000.

Example 5.3

Darren and Emily are married and have three children. Assume the amount of the gift tax annual exclusion is $13,000. Darren can give each child $13,000. So can Emily. Or Darren can give each child $26,000 if Emily agrees to split the gifts. But Darren cannot give each child $26,000 and have Emily do the same and claim that the total—$52,000 to each child—is sheltered by the split gift provision in § 2513.

C.   PRESENT VERSUS FUTURE INTERESTS

1.   Outright Gifts

a.   Present Interest Defined

The annual exclusion is only available for gifts of present, rather than future, interests. A present interest is one that gives the recipient the unrestricted right to the immediate use, possession, or enjoyment of the property. Regulation § 25.2503–3(b). Congress included this requirement to avoid the need for determining the ultimate number of donees or the value of their rights.

b. **Gifts with Delayed Financial Benefits**

Outright gifts qualify as present interests. Even gifts that delay financial benefit may qualify if it is the nature of the property itself, rather than the method of transfer, that imposes the restriction.

Example 5.4

Evan transfers a life insurance policy to his son, Sidney. Even though that policy will not pay benefits until Evan dies, the gift is one of a present interest. Regulation § 25.2503–3(a).

The same is true of a bond, a promissory note with a maturity date in the future, or payments under an installment contract. In all these situations, the gifts qualify for the annual exclusion because it is the nature of the asset itself, not any restrictions imposed by the donor that delays the financial benefit. If that benefit is delayed because of the form of the gift, *e.g.*, a gift in trust, the gift will not qualify for the annual exclusion.

Example 5.5

Evan creates an irrevocable, inter vivos trust with Friendly National Bank as the trustee for the benefit of his son, Sidney, and Sidney's issue. Evan transfers a life insurance policy to the trust. The gift does not qualify for the annual exclusion because it is a future interest. Regulation § 25.2503–3(c), Ex. (2).

---

c. **Gifts of Stock**

Ordinarily, a gift of stock in a publicly traded corporation will qualify for the annual exclusion. If the corporation is closely-held, it might not pay dividends. This alone should not prevent the gift from being a present interest. If the stock is subject to transfer restrictions, the recipient might not have the *immediate* right to use, possess, or enjoy that property since she cannot sell, gift, or otherwise transfer it. In these cases, the stock would not be a present interest and would not qualify for the annual exclusion. Revenue Ruling 76–360, 1976–2 C.B. 298.

107

d. Gifts of Partnership and Limited Liability Company Interests

The same rules apply to other business interests. Even though income might not be distributed on a regular basis and even though a general partner or manager might control the flow of the income, these business interests generally qualify as present interests. If, however, the interest is significantly restricted, it will not be a present interest.

Illustrative Case

In *Hackl v. Commissioner*, 118 T.C. 279 (2002), the taxpayers made gifts of membership units in a limited liability company that had been organized to hold and operate tree farming properties. The court used a three-part test, articulated in *Calder v. Commissioner*, 85 T.C. 713 (1985), that requires the taxpayer to prove, based on all the facts and circumstances, "(1) that the trust will receive income, (2) that some portion of that income will flow steadily to the beneficiary, and (3) that such portion can be ascertained." *Id.* at 727–28. The court found that the recipients in *Hackl* did not receive a *substantial present economic benefit* because the primary purpose of the company was to hold and acquire timberland for long-term development, and it would not make any distributions for a number of years. Moreover, the recipients could not compel distributions, could not withdraw their capital accounts without managerial consent, and could not transfer their interests freely. As a result, the gifts did not qualify for the annual exclusion.

---

2. Gifts In Trust: General Principles

a. Gifts are to Beneficiaries, not the Trustee

Gifts in trust have been a fertile source of controversy over qualification for the annual exclusion. The most basic issue is whether the donor who makes a gift in trust makes a transfer to the trustee or to the beneficiaries. In *Helvering v. Hutchings*, 312 U.S. 393 (1941), the Supreme Court held that the beneficiary, not the trustee, was the donee. As a result, each interest must be examined to determine if it is a present interest.

b. Future Interests

Future interests are those that commence in use, possession, or enjoyment at some time in the future. Regulation § 25.2503–3(a). This includes reversions, remainders, and similar interests, whether vested or contingent. *Id.*

> **Example 5.6**
>
> Dexter establishes an irrevocable, inter vivos trust to pay the income to Alex for 20 years, then to pay the income to Brian until his death, and then to distribute the trust property to Clark or his estate. Clark's interest is a vested remainder. Despite the fact that the remainder is vested and can be valued actuarially, it is a future interest. Brian's life estate is also a future interest because Brian must wait 20 years before enjoying the trust income. Neither Clark nor Brian has the *immediate* use, possession or enjoyment of the property. Their interests, therefore, do not qualify for the annual exclusion.

3. Gifts In Trust: Mandatory Payment of Income

a. General Rule

If the trustee is required to distribute all income at least annually to the beneficiary, the value of the income interest qualifies as a present interest. Alex's income interest in Example 5.6 might be a present interest. If the trustee must accumulate income or has the discretion to do so, the income interests will not qualify. In such cases the beneficiaries do not have an unrestricted right to the *immediate* possession or enjoyment because the income may not be distributed until some time in the future, if at all.

b. Property Must Produce Income

In addition, the trust property must produce income. When non-income producing property, such as unimproved real property or stock in a company that has never paid dividends and is unlikely to do so in the future, is transferred into trust, there will be no annual exclusion for the income interest. There must be a definite value in order to calculate the annual exclusion. When the value is nebulous or nonexistent, there is no exclusion available.

c. Trustee Discretion or Delay

If the trustee has discretion to accumulate or distribute income, the income interest is not a present interest. The donor may have imposed a delay in distributions, for example, until the beneficiary graduates from college or until the beneficiary is married or until the beneficiary is age 30. In all these cases, the beneficiary has a future interest because she does not have an *immediate* right to use, possess, or enjoy the property.

109

d. Spendthrift Provision

A spendthrift provision prevents a beneficiary from anticipating or assigning her interest. Such a restriction will not prevent the income interest from being classified as a present interest because the beneficiary will enjoy the use, possession, or enjoyment of the income as soon as it becomes available. Revenue Ruling 54–344, 1954–2 C.B. 319.

e. Discretion Limited by a Standard

If the trustee has discretion to distribute income for the health, education, support or maintenance of a beneficiary, it is not always clear that the income interest will be considered a present interest. While an ascertainable standard imposed on a donor-trustee will mean that the donor no longer has control and, thus, the gift is complete, that same standard will not necessarily qualify the gift as one of a present interest. It must be clear from the moment of the transfer into the trust that there will be substantial income distributions that can be valued. On the other hand, where the facts make it uncertain that any income will in fact be distributed, the annual exclusion will be denied. In this latter case the value of the income interest is too uncertain; it might have no value at all.

Illustrative Case

In *Morgan v. Commissioner*, 42 T.C. 1080 (1964), *aff'd per curiam* 353 F.2d 209 (4th Cir. 1965), the taxpayer established a trust for a disabled child. The trustee had the sole discretion to "make such disbursements of this income as will best provide for the health, comfort, maintenance and education" of the child. *Id.* at 1083. Any income not distributed was accumulated for her needs in later years. The court held that the gift qualified for the annual exclusion because the child lived in a home for disabled children, and there was an immediate need for a substantial amount of income to be actually expended for the child. The court noted that the words "present interest" were not "words of art . . . but connote the right to substantial present economic benefit. The question is of time, not when title vests, but when enjoyment begins." *Id.* at 1090.

Illustrative Case

In *Commissioner v. Disston*, 325 U.S. 442 (1945), the taxpayer established trusts for his minor children. The trustee had discretion to accumulate the income or to distribute it "as may be necessary for the education, comfort and support" of the children. *Id.* at 444. The Court held that the income interest was not a present interest because it could not be determined how much of the income might be necessary to meet this standard. "In the absence of some indication from the face of the trust or surrounding circumstances that a steady flow of some ascertainable portion of income to the minor would be required, there is no basis for a conclusion that there is a gift of anything other than [a future interest]." *Id.* at 449.

---

f. Multiple Income Beneficiaries

The ability to value the flow of income to the beneficiary is critical whenever there is more than one income beneficiary. As long as the number of beneficiaries and their respective shares are fixed, the income interest of each can be valued. Once valued, the interest qualifies for the annual exclusion. If the number of beneficiaries is fixed, but the trustee has discretion to sprinkle income (determine how much each beneficiary will receive), the ability to value each interest disappears and along with it, the annual exclusion.

g. Discretion to Invade Principal

The final obstacle to allowing an annual exclusion is the trustee's ability to invade the principal. If the power to invade is for the benefit of the income beneficiary, the annual exclusion will still be allowed. Under these circumstances, exercise of the power to invade will simply alter the time and manner of the beneficiary's enjoyment; it will not alter the fact of that enjoyment. If the power to invade is for the benefit of someone other than the income beneficiary, however, the exercise of the power would deprive that beneficiary of the property's income, for once the property is distributed to another, the income follows the property. This power to invade principal for the benefit of another makes the value of the income interest unascertainable and results in a denial of the annual exclusion. The power to invade principal for the benefit of either of two income beneficiaries would appear to render both income interests incapable of valuation and thus ineligible for the annual exclusion.

4. **General Powers of Appointment:** *Crummey* **Powers**

   a. **General Principles**

   Frequently donors do not want to be restricted to mandatory payments of income to all the possible income beneficiaries; rather donors greatly prefer a trust that allows the trustee to accumulate or sprinkle trust income among a group of beneficiaries. The desire to achieve both tax benefits and flexibility in estate planning has led many donors to incorporate powers of appointment into trusts. A general power of appointment allows the power holder to withdraw trust property for her own benefit. This gives the power holder the *immediate* right to use, possess, or enjoy the trust property. In other words, it creates a present interest in the power holder.

   Example 5.7

   Bonnie establishes an irrevocable, inter vivos trust with Friendly National Bank as trustee. The trustee has discretion to distribute income to any of Bonnie's children or to accumulate it. The trust property will be distributed to Bonnie's descendants after the death of her last child. Bonnie gives each of her four children the right to withdraw the lesser of (1) their pro rata share of a trust contribution or (2) the amount of the gift tax annual exclusion. If the child does not exercise the right to withdraw within 30 days of notice of the contribution, the power to withdraw terminates. The right to withdraw is non-cumulative.

   Assume that Bonnie transfers $52,000 to the trust in a year when the amount of the gift tax annual exclusion is $13,000. The entire $52,000 will qualify for the gift tax annual exclusion. Each of her four children has a general power of appointment over $13,000, creating a present interest in each of them to that extent.

   ---

   b. **Limited Amount**

   Often donors do not intend that power holders exercise their powers to withdraw. Consequently, donors will limit the amount that the power holder can withdraw to the amount necessary to qualify for the annual exclusion. This can create a tension with the potential gift tax consequences to the power holder.

   c. **Limited Time to Withdraw**

   Donors also will limit the amount of time that a power holder has to exercise his power to withdraw. Thirty days is generally considered sufficient although the power holders in *Estate of Cristofani v. Commissioner*, 97 T.C. 74 (1991) had only 15 days to withdraw and the court held that their powers were valid.

d. Power is Non–Cumulative

Most *Crummey* powers are non-cumulative. This means that if the power holder does not withdraw the stated amount in year 1, the ability to do so terminates.

Example 5.7 Revisited

Bonnie's children must exercise their powers within 30 days or those powers lapse, *i.e.*, they terminate. Assume that Bonnie transfers $52,000 to the trust each year. If a child fails to withdraw $13,000 in year 1, that child cannot withdraw $26,000 in year 2. The child's power is non-cumulative, meaning the child is limited to withdrawing that amount only in that year.

---

e. Notice

Power holders must be given notice of their right to withdraw. They must also be given notice of contributions to the trust that trigger their right to withdraw.

f. Power Holders

Power holders need not be trust beneficiaries, although they usually are. Minor children may be power holders. The court in *Crummey v. Commissioner*, 397 F.2d 82 (9th Cir. 1968), so held. See section D.7. below. General powers of appointment that are designed to qualify transfers for the annual exclusion are commonly referred to as *Crummey* powers whether the power holder is a child or an adult.

g. Contingent Beneficiaries

Contingent beneficiaries can be given *Crummey* powers.

Illustrative Case

In *Estate of Cristofani v. Commissioner*, 97 T.C. 74 (1991), the donor created a trust for the benefit of her two children. They were to receive the income from the trust until the donor died. At that time, the trust was to terminate and the property distributed to the

---

children if they were living. The trustees could also distribute trust principal to the children for their health, education, maintenance, or support. The donor's five grandchildren were contingent beneficiaries, *i.e.*, they would receive their parent's share of the trust property if their parents died before the donor. Both children and all five grandchildren were given the right to withdraw an amount equal to the gift tax annual exclusion within 15 days of a transfer by the donor. The IRS challenged the validity of the powers in the grandchildren but lost. The court found that the donor had intended to benefit her grandchildren and that there was no agreement that the grandchildren would not exercise their powers to withdraw.

The IRS acquiesced in the result in *Cristofani* but not its rationale. It continued to challenge withdrawal powers given to anyone other than the primary beneficiaries of a trust, and courts continued to reject those challenges. *See, e.g., Estate of Kohlsaat v. Commissioner*, 73 T.C.M. (CCH) 2732 (1997); *Estate of Holland v. Commissioner*, 73 T.C.M. (CCH) 3236 (1997).

h. Gift Tax Consequences to Holders of *Crummey* Powers

(1) Appointment to Self or Others

Crummey powers are general powers of appointment because the power holder can appoint property to himself. § 2514(c)(1). If the power holder does so, there are no gift tax consequences because there is no transfer. If, on the other hand, the holder of a general power transfers property to someone else pursuant to that power, the holder has made a gift. § 2514(b).

(2) Lapse

If a power holder fails to exercise a *Crummey* power that is non-cumulative, that power lapses, *i.e.*, it terminates. The lapse of a general power of appointment is treated as a release of that power. § 2514(e). And a release of a power is treated as a transfer of property. § 2514(b). The result is that a failure to exercise a *Crummey* power will be treated as a transfer of property by the power holder to the trust beneficiaries.

(3) Limitation on Lapse

Section 2514(e) limits the gift tax consequences. It provides that a lapse is only a release to the extent that the property which could have been appointed under the power exceeds the greater of (1) $5,000 or (2) 5 percent of the trust property. If the power holder is limited to appointing that amount, the failure to so appoint is not a lapse and not a release and, therefore, not a gift.

Example 5.8

Robin creates an irrevocable, inter vivos trust with Friendly National Bank as trustee. The trustee has discretion to distribute income to Ethan or to accumulate it. At Ethan's death, the trust property will be distributed to his issue. Ethan has the power to withdraw the amount contributed to the trust within 30 days of notice of a contribution. His power is non-cumulative. Robin transfers $13,000 to the trust; there is no other property in the trust. Ethan fails to withdraw. This failure is a lapse. This lapse is a release of the power only to the extent of $8,000 ($13,000 minus $5,000). He is treated as making a transfer to the trust of that $8,000. The portion of that $8,000 that is attributable to the remainder is a gift by Ethan. Because it is a remainder interest, it is a future interest.

Example 5.9

Roy creates an irrevocable, inter vivos trust with Friendly National Bank as trustee. The trustee has discretion to distribute income to Evelyn or to accumulate it. At Evelyn's death, the trust property will be distributed to her issue. Evelyn has the power to demand the amount contributed to the trust or the amount of the gift tax annual exclusion, whichever is less, within 30 days of notice of a contribution. Evelyn's power is non-cumulative. Assume the gift tax annual exclusion amount is $13,000. Roy transfers $260,000 to the trust in year 1 and $13,000 in year 2. Evelyn does not make a demand in either year. Her failure to make a demand in each year is a lapse of the power. Each lapse, however, is *not* treated as a release because it is limited to five percent of the trust property. (Five percent of $260,000 is $13,000.) As a result, there are no gift tax consequences to Evelyn.

---

5. **Exam Strategy**

To qualify for the annual exclusion, the gift must give the recipient the right to *immediate* use, possession, or enjoyment. If the gift is not in trust, look for any restrictions imposed on the ability to transfer the asset. If the gift is in trust, only the income interests will qualify as present interests. Remember: there must be (1) mandatory payments of income, (2) income producing property, and (3) no restrictions on distributions. If there are not mandatory payments of income, the beneficiary (or beneficiaries) must have a right to demand trust property, *i.e.*, a *Crummey* power.

D. GIFTS TO MINORS

1. Outright Gifts

Gifts to minors present special problems for donors wishing to take advantage of the annual exclusion. For small items such as birthday presents, outright transfers make sense. No one, however, wants to give a minor child unfettered access to significant amounts of money. Moreover, a minor cannot buy, sell, or otherwise manage other types of property during minority. Outright transfers to minors, therefore, play a very modest role in most donors' estate plans.

2. Joint Bank Accounts

Donors, particularly parents, may create joint bank accounts with their minor children. Such accounts are often used to manage small amounts of cash such as allowances, birthday gifts, or holiday gifts; they are rarely used to transfer significant amounts. Transfers into joint bank accounts are revocable transfers as either the parent or the child can withdraw the full amount in the account. Regulation § 25.2511–1(h)(4). As a result, if a parent transfers money into a joint bank account with a child, the transfer will not qualify for the annual exclusion because it is not a completed gift until the child withdraws the money. If and when the child withdraws, there is a completed gift that will qualify for the gift tax annual exclusion.

3. Gifts to Legal Guardians

To overcome the problems of the minor's legal disabilities, a donor can transfer property to a guardian for the benefit of the minor. Such a gift is also considered a gift of a present interest qualifying for the annual exclusion. Guardianships, however, present their own set of problems. A guardian must usually obtain court approval for any transaction, and the guardian's investment powers may be severely restricted.

4. Gifts to Custodians: Uniform Transfer to Minors Act

a. Advantages

To avoid these problems, donors often make gifts pursuant to the Uniform Transfers to Minors Act (UTMA), which gives the custodian broad powers to deal with the gift property without court supervision and allows investment decisions to be governed by the prudent person rule. Transfers under this act may be as simple as "to A as custodian for X (the minor)." Such transfers are completed gifts of present interests that qualify for the annual exclusion. Revenue Ruling 59–357, 1959–2 C.B. 212; Revenue Ruling 73–287, 1973–2 C.B. 321.

b. Disadvantages

Transfers pursuant to UTMA also have disadvantages. The property must be distributed to the beneficiary at the age of 21. If the custodian actually uses the property for the support of the minor child, the parent (even if not the donor or the custodian) will be taxed on the income from that property.§ 677(b). Moreover, if the donor is the custodian and dies before the minor reaches the age of majority, the property will be in the donor's gross estate under § 2036 or § 2038 because the custodian has broad powers to use the property for the benefit of the minor. If the custodian is not the donor but is the parent of the minor beneficiary, and if the custodian dies before the minor reaches the age of majority, the property will also be in the parent-custodian's gross estate under § 2041. Section 2041 applies because the custodian's powers are the equivalent of a general power of appointment. Because the parent is legally responsible for supporting the child, distributions benefit the parent. This is the same as a distribution to a creditor of the parent.

5. Mandatory Payment of Income Trusts

Because of the disadvantages of, and limitations on, outright gifts or gifts to custodians, most donors will prefer to create trusts for the benefit of minor children. Trusts allow greater flexibility, but they still present challenges. A minor child can be an income beneficiary of a trust with mandatory payments of income. See section C.3. above. The value of the income interest will be a present interest that qualifies for the annual exclusion. Most donors will not want mandatory distributions of income to a minor child because of the inability of that child to hold or manage the money.

6. Section 2503(c) Trusts

a. Requirements

Section 2503(c) provides that *no part* of a gift to a minor will be considered a future interest if two conditions are met. First, the property and its income must be distributed to or for the benefit of the donee before age 21 or accumulated and made available to the donee at age 21. Second, if the donee dies before 21, the property and accumulated income must be payable to the donee's estate or as the donee appoints under a general power of appointment. Under this section, the entire value of the property, not just the value of the income interest, will qualify for the gift tax annual exclusion.

b.   Property and Income for the Benefit of the Minor

Section 2503(c) applies if the property and income therefrom may be expended by, or for the benefit of, the donee before his attaining the age of 21 years. The courts have interpreted this language to mean that the income and the principal are separate property interests. *Commissioner v. Herr*, 303 F.2d 780 (3d Cir. 1962). As a result, a donor can make only the income available during minority and, to the extent not expended during that time, have the income distributed to the beneficiary at age 21. The value of the income interest then qualifies as a present interest under § 2503(c). The remainder interest can be distributed at some later date or not at all, although the value of the remainder interest will then constitute a taxable gift of a future interest.

Illustrative Case

In *Estate of Levine v. Commissioner*, 526 F.2d 717 (2d Cir. 1975), the trust instrument provided that the trustee had discretion to distribute income for the benefit of the child until age 21, and to the extent not so expended, the income was to be accumulated and paid to the child at age 21. The trust continued until the child's death with mandatory payments of income after age 21. The court held that the donor had created three interests—(1) the income interest until age 21; (2) the income interest after age 21; and (3) the interest in the principal. The income interest until age 21 was a present interest under § 2503(c). The income interest starting at age 21, although mandatory, was held to be a future interest because it did not begin in use, possession, or enjoyment until the beneficiary became 21. As a result, it did qualify for the gift tax annual exclusion.

---

c.   No Substantial Restrictions

Transfers to a § 2503(c) trust will not qualify as present interests if there are substantial restrictions on the trustee's ability to use the property for the child's benefit. Regulation § 25.2503–4(b)(1).

Restrictions that give the trustee only the powers that state law accords guardians will not disqualify the trust, but other limitations could result in a denial of the annual exclusion. For example, the trustee's discretion to distribute trust funds only upon the "illness, infirmity, or disability" of the beneficiary, *Pettus v. Commissioner*, 54 T.C. 112 (1970), or upon the happening of an "accident, illness, or other emergency," *Faber v. United States*, 439 F.2d 1189 (6th Cir. 1971), is too restrictive. The discretion to distribute for the beneficiary's "support, care, education, comfort and welfare" is not. Revenue Ruling 67–270, 1967–2 C.B. 349. The discretion to distribute funds for the beneficiary's "care, support, education, and welfare" is too restrictive if the trustee must consider other resources available to the beneficiary before making a distribution. Revenue Ruling 69–345, 1969–1 C.B. 226. Finally, the ability of the trustee to sprinkle income among beneficiaries will defeat the annual exclusion. Regulation § 25.2503–3(c), (Ex. 3).

d. Power in Child to Withdraw at Age 21

To qualify under § 2503(c), the trust must provide that the property and accumulated income will pass to the donee at age 21. Often donors do not want the property to be distributed to the child at that age. A long as the child has the power to obtain the property at age 21 (for example through a demand provision), the trust can be drafted to continue past 21 and yet qualify under § 2503(c). Revenue Ruling 74–43, 1974–1 C.B. 285. This power, much like a *Crummey* power, can be limited to a reasonable amount of time, such as 30 days, so long as the beneficiary has actual notice of the existence of the power.

e. Distribution to Donee's Estate

The trust must also provide that the property and accumulated income are payable to the estate of the donee or is subject to her general power of appointment should the donee die before age 21. Strict adherence to this language is required. A gift to the donee's heirs at law rather than the donee's estate, for example, is not sufficient. *Ross v. Commissioner*, 652 F.2d 1365 (9th Cir. 1981).

f. General Power of Appointment Alternative

On the other hand, giving the donee a general power of appointment with a gift to others in default of the donee's exercise of the power is sufficient even though the donee has no opportunity to exercise the power before death. Regulation § 25.2503–4(b); Revenue Ruling 75–351, 1975–2 C.B. 368. The limitations imposed by state law, *i.e.*, the inability of a minor to exercise the power because the minor cannot execute a will, do not disqualify the interest. Giving the donee a general power with a gift in default is generally better because it allows the donor to direct the property to other beneficiaries and prevents the property from returning to the donor in the event of the donee's untimely demise.

7. **General Powers of Appointment:** *Crummey* **Powers**

A withdrawal power (discussed at section C.4.) given to a minor child is valid as long as the child has the legal ability to exercise the power either directly or through a legal guardian.

Illustrative Case

In *Crummey v. Commissioner*, 397 F.2d 82 (9th Cir. 1968), the donor created trusts giving withdrawal powers to his four children, aged 11, 15, 20, and 22. The Commissioner claimed that the powers in the three minor children (21 was then the age of majority) were not valid. The Tax Court disagreed and held that the power in the 20–year-old was valid because she was able to make contracts and thus could make an effective demand. The Ninth Circuit found that distinction artificial and held that the powers in all four children created present interests because the parents, as legal guardians, could make a demand on behalf of a minor child and there was no showing that such a demand could have been resisted.

All of the rules discussed at section C.4. also apply to withdrawal powers in minor children. And, although the *Crummey* case dealt only with gifts to minors, withdrawal powers in beneficiaries of all ages are commonly referred to as *Crummey* powers.

---

8. **Exam Strategy**

Gifts to minors are subject to the same rules as gifts to adults. In addition, gifts to guardians, gifts to custodians pursuant to the Uniform Transfers to Minors Act, and gifts to § 2503(c) trusts will qualify as present interests. Section 2503(c) requires that the property be either (1) payable to the beneficiary's estate or (2) subject to a general power of appointment in the beneficiary if the beneficiary dies before age 21. Gifts to "heirs," "next of kin," or the like do not qualify.

PART III

THE ESTATE TAX

CHAPTER 6

PROPERTY OWNED AT DEATH

A. GENERAL PRINCIPLES

1. Nature of the Tax

The estate tax, like the gift tax, is a tax on the *transfer of property*. It is imposed on all citizens and residents of the United States (§ 2001(a)), and it is imposed on "all property, real or personal, tangible or intangible, wherever situated." § 2031(a). The executor is required to file an estate tax return whenever the gross estate exceeds the applicable exemption amount. § 6018(a)(1).

2. The Gross Estate

Section 2031 defines the gross estate as the value of all property "to the extent provided in this part." There is no broad, all-encompassing definition of the gross estate. Instead, sections 2032 through 2046 are specific provisions governing different types of property. Although the estate tax is a federal law, it relies on state law to create the property interests. Reliance on state law, however, does not mean that the estate tax is limited to property interests that are included in the decedent's probate estate.

B. PROPERTY IN WHICH DECEDENT HAD AN INTEREST: § 2033

1. General Rule

Section 2033 includes in the gross estate all property interests to the extent of the decedent's interest at the time of her death. This definition encompasses all the decedent's probate property, and it extends beyond that to any interest that passes from the decedent to another as a result of her death. Property interests that terminate at death are not included. Section 2033 applies if (1) the decedent had a property interest immediately before death and (2) that property interest passed *from decedent to others* as a result of death.

123

2.   Specific Property Interests

a.   Outright Ownership/Fee Interest

Property that a decedent owns outright or in fee will be included in her gross estate under § 2033. Such property passes from decedent to others either by her will or through intestacy.

b.   Tenancy in Common

Decedent's interest as a tenant in common is also included in her gross estate under § 2033. There is no survivorship interest in a tenancy in common. The decedent's interest passes from decedent to another either under her will or by intestacy.

c.   Reversions

Reversions are future interests retained by a transferor. For example, Owen creates a trust to pay the income to Craig for 15 years. Whether Owen explicitly retains the right to the property after Craig's income interest terminates or state law implies it, Owen has a reversion. If Owen dies while Craig is receiving income, Owen's reversion will be in his gross estate pursuant to § 2033. That interest will pass from him to others either under his will or by intestacy. Whoever receives the reversion from Owen will receive the trust property at the end of the 15 years.

d.   Remainders

Remainders are future interests created by others. They can be vested or contingent, depending on the terms of the trust or deed creating them as well as on state law. Contingent remainders and other defeasible interests are property interests that are included in the gross estate pursuant to § 2033 unless the interest is contingent on survival until the time of possession. Revenue Ruling 67–370, 1967–2 C.B. 324; Revenue Ruling 54–438, 1955–2 C.B. 601. Any contingencies will affect the value of the interest, not its inclusion in the gross estate.

Example 6.1

Tim creates a trust to pay the income to Sarah for her life and the remainder to Max. Unless state law makes Max's remainder contingent upon survival until the time of possession, Max has a

---

> vested remainder. If Max dies before Sarah, Max can transfer his interest in his will or by intestacy. As a result, it is included in his gross estate pursuant to § 2033.

e. Life Insurance on the Life of Another

Insurance on the life of the decedent and owned by the decedent is governed by § 2042. If the insured is not the owner of the policy and the owner dies before the insured, the insurance policy is an asset of the owner's estate. It is included in the owner's gross estate pursuant to § 2033. The value of the policy will depend on its nature and its terms.

Example 6.2

Tom bought a life insurance policy on his own life with a face amount of $500,000. Tom transferred that policy to his wife, Linda. Linda died survived by Tom. The life insurance policy is in Linda's gross estate pursuant to § 2033. It will pass from Linda to someone else under her will or by intestacy.

---

f. Copyrights, Patents, the Right to Publicity, and Similar Rights

State law, either by statute or judicial decision, may recognize the right of a celebrity to control the use of her name or likeness. This right may extend beyond death and pass to designated beneficiaries under a will or to heirs in intestacy. This is a property right akin to a copyright or a patent. All are property interests that would be included in the decedent's gross estate pursuant to § 2033.

Illustrative Case

Estate of Andrews v. United States, 850 F.Supp. 1279 (E.D. Va. 1994), concerned an author's name, not the right to publicity. The author, V.C. Andrews died on December 19, 1986. Although she had achieved international recognition for her fiction, her death went largely unnoticed by the media. Her publisher and her estate hired a ghost writer to complete two books that Andrews had been under contract to write at the time of her death. When those books became commercial successes, the publisher and the estate signed

---

two further contracts with the same writer. The estate did not list Andrews' name as an asset of the estate, but the estate did not dispute that it was includible. Instead, the issue before the court was how to value that name. The court ultimately decided that only the first post-death contract was relevant and that only the advance to the ghost writer, minus certain expenses, should be considered. The court then applied a 33 percent discount factor for the risk associated with using a ghost writer to arrive at a value of $703,500.

g. **Causes of Action**

If the decedent has a cause of action pending at death (other than a wrongful death suit) and if state law allows that cause of action to survive death, that cause of action is an interest in property included in the gross estate pursuant to § 2033. The interest will be valued as of the date of decedent's death, taking into account all the relevant facts and circumstances.

h. **Stolen Property**

All interests in property are included in the decedent's gross estate if the decedent possessed the use and economic benefit of that property even though the decedent did not have actual legal title to the property.

Example 6.3

Lewis served in the army during World War II. While stationed in Europe, he stole various art objects and smuggled them home. Lewis had the exclusive possession and enjoyment of these art objects until his death. He sold some of them during his life to provide funds for his own support. At his death, those art objects passed from Lewis to his brother, John. Although Lewis did not have legal title to the art objects, they will be in his gross estate pursuant to § 2033. Technical Advice Memorandum 9152005.

The result in example 6.3 is in accord with the general principles of § 2033. Lewis had a property interest recognized by state law in the art objects immediately before his death. Those art objects passed from him to others as a result of his death. If these objects were not included in his gross estate, he would profit from his criminal activity.

---

i. Illegal Goods

Including illegal goods, such as drugs, in the gross estate is more dubious. In Technical Advice Memorandum 9207004, the IRS ruled that illegal drugs in a decedent's possession at the time of his death were included in his gross estate under § 2033 because he had exclusive possession and control over the drugs and was to receive their economic benefit. The government, however, seized those drugs and, thus, they did not pass from decedent to anyone else as a result of his death. Nonetheless, the IRS ruled that they were included in his gross estate under § 2033. The IRS also denied a deduction even though the drugs were forfeited because to do so would have frustrated the clearly defined public policy against drug trafficking. While the result in this case might be good policy, it does not meet the second-prong of the § 2033 test.

3. Right to Income

a. Salary

A taxpayer who dies while still employed will undoubtedly be owed salary at the date of death. The decedent has a property interest in that salary, and that interest transfers from the decedent to another as a result of her death. That property, therefore, is included in the gross estate under § 2033. That salary is also income and must be reported by the recipient on the recipient's income tax return. (This is called income in respect of a decedent or IRD. § 691.) The recipient will receive an income tax deduction for the estate tax attributable to that item of income. § 691(c).

b. Bonuses

A bonus that is earned before death but not awarded until after death is included in the gross estate under § 2033 just like salary. Revenue Ruling 65–217, 1965–2 C.B. 214. If a bonus is awarded after death and that bonus is within the discretion of the decedent's employer, that bonus will not be included in the gross estate under § 2033. *Id.* A bonus may simply be a death benefit paid to the decedent's spouse or designated beneficiary. See subsection 3.e.

c. Fees of Attorneys

If decedent is an attorney, amounts earned before death will be included in the gross estate even though the amounts are not paid until after death.

Illustrative Case

In *Estate of Curry v. Commissioner*, 74 T.C. 540 (1980), the decedent had signed an agreement with another attorney to receive a stated percentage of any fees award in a list of cases pending before the Indian Claims Commissioner. The court held that the date of death value of his right to receive those fees was a property interest included in his gross estate. The issue was only how to value those potential fees. The court noted that decedent's past success in prosecuting such cases, the delays in this type of litigation, and the fact that others claimed a portion of the fee awards in all but two cases were factors to be considered in establishing the value. *Id.* at 551.

Attorneys often work on a contingent fee basis. If the value of a potential fee is too uncertain and the estate could not sue for the value of the decedent's services, *i.e.*, make a *quantum meruit* claim, nothing will be in decedent's gross estate. *Estate of Nemerov v. Commissioner*, 15 T.C.M. (CCH) 855 (1956).

d.   Deferred Compensation

If decedent's employer has a deferred compensation plan, amounts due to the decedent will be in his gross estate either under § 2033 or § 2039. See chapter 9 for a discussion of § 2039. Section 2033, rather than § 2039, will apply when the compensation is paid to the decedent's estate rather than a designated beneficiary.

Illustrative Case

In *Goodman v. Granger*, 243 F.2d 264 (3d Cir. 1957), decedent's employer agreed to pay him $2,000 a year for 15 years after he terminated his employment. The employer was required to pay only if decedent's performance was satisfactory and he did not compete with his employer for a period of time after terminating his employment. Decedent died while still employed, and his employer made the payments to his estate. The only question was the value to be reported. The court rejected the estate's argument that the right to the payments as of the date of death had no value because of the contingencies in the contract. Instead, it held that since death ripened the interest into an absolute one, the right to payments would be valued without consideration of the contingencies.

---

e. **Death Benefits**

An employer may pay a death benefit, over and above any earned salary and bonus, to the decedent's estate. If the decedent has a contractual right to the payment, it is included in his gross estate under § 2033. If the decedent has only a mere hope or promise and not a contractual right, the benefit will not be in the decedent's gross estate. *Estate of Barr v. Commissioner*, 40 T.C. 227 (1963). See section C of chapter 9 for a further discussion of these benefits. *See also Estate of DiMarco v. Commissioner*, discussed at section C.3. of chapter 4 for a discussion of possible gift tax consequences of such benefits.

f. **Rent and Other Contractual Payments**

Any payments that are due to the decedent under contracts, whether written or oral, will be in her gross estate as long as the right to those payments has accrued at the moment of death. Future payments are not included.

Example 6.4

Anna owned an apartment building consisting of ten units. Rent was due on the first day of the month. Anna died on August 2. She had received the rent from six of the units on August 1 and deposited those checks in her bank account. The value of the rent from the remaining four tenants that was due on August 1 is an asset of her estate.

Rent for September, October, and other months will be collected by her estate. That rent will be income to her estate, but those payments will not be included in her gross estate. Instead, the fair market value of the apartment building will be in her gross estate. The value of that building will be determined, at least in part, by the rental income that it generates. The apartment building is analogous to an apple tree with the future rent being the not yet ripe apples.

Example 6.5

Earlene had also owned an apartment building, but she sold it five years before her death to Devon. Earlene agreed to an installment sale with quarterly payments due for ten years. Earlene died on

---

> April 3 without having received the payment due on April 1. The value of that payment will be included in her gross estate because it is a property interest that was due and payable at the moment of her death.
>
> The fair market value of the remaining payments, *i.e.*, the fair market value of the installment contract, will also be in her gross estate under § 2033. The individual quarterly payments due after her death will not.

4. Interests Excluded

a. Powers of Appointment

It is often said that a general power of appointment exercisable during life is almost the same as fee simple ownership because all that the power holder has to do is ask for the property. The original estate tax included all property that was "subject to the payment of charges against [the decedent's] estate." In *United States v. Field*, 255 U.S. 257 (1921), the Supreme Court refused to apply this language to property that passed pursuant to the exercise of a general power of appointment because that property was not in the decedent's probate estate and, thus, not subject to the claims of the decedent's creditors. Although § 2033 is broader than its predecessor, other provisions now govern powers of appointment (§ 2041) and other non-probate property such as joint tenancy property (§ 2040) and life insurance proceeds (§ 2042).

b. Wrongful Death Proceeds

The proceeds of a wrongful death action brought by decedent's estate are not in the gross estate. The decedent did not have a property interest in that cause of action immediately prior to death; instead, the cause of action arose *because of* death. It does not matter if the proceeds are receivable by the decedent's beneficiaries or the decedent's estate. *Connecticut Bank and Trust Co. v. United States*, 465 F.2d 760 (2d Cir. 1972); Revenue Ruling 54–19, 1954–1 C.B. 179.

Any recovery for pain and suffering or for expenses incurred before death is, however, included in the gross estate pursuant to § 2033 because the decedent would have been entitled to these amounts if she had in fact survived. Revenue Ruling 69–8, 1969–1 C.B. 219; Revenue Ruling 75–127, 1975–1 C.B. 297.

c. **Social Security Benefits**

A lump sum benefit paid to a decedent's surviving spouse under the Social Security Act is not included in her gross estate pursuant to § 2033. That benefit passes to the spouse, not from the decedent, but from the government. The decedent has no control over who would receive it. Revenue Ruling 55–87, 1955–1 C.B. 112. This rationale will also apply to other statutory benefits.

5. **Exam Strategy**

There are two prongs to a § 2033 analysis: (1) Did the decedent own a property interest at the moment immediately before death? and (2) Did that property interest transfer *from the decedent* to another person? Look to state law for what is, or is not, a property interest. If that property interest passes by intestacy or by will, it will be included in the gross estate by § 2033.

C. MARITAL INTERESTS IN PROPERTY: § 2034

1. **General Principles**

In common law property jurisdictions, a surviving spouse has a legal right to a share of the decedent's estate. This right is reflected both in the intestacy statues and in the elective share statutes. These rights, however, do not reduce the value of the decedent's gross estate. Section 2034 so provides.

Example 6.6

Drew lives in a common law property jurisdiction. He owns the family home in his own name (fair market value $600,000); a car, bank accounts and personal property (fair market value $100,000); and investments (fair market value $4,300,000). All of these assets are in his gross estate pursuant to § 2033 because he owns them in fee simple. Drew is married to Clara. State law provides that she has a right to one-half of the decedent's net probate estate. Nonetheless, because of § 2034, Drew's gross estate is valued at $5,000,000. Clara's rights do not diminish the value of his gross estate.

If Clara exercises her right to one-half of Drew's property, she will receive $2,500,000, and his estate will be entitled to a marital deduction of that amount. Assuming no other deductions, his taxable estate will be $2,500,000. The same result occurs if Drew leaves one-half his property to Clara in his will. If he leaves her all of his property, the marital deduction would be $5,000,000 and his taxable estate will be $0.

2. Exam Strategy

Do not decrease the value of decedent's gross estate due to the rights of a surviving spouse. The marital deduction will apply to any interests going to the surviving spouse whether in intestacy, under the will, or pursuant to state law.

CHAPTER 7

JOINTLY OWNED PROPERTY

A. GENERAL PRINCIPLES

1. Forms of Concurrent Ownership

Taxpayers can own concurrent interests in property as tenants in common, joint tenants with the right of survivorship and, in some jurisdictions, as tenants by the entirety. The presumption in most, if not all, jurisdictions is that property deeded, given, devised, or transferred through intestacy to two or more individuals results in a tenancy in common. There must be specific language creating a joint tenancy with the right of survivorship or a tenancy by the entirety. A tenancy by the entirety applies only to spouses, and the transfer tax consequences are the same as those of joint tenancy with the right of survivorship.

2. Transfer on Death

A taxpayer can transfer an interest as a tenant in common by will or through intestacy. The taxpayer's interest, therefore, is brought into his gross estate by § 2033. When a joint tenant dies, that interest passes automatically to the surviving joint tenant by operation of law. The transfer tax consequences depend on whether the only joint tenants are spouses, in which case § 2040(b) applies, or whether the joint tenants include non-spouses, in which case § 2040(a) applies.

B. SPOUSAL JOINT TENANCIES: § 2040(b)

1. General Rule

If the joint tenants own a qualified joint interest, then only one-half of the value of the joint tenancy interest is included in the gross estate of the first joint tenant to die. § 2040(b)(1). **A qualified joint interest** is one that is owned either (1) as tenants by the entirety, which applies only to spouses, or (2) as joint tenants with the right of survivorship but only if the decedent and the surviving spouse are the only joint tenants. The rule of § 2040(b) means that a married couple does not need to keep records to establish who paid what portion of the consideration for the property.

2. Marital Deduction

The one-half interest of the decedent in joint tenancy property qualifies for the marital deduction. It is included in the gross estate of the decedent (§ 2040(b)), and it passes from the decedent to the surviving spouse (§ 2056(c)(5)). As a result, there will be no estate tax on joint tenancy interests passing from the decedent to the surviving spouse.

3. Surviving Spouse's Basis

A beneficiary receives a date-of-death value as her basis in property received from a decedent. § 1014. For property that has appreciated in value, this means the beneficiary receives a stepped-up basis and will have no income tax consequences if she sells the property immediately after decedent's death. When only one-half of the value of joint tenancy property is included in the decedent's gross estate under § 2040(b), only that one-half of the property will receive a stepped-up basis under § 1014.[1]

4. Exam Strategy

Section 2040(b) only applies to joint tenancy property owned by a married couple and to tenancy by the entirety property. This rule does not currently apply to a same-sex couple, even though legally married, because of the Defense of Marriage Act, 1 U.S.C. § 7. If § 2040(b) applies, only one-half the value of the joint tenancy property is in the decedent's gross estate regardless of who provided what portion of the consideration.

C. NON–SPOUSAL JOINT TENANCIES: § 2040(a)

1. General Rule

Section 2040(a) governs joint tenancies that are not spousal joint tenancies. This subsection provides that the full value of joint tenancy held property is to be included in the gross estate of the first joint tenant to die except "that part thereof as may be shown to have originally belonged to

---

1. Section 1014 does not apply to estates of decedents dying in 2010. Instead, § 1022 applies a carryover basis rule, *i.e.*, the estate and ultimately the beneficiary takes the decedent's basis in the property. Section 1022 includes a step-up in basis of $1.3 million plus an additional $3 million for property transferred to a surviving spouse.

[the surviving joint tenant].” This language creates a presumption that the first joint tenant to die provided all the consideration for the purchase of the jointly owned property. The survivor must establish her contribution toward the purchase of the property.

Example 7.1

Colin and Bronwyn are siblings and own Blackacre as joint tenants with the right of survivorship. Colin dies when Blackacre has a fair market value of $100,000. The full $100,000 will be in Colin's gross estate unless Bronwyn can establish her contribution to the purchase price.

Assume that the original cost of Blackacre was $50,000 and that Colin paid $30,000 while Bronwyn paid $20,000. In this situation that portion of the purchase price, *i.e.*, $20,000/$50,000 or 40 percent, which originally belonged to Bronwyn, the survivor, is excluded from Colin's gross estate. As a result, only $60,000 is included in Colin's gross estate.

---

2. Gifts or Bequests to Individuals as Joint Tenants

A different rule applies when all the joint tenants acquire their interests as gifts or bequests from someone else. In these cases, the interest of the deceased joint tenant is his fractional interest in the property.

Example 7.2

Assume that Colin and Bronwyn from example 7.1 did not purchase Blackacre, but instead their mother, Sharon, devised it to them as joint tenants in her will. Colin dies when Blackacre has a fair market value of $100,000. In this case, only one-half the value, Colin's fractional interest, will be in his gross estate because neither Colin nor Bronwyn paid any part of the consideration for the purchase of Blackacre.

---

3. Consideration

a. Paid by the Surviving Joint Tenant

Section 2040(a) excludes that portion of the value that is attributable to the consideration paid by the surviving joint tenant. The exclusion can be represented by the following fraction:

consideration paid by the surviving joint tenant

total consideration paid for the property

Example 7.3

Colin and Bronwyn, who are siblings, purchase Whiteacre. The cost is $100,000. Colin pays $25,000 and Bronwyn pays $75,000. Colin dies when Whiteacre has a fair market value of $200,000. The amount excluded is:

$75,000 (*i.e.*, the consideration paid by Bronwyn, the survivor)

$100,000 (*i.e.*, the total consideration for the purchase of Whiteacre)

This is 75 percent; so 75 percent of the date of death value ($150,000) is excluded from Colin's gross estate. The result is that $50,000 ($200,000—$150,000) is included in Colin's gross estate.

---

b. Received from the Decedent

It would be easy to avoid the rule in § 2040(a) simply by having the decedent give part of the consideration to the surviving joint tenant prior to the acquisition of the property.

Example 7.4

Mother plans to purchase Greenacre and take title with Son as joint tenants with the right of survivorship. The purchase price of Greenacre is $40,000. Mother gives Son $20,000. Then they purchase Greenacre, each contributing $20,000. Twenty years later, when Greenacre has a value of $100,000, Mother dies. Arguably, only $50,000 is in her gross estate because Son provided one-half the consideration for the purchase of Greenacre.

Section 2040(a) prevents this blatant attempt at tax avoidance. It excludes consideration that was "received or acquired by the [surviving joint tenant] from the decedent for less than an adequate and full consideration in money or money's worth." As a result, the full date of death value of Greenacre will be in Mother's gross estate.

---

c. What Qualifies, or Not, as Consideration

Any amount that the surviving joint tenant pays for the acquisition or improvement of the property qualifies as consideration unless, of course, that amount had been gifted to the survivor by the decedent. Paying part of the down payment, making mortgage payments, and paying for improvements on the property qualify. Income earned on the property that is taxed to survivor as income and then used to purchase additional joint tenancy property qualifies as the survivor's contribution. The same rule applies to appreciation in value that is recognized by the survivor for purposes of the income tax.

Example 7.5

Mother and Son purchase Greenacre for $40,000. Mother contributes the entire purchase price. Greenacre is commercial real estate, and Mother and Son each report one-half of the net rental income on their income taxes. Mother and Son then purchase Greyacre for $50,000, with each paying $25,000. Son uses the rental income from Greenacre as his contribution toward the purchase of Greyacre. Mother dies when Greyacre has a fair market value of $80,000. Only $40,000 will be included in Mother's gross estate because the $25,000 paid by Son will be sufficient consideration.

Example 7.6

Same basic facts as example 7.5. Mother contributes the entire purchase price of Greenacre. Now assume that Mother and Son sell Greenacre for $50,000. Each reports $25,000 as their amount realized and pays income tax on their share of the appreciation (*i.e.*, $5,000). Son uses his half of the proceeds, $25,000, to purchase Greyacre with Mother as joint tenants. The cost of Greyacre is $50,000. Mother dies when Greyacre has a fair market value of $80,000. The amount excluded will be:

$$\frac{\$5,000 \text{ (amount of taxable gain to Son)}}{\$50,000 \text{ (cost of Greyacre)}}$$

This is ten percent. So ten percent of the value of Greyacre or $8,000 will be excluded. As a result, $72,000 ($80,000—$8,000) will be included Mother's gross estate. Only the amount of the taxable gain and not the full amount realized is treated as Son's contribution. The other $20,000 that he paid is consideration that was received "from the decedent for less than an adequate and full consideration in money or money's worth." *Estate of Goldsborough v. Commissioner*, 70 T.C. 1077, 1081 (1978); Revenue Ruling 79–372, 1979–2 C.B. 330.

Example 7.7

Same basic facts as example 7.5. Mother contributes the entire purchase price of Greenacre, *i.e.*, $40,000. When Greenacre has a fair market value of $50,000, Mother and Son exchange Greenacre for Whiteacre in a like-kind exchange that qualifies for non-recognition under § 1031. Mother dies when Whiteacre has a fair market value of $80,000. The entire date of death value will be in Mother's gross estate because Son has not contributed any of the consideration for its purchase. His contribution was his share of Greenacre, which he had received from Mother for less than an adequate and full consideration in money or money's worth.

---

   d.   **Services**

   Services can qualify as consideration. This is particularly true in a business context between unrelated parties, and it is also true in a business context between related parties. In such cases, the courts will usually find that there is a joint venture. *See, e.g., United States v. Neel*, 235 F.2d 395 (10th Cir. 1956), where a husband and wife each made significant contributions of labor and services to joint undertakings in farming, business, and the practice of law.

   When services are rendered in a family context, there will be a presumption that such services are gratuitous. The survivor will have the burden of proving that there was an agreement that services would be treated as consideration. *See, e.g., Campana v. Commissioner*, 26 Mass.App.Ct. 105, 524 N.E.2d 113 (1988), where son lived with mother following his father's death, looked after her and her investments, helped with maintenance of the house, and accompanied her to social, church, and political events. The court held that mother's transfer of the house to herself and son was gratuitous and not for services rendered.

3.   **Exam Strategy**

   Begin with the presumption that the decedent paid all the consideration. Then look for any consideration, money, property, or services contributed by the survivor. The amount excluded is the percentage of the cost of the property paid by the survivor.

D. VALUATION OF JOINT TENANCY PROPERTY

When the decedent owns a minority interest in a business, a discount may be applied to reflect that fact. Regulation § 20.2031–2(e). No minority interest or fractional interest discount is allowed for joint tenancy property. *Estate of Young v. Commissioner*, 110 T.C. 297 (1998); *Estate of Fratini v. Commissioner*, 76 T.C.M. (CCH) 342 (1998). The rationale is twofold. First, the statute requires that *the entire value* be included, less any portion attributable to the survivor's contribution. Second, each joint tenant owns an undivided interest in the property.

CHAPTER 8

RETAINED INTERESTS

A. GENERAL PRINCIPLES

Sections 2035 through 2038 are referred to as the retained interest sections because, with limited exceptions, these sections only apply if the decedent owned property and made a transfer of that property or an interest in that property during his life. These sections were one sentence in the original estate tax statute, which included all property to the extent "of any interest therein of which the decedent has at any time made a transfer . . . in contemplation of or intended to take effect in possession or enjoyment at or after his death." Revenue Act of 1916, § 202(b). If the current sections cause confusion, return to this language and ask, "Is this the type of transfer that is intended to take effect at or after death?" That is, is it testamentary in nature? If the answer is "yes," the interest is likely to be brought into the gross estate by one of the retained interest sections.

B. LIFE ESTATES AND THE RIGHT TO ENJOYMENT OF PROPERTY: § 2036(a)(1)

1. General Rule

Section 2036(a)(1) includes in the decedent's gross estate the value of all property to the extent of any interest in that property which the decedent has transferred during his life if the decedent retained either (1) a right to the income or (2) the use, possession, or enjoyment of the property. There are two different components. One is the **right to the income** whether or not the decedent is actually receiving the income at his death. The other is **actual use, possession, or enjoyment** of property even if the decedent does not have a legal right to the property.

2. Period for Which Interest is Retained

The decedent must retain either the right to income or the use of the property for: (1) his life; (2) a period which does not in fact end before his death; or (3) a period which is not ascertainable without reference to his death.

a. For Life

The first rule is relatively easy. The decedent must retain the right to the income or the possession of the property for his life. If the decedent is receiving the income or has possession of the property at the time of his death, this requirement is met.

Example 8.1

Trent created an irrevocable, inter vivos trust with Friendly National Bank as trustee, to pay the income to himself for his life and the remainder to his children. When Trent dies, the full value of the trust property as of the date of his death will be in his gross estate pursuant to § 2036(a)(1) because Trent had the right to income from the entire trust property for his life.

---

b. For a Period Which Does Not in Fact End Before Death

The second rule applies when the decedent has retained a term of years or a term certain and dies before the end of the term.

Example 8.2

Trent creates an irrevocable, inter vivos trust with Friendly National Bank as trustee, to pay the income to himself for 10 years and then to distribute the trust property to his children. Trent dies in the seventh year of the trust. The full value of the trust property as of the date of his death will be in his gross estate pursuant to § 2036(a)(1) because Trent had the right to income for a period which did not in fact end before his death.

If Trent had lived for 11 years, he would not have been receiving income from the trust at the time of his death. As a result, nothing would be in his gross estate. This is, in fact, the strategy employed by grantor retained interest trusts (GRITs). It is always a gamble. Sometimes the decedent wins the gamble; other times not. If the decedent wins, nothing is in his gross estate. If the decedent loses, the fair market value of the trust property on the date of death is in his gross estate pursuant to § 2036(a)(1).

---

c. For a Period Which is Not Ascertainable Without Reference to Death

The third rule exists to prevent tax avoidance through clever schemes.

> **Example 8.3**
>
> Having been told that he cannot retain the right to income for his life or a period that does not in fact end before his death, Trent drafts his irrevocable, inter vivos trust to provide for the right to income "up until the quarterly distribution for the quarter that ends before my death and any income earned after that distribution will be accumulated and distributed with the trust principal." If quarterly payments are made on April 1, July 1, September 1, and January 1, and Trent dies on June 15, he would not have a right to the income earned after March 31. So, he has no right to income at the time of his death.
>
> Section 2036(a)(1), however, includes the date of death value of the trust principal in his gross estate because he has retained the right to the trust income for a period that is not ascertainable without reference to his death. In other words, his right to income cannot be determined until the date of his death is established.

3. Right to Income From Property

Section 2036(a)(1) applies if the decedent had the right to the trust income. See examples 8.1, 8.2, and 8.3 above. It does not matter that the decedent is not in fact receiving the trust income as long as he has the legal right to receive it.

4. Trustee Discretion to Distribute Income to the Donor

Section 2036(a)(1) will not apply to a trust if the trustee has absolute discretion to distribute income to the decedent. In that case, the decedent does not have a legally enforceable right to the income. Taxpayers can easily avoid this rule, so it will not apply if:

a. there is an explicit, or even implicit, understanding between the decedent and the trustee that the trustee will in fact distribute trust income to the decedent whenever he wants it;

b. state law provides that the decedent's creditors can reach trust income despite the trustee's sole and absolute discretion, which can occur in states that have not adopted legislation permitting self-settled asset protection (or spendthrift) trusts; or

c.   the trustee's discretion is limited by an ascertainable standard relating to health, education, maintenance, or support in which case the decedent, not the trustee, is actually in control of the flow of trust income.

Example 8.4

Trent creates an irrevocable, inter vivos trust with Friendly National Bank as trustee. The trustee has sole and absolute discretion to distribute trust income to Trent during his life. Any income not distributed will be accumulated and added to principal. Trust principal will be distributed to Trent's surviving issue. Assume that Friendly National Bank makes regular distributions of trust income to Trent during the term of the trust. When Trent dies, the trust property will be included in his gross estate pursuant to § 2036(a)(1) because the pattern of trust distributions indicates a strong likelihood that there was an agreement, either express or implied, that the trustee would in fact distribute income to Trent during his life.

Example 8.5

Trent creates an irrevocable, inter vivos trust with Friendly National Bank as trustee. The trustee has discretion to distribute trust income to Trent for his health or support or in an emergency. "Health or support" and "an emergency" are both ascertainable standards. Regulations §§ 2041–1(c)(2), 25.2511–1(g)(2), 25.2514–1(c)(2). As a result, the full value of the trust property, as of the date of Trent's death, will be in his gross estate. Because the trustee's discretion is limited by an ascertainable standard, Trent controls whether or not there is a distribution of income and, thus, he has a right to trust income.

---

5.   Secondary Life Estate

Section 2036(a)(1) also applies when the decedent retains a right to income following an income interest in another person. The decedent does not need to be actually receiving income at the moment of death as long as he has *the right* to the income.

Example 8.6

Tracy creates an irrevocable, inter vivos trust with Friendly National Bank as trustee to pay the income to George for his life, then to pay the income to Tracy for her life, and then to distribute the remainder to Tracy's descendants. Tracy dies before George. The value of the trust as of the date of her death less the value of George's life estate will be in her gross estate. Regulation § 20.2036–1(b)(1)(ii).

---

6. Retained Enjoyment of Property

a. General Principle

Section 2036(a)(1) also includes in the decedent's gross estate property transferred during life if the decedent is in fact in possession of that property at his death. This issue often arises when a decedent gives her residence to her child but is living in the residence at the time of her death.

Illustrative Case

In *Estate of Rapelje v. Commissioner*, 73 T.C. 82 (1979), the decedent transferred his residence to his two daughters on August 11, 1969, and reported the transfer as a gift. Decedent traveled to Florida in November 1969 for a vacation. Although he considered purchasing a house there, he did not do so and returned to his former residence in May 1970. Decedent lived at his residence until his death on November 18, 1973. Even though there was no explicit agreement allowing decedent to retain the possession and enjoyment of the residence, the court determined that there was an implicit agreement and included the residence in decedent's gross estate. The court found that the decedent's exclusive possession and his withholding possession from the donees were particularly significant. The court found decedent's search for a residence in Florida to be of little weight because he had made identical trips to Florida, although without looking at houses, for ten years. Moreover, the decedent paid no rent and he continued to pay the real estate taxes and most of the costs of maintaining the house. Finally, the donees did not make any attempt to sell their own homes or to occupy decedent's house.

---

b. Payment of Rent

If decedent pays the donees fair market rent and all parties treat decedent like a tenant rather than an owner, the decedent may be able to avoid § 2036(a)(1). The result in any particular case will depend on all the facts and circumstances.

Illustrative Case

In *Estate of Barlow v. Commissioner*, 55 T.C. 666 (1971), decedent gave his four children parcels from a 372–acre farm. The decedent recorded the deeds and filed gift tax returns. At the same time, decedent and his children executed leases on each of the parcels that allowed decedent to rent each parcel at its fair rental value. The leases were recorded and required decedent to pay the property taxes and to cultivate the land "in a good, careful, and farmerlike manner." *Id.* at 667. The court held that the property was not in decedent's gross estate, relying on the form of the transaction. It noted that the right to receive rent was the most valuable of the incidents of ownership and that "[h]e who receives the rent in fact enjoys the property." *Id.* at 671. The children had the right to the rent and were entitled to terminate the lease and evict the decedent if the rent was not in fact paid.

Illustrative Case

In *Estate of Maxwell v. Commissioner*, 3 F.3d 591 (2d Cir. 1993), the decedent sold her residence to her son and his wife but she continued to occupy the house until her death two years later. Decedent forgave $20,000 (the amount of the gift tax annual exclusion was then $10,000 per donee) of the $250,000 purchase price at the time of the sale, and she forgave $20,000 of the mortgage principal each year. In her will, she forgave the remaining debt. The decedent did pay her son rent in each of the three years she occupied the house after the sale, and her son paid interest on the mortgage in each of those years. The rent paid in each year was approximately equal to the interest due in each year. The parties stipulated that the fair market value of the house at the time of the sale was $280,000, but the donees sold the house two and one-half years later, shortly after decedent's death, for

---

$550,000. The court held that the mortgage and promissory note signed by the decedent's son and his wife were not adequate and full consideration for the transfer because decedent had never intended to collect on that note. As a result, the court characterized the initial transaction as a gift and held that decedent's retained possession of the house until her death required its inclusion in her gross estate pursuant to § 2036(a)(1). The most significant factor in this case may have been the testimony of decedent's attorney that the donor had no intention of collecting on the debt. Moreover, there was no evidence that the rent charged had any relationship to the fair rental value of the house.

c. Substantial Economic Benefit

In other contexts, such as Family Limited Partnerships (discussed in section E.3.), courts look to see if the decedent has retained a substantial present economic benefit from the property.

7. Legal Obligation of Support

A decedent has a legal obligation to support her spouse and her minor children. If property is used to satisfy this obligation, it may be included in decedent's gross estate pursuant to § 2036(a)(1). Regulation § 20.2036–1(b)(2). There are two different rules.

a. Decedent as Trustee

If the decedent is the trustee of a trust and has discretion to use the income or principal or both for the support of her children (or spouse), the trust will be in the decedent's gross estate if she dies while the children are minors (or she is married). Because the decedent is the trustee, she is in control and can decide whether or not to use the trust property to discharge her legal obligation.

b. Independent Trustee

If the trustee is an independent trustee, *i.e.*, one that is not related or subordinate to the decedent, the trust property will be in the decedent's gross estate only if the trustee is required to distribute trust income (or principal) for the support of decedent's minor children (or spouse) or if the trustee is in fact doing so.

Illustrative Case

In *Estate of Gokey v. Commissioner*, 72 T.C. 721 (1979), the decedent created a trust for the benefit of his children. He died when two of his children were aged 15 and 13. The trust provided that "the Trustee shall use such part or all of the net income of . . . the trust for the support, care, welfare, and education" of the beneficiaries. *Id.* at 722. The court first held that the word "shall" required the trustee to distribute income for the stated purposes. It then held that the phrase "support, care, welfare, and education" was equivalent to an ascertainable standard for the support of the beneficiaries. *Id.* at 726. Because the trust income was required to be used to satisfy the decedent's legal obligation of support, the court held that the trust property was included in his gross estate pursuant to § 2036(a)(1).

8. Exam Strategy

Do a three-step analysis. First, determine if the decedent owned a property interest. Second, determine if the decedent made a transfer of that property interest. Third, determine if the decedent retained a right to the income from that property. This includes: (1) the immediate right to the income; (2) the right to the income after someone else's death or a term of years; and (3) the ability to have the income used to discharge the decedent's support obligation. If the decedent does not have a right to the income, then look to see if the decedent has the use, possession, or enjoyment of the property at the time of her death even if she does not have a legal right to it. As long as she has a substantial economic benefit, she will be deemed to have enjoyment of the property.

C. RETAINED POWER TO DESIGNATE ENJOYMENT OF PROPERTY: §§ 2036(a)(2) and 2038

1. Powers in General

When the decedent has the power to control the beneficial enjoyment of property, that property will be included in her gross estate under § 2036(a)(2) or § 2038(a)(1) or both. In most cases, the power will cause inclusion under both sections. In some cases, only one of the sections will apply. And in still other cases, one section will bring only a portion of the property into the gross estate while the other section will bring the entire property into the gross estate. The provision that will cause the greatest value to be included will control, but there will never be more than 100 percent of the value of the property in the gross estate.

a. Section 2036(a)(2)

This section brings into the gross estate:

(1) property transferred by the decedent;

(2) if the decedent retained the right to determine who will enjoy the property or the income from it; and

(3) the decedent retained the power (a) for life, (b) for a period which did not in fact end before death, or (c) for a period that is not ascertainable without reference to death.

This includes the power to determine beneficial enjoyment even when the property cannot return to the decedent.

Example 8.7

Carl creates an irrevocable inter vivos trust. The trustee has the power to distribute income among Carl's children. At the death of the last child, the trust property will be distributed to Carl's descendants. Carl is serving as the trustee at his death. Because Carl has the power to determine who will receive trust income and his power extends over the entire trust income, the value of the trust property will be included in his gross estate pursuant to § 2036(a)(2).

---

b. Section 2038(a)(1)

This section brings into the gross estate:

(1) property transferred by the decedent;

(2) if the decedent had the power to alter, amend, terminate, or revoke; and

(3) the decedent had the power at the moment of his death.

This includes a power that is exercisable only in the decedent's will.

Example 8.8

Karen creates an irrevocable inter vivos trust with Friendly National Bank to distribute income to her children and grandchildren. Karen reserves the right to designate who will receive the trust property in her will. Only § 2038(a)(1) will apply in this situation because Karen has not retained the power for her life. Section 2038(a)(1) will only include the remainder in her gross estate because she does not have the power to alter or amend the income interest.

If Karen had the power, exercisable only in her will, to add or eliminate income beneficiaries as well as remaindermen, then the entire date of death value of the trust property will be in her gross estate pursuant to § 2038(a)(1).

---

2.   **Ascertainable Standards**

Powers that are limited by an ascertainable standard relating to health, education, maintenance, or support will not cause inclusion under either § 2036(a)(2) or § 2038(a)(1). Although neither the Internal Revenue Code nor the regulations refers to this principle, it is well established in judicial decisions. The rationale is that the decedent is not in *control* when the power is limited by an ascertainable standard because the beneficiary can go to court to enforce the power.

a.   **Powers Limited by an Ascertainable Standard Include:**

   (1)   to maintain the beneficiary in his accustomed standard of living, Jennings v. Smith, 161 F.2d 74 (2d Cir. 1947);

   (2)   in the case of prolonged illness or financial misfortune, Jennings v. Smith, 161 F.2d 74 (2d Cir. 1947);

   (3)   in the case of sickness or if desirable in view of changed circumstances, Old Colony Trust Co. v. United States, 423 F.2d 601 (1st Cir. 1970).

b.   **Powers Not Limited by an Ascertainable Standard Include:**

   (1)   the best interests of the beneficiary, Old Colony Trust Co. v. United States, 423 F.2d 601 (1st Cir. 1970);

(2) if necessary and proper, Leopold v. United States, 510 F.2d 617 (9th Cir. 1975).

c. Administrative Powers

Trustees have broad administrative and management powers over trust property. This includes the power to invest the trust property, to buy and sell trust property, to allocate receipts between income and principal, to borrow money, and the like. These powers, while they can affect the beneficial enjoyment of the trust property, will not cause the trust property to be included in the decedent's gross estate pursuant to either § 2036(a)(2) or § 2038(a)(1). *Old Colony Trust Co. v. United States*, 423 F.2d 601 (1st Cir. 1970). The rationale is that the decedent as trustee is bound by fiduciary obligations in exercising these powers and is subject to review and control by the court. As a result, the decedent does not have unfettered control to determine beneficial enjoyment. *Id.*

3. Power to Appoint Trustees

If the decedent is not the trustee but has the power to replace the trustee, will the trustee's powers be imputed to the decedent? The IRS initially took the position that the trustees' powers would be imputed to the decedent even when the decedent could not become the trustee. The Tax Court rejected this argument in *Estate of Wall v. Commissioner*, 101 T.C. 300 (1993), because a trustee would violate its fiduciary obligations to the beneficiaries if it acceded to any and all requests of the decedent/grantor of the trust. The IRS conceded defeat in Revenue Ruling 95–58, 1995–2 C.B. 191 and will not impute the trustees' powers to the decedent if the decedent can only replace the existing trustee with one that is neither related nor subordinate. A related or subordinate trustee is someone that does not have a substantial beneficial interest in the trust that would be adversely affected by the exercise of the power and who is (1) the grantor's spouse (if living with the grantor), parent, issue, sibling, or employee; (2) a corporation or employee of a corporation in which the grantor has significant voting control; or (3) a corporation or employee of a corporation in which the grantor is an executive. *Id. See also* § 672(a), (c).

4. Joint Powers

Both § 2036(a)(2) and § 2038(a)(1) apply where the decedent has the power alone or in conjunction with any other person. Unlike the income tax (§ 672(a)) or the gift tax (Regulation § 25.2511–2(e)), there is no safe harbor if that other person has a *substantial adverse interest*. The retained interest sections apply when the other person has (1) no interest in the property, (2) an interest that is not adverse to the exercise of the power, or (3) an interest that is adverse to the exercise of the power.

Example 8.9

Gerald creates an irrevocable, inter vivos trust and is serving as trustee. The trustee has discretion to accumulate income or distribute it among Gerald's children, but only with the consent of Gerald's wife, Wilma. Gerald dies while serving as trustee. The trust property will be in his gross estate pursuant to both § 2036(a)(2) and § 2038(a)(1) even though he must obtain the consent of Wilma. The same result applies if Wilma is an income beneficiary and has an interest that is substantial and adverse to the distribution of income to others.

---

5. Contingent Powers

Section 2038(a)(1) will not apply to a power that can only be exercised if a specific contingency occurs; § 2036(a)(1), however, is not so limited. *Compare* Regulation § 20.2038–1(b) *with* Regulation § 20.2036–1(b)(3).

Example 8.10

Michelle creates an irrevocable, inter vivos trust and is serving as the trustee at the time of her death. The trustee is to distribute the income quarterly to Michelle's daughter, Rowan, and the trustee also has the power to distribute trust principal to Rowan but only if her husband, Richard, has died or they are divorced. At Michelle's death, Rowan is still married to Richard. The trust property will not be included in Michelle's gross estate under § 2038(a)(1) because her power is subject to a contingency that did not in fact occur. It will be included under § 2036(a)(2), however, because that section applies even where "the exercise of the power was subject to a contingency beyond the decedent's control which did not occur before [her] death." Regulation § 20.2036–1(b)(3).

---

6. Exam Strategy

Analyze § 2036(a)(2) and § 2038(a)(1) separately. Always consider both sections. Section 2036(a)(2) requires: (1) that decedent owned the property; (2) that decedent made a transfer; and (3) that decedent retained the power to control beneficial enjoyment. Section 2038 requires: (1) that decedent owned the property; (2) that decedent made a transfer; and (3) that the decedent had the power to alter, amend, revoke, or terminate at the time of her death. For § 2038 to apply, the decedent need not have the power between the time of the transfer and the time of her death.

D. RECIPROCAL TRUSTS

1. General Rule

The decedent cannot avoid application of §§ 2036 and 2038 by creating reciprocal trusts with his spouse, his sibling, or any other person. There does not need to be an explicit, or even implicit, agreement between the parties. It is enough that the trusts (1) are inter-related and (2) leave the parties in the same economic position they would have been in if they had created trusts for themselves. *United States v. Estate of Grace*, 395 U.S. 316 (1969).

Example 8.11

Henry and Wanda are married. Henry creates an irrevocable, inter vivos trust with Friendly National Bank as trustee to pay the income to Wanda for life and the remainder to their descendants. Wanda also creates an irrevocable, inter vivos trust with Friendly National Bank as trustee to pay the income to Henry for life and the remainder to their descendants. Henry dies. The value of the trust established for his benefit will be included in his gross estate pursuant to § 2036(a)(1).

---

2. Exam Strategy

The reciprocal trust doctrine can be extended to transfers that are not in trust. There does not need to be an agreement, only inter-related transfers that leave the parties in approximately the same economic position as if they had made the transfer themselves.

E. RETAINED BUSINESS INTERESTS

1. Right to Vote Stock: § 2036(b)

Does the right to vote stock give a decedent the power to control the beneficial enjoyment of the stock? The Supreme Court held "no" in *United States v. Byrum*, 408 U.S. 125 (1972), because the decedent had fiduciary obligations to the minority shareholders and because he was not trustee and, thus, could not control the distributions from the trust. Congress overruled *Byrum* in § 2036(b) and provided that the right to vote *will be* retention of the enjoyment of the transferred property if the corporation is controlled by the decedent. Control means that the decedent, during the three-year period ending on the date of his death, owned or had the right to vote stock possessing at least 20 percent of the total combined voting power of all classes of stock. The attribution rules of § 318 apply to determine decedent's ownership of the stock.

2. Applicable Retained Interests: § 2701

a. The Problem

Assume that decedent owns all the stock in a corporation and wants to transfer ownership of the corporation to his daughter with the least possible gift and estate taxes. Decedent transfers his common stock back to the corporation and receives in return two classes of stock: (1) preferred stock and (2) common stock. Decedent structures the preferred stock to absorb most, if not all, of the current value of the corporation. Decedent then transfers the common stock, and with it all future appreciation in the value of the corporation, to his daughter. With little or no value in the common stock, the decedent will pay no gift taxes. When the decedent dies, only the value of the preferred stock will be in his gross estate under § 2033. The decedent has frozen the value of this asset at its value at the time of the gift to his daughter. If the decedent does not enforce his right to dividends on the preferred stock, he can shift additional value to his daughter at no transfer tax cost.

b. The Solution

Section 2701 now blocks this estate freezing technique. If a transferor transfers an interest in a corporation or a partnership to a member of his family and either he, or an applicable family member, retains an interest, the value of the retained interest has no value unless it is a qualified payment. A qualified payment is a dividend payable on cumulative preferred stock at a fixed rate. § 2701(c)(3)(A). This ensures that the decedent does not shift economic benefit through failure to collect dividends. Section 2701(a)(4) requires that the junior equity, the common stock transferred to the next generation, have a value equal of greater than ten percent of all equity interests plus any debt owed the transferor or an applicable family member. This prevents decedent from shifting all future appreciation to the next generation at no gift tax cost.

3. **Family Limited Partnerships**

   a. **Discounts for Minority Interest and Lack of Marketability**

   Because minority interests in a business may be entitled to a discounted value to reflect that minority status, taxpayers transfer their property to a family limited partnership or limited liability company. When the taxpayer transfers interests in the entity to his children, those gifts will have a discounted value because they represent only a minority interest in the entity. If decedent is successful in transferring a significant percentage of the entity in this way, he will only own a minority interest at death and again receive a minority discount. If interests in the entity are subject to restrictions on transferability, they will enjoy further discounts.

   b. **Form versus Substance**

   This estate planning technique tends to elevate form over substance. Courts will disregard the form and tax the substance when the taxpayer ignores the formalities and treats the partnership property as his own. Courts will also disregard the form and tax the substance when the taxpayer is too greedy, for example, by transferring all of his assets, often including his personal residence, into the partnership. Courts will also disregard the form when there is no legitimate business purpose, other than tax avoidance, for creating the partnership.

   c. **Application of § 2036(a)(1)**

   When the decedent creates a family limited partnership or limited liability company, the court will apply § 2036(a)(1) to determine if the decedent has retained use, possession, or enjoyment of the property. The court will find such retention where the decedent has retained a substantial economic benefit from the transferred property. That benefit exists if there is either an express or an implied agreement that the transferred property will be used for the decedent's benefit.

   d. **Bona Fide Sale for Adequate and Full Consideration**

   The decedent can avoid application of § 2036(a)(1) if the transfer is a bona fide sale for adequate and full consideration. The courts have held that the consideration is adequate and full if decedent receives partnership or limited liability member units proportionate to his contribution to the business. The bona fide sale requirement is only met if the decedent has a legitimate, nontax business reason for

155

creating the company. All the facts and circumstances are relevant in determining whether or not such a reason exists, and each case is decided on its own merits. It is, therefore, difficult to make any generalizations.

(1) Sufficient Nontax Business Reasons

(a) In Estate of Stone v. Commissioner, 86 T.C.M. (CCH) 551 (2003), the decedent created family limited partnerships with his children and transferred ongoing businesses to each of them. The decedent created the partnerships to transfer management of the businesses to the children and to settle disputes among the children regarding the operation of the businesses. The children had been active in the businesses before the transfers and assumed more significant management responsibilities afterwards.

(b) In Kimbell v. United States, 371 F.3d 257 (5th Cir. 2004), the decedent transferred working interests in oil and gas properties that required active business management and other assets to a family limited partnership. Other justifications for the transfer included protection from creditors, centralizing management of investment assets, and preserving property as separate family property.

(c) In Estate of Schutt v. Commissioner, 89 T.C.M. (CCH) 1353 (2005), the decedent transferred DuPont and Exxon stock, which were a significant portion of the family wealth, to a family limited partnership in order to retain those holdings and to perpetuate his "buy and hold" investment philosophy.

(d) In Estate of Bongard v. Commissioner, 124 T.C. 95 (2005), the court held that creation of a holding company to facilitate corporate liquidity and pooling of investment assets was sufficient.

(e) In Estate of Mirowski v. Commissioner, 95 T.C.M. (CCH) 1277 (2008), decedent created a limited liability company after her husband's death when royalties from his invention increased to millions of dollars per year. The Tax Court held that her interest in jointly managing assets with her daughters, the creation of a single pool for investment opportunities, and providing for each of her three daughters on an equal basis were legitimate and significant nontax business purposes.

(f) In Estate of Miller v. Commissioner, 97 T.C.M. (CCH) 1602 (2009), the decedent's desire to have her marketable securities managed according to her husband's investment philosophy of charting stocks was a sufficient nontax business purpose.

(2) Insufficient Nontax Business Reasons

(a) In Strangi v. Commissioner, 417 F.3d 468 (5th Cir. 2005), the decedent transferred almost all of his assets to the partnership. The court rejected every claimed justification for creation of the partnership, finding no need for protection against a potential will contest by decedent's stepchildren or against a potential claim by his housekeeper. The court also found that the partnership was not justified either as a joint venture or by the need for centralized and active management of investments. The primary assets contributed to the partnership were brokerage accounts that continued to be managed in the same way after creation of the partnership as before.

(b) In Estate of Bigelow v. Commissioner, 503 F.3d 955 (9th Cir. 2007), there was no pooling of assets and no change in management of decedent's assets. The court also rejected the argument that facilitation of decedent's gift-giving program was a nontax business purpose.

(c) In Estate of Rosen v. Commissioner, 91 T.C.M. (CCH) 1220 (2006), the assets contributed to the partnership were marketable securities and cash, and the partnership engaged in minimal business or investment activities. The court again rejected the argument that there was a sufficient nontax business purpose for creation of the partnership. The court emphasized that decedent was 88 years old and suffering from Altzheimer's disease when she created the partnership, that she transferred almost all her assets to it, and that she remained financially dependent on those assets.

(d) In Estate of Hurford v. Commissioner, 96 T.C.M. (CCH) 422 (2008), the decedent created three family limited partnerships. The court found no legitimate, significant nontax business purpose for any of the three, holding that there needed to be either a functioning business or some meaningful economic activity. One partnership held only cash and marketable securities and all investment decisions continued to be made by Chase Bank, which had been making those investments before the creation of the partnership. One partnership held only Hunt Oil phantom stock, which by its nature could only be held or cashed out. And, while the third partnership held real estate, the partnership only collected rents because the decedent had leased all of the real estate prior to creation of the partnership.

4. Exam Strategy

Section 2036 may apply to the transfer of a business if the decedent retains either the right to vote the stock or the right to preferred stock. It may also apply to a family limited partnership or limited liability company if there is not a substantial nontax business reason for creation of that entity. Always examine both the form of the transaction as well as the substance. While it is important to observe the formalities, doing so will not necessarily preclude inclusion of the transferred interest in the gross estate.

F. REVERSIONS: § 2037

1. Definition

A reversion is a future interest in property that is retained by the transferor. There are two sections that govern reversions: § 2033 and § 2037.

2. Section 2037

Section 2037 only applies if:

a. the decedent made a transfer and retained a reversion that exceeds five percent of the value of the trust property immediately before death, and

b. another person can obtain possession or enjoyment of the property only by surviving the decedent.

Example 8.12

Dwight creates an irrevocable, inter vivos trust to pay the income to Adam for life. At Adam's death, the trustee is to distribute the trust property to Dwight if he is living, otherwise to Ben. Dwight predeceases both Adam and Ben. The value of the trust property minus the value of Adam's life estate will be in Dwight's gross estate pursuant to § 2037 if his reversion, valued under the applicable valuation tables, exceeds 5 percent of the value of the trust property. In this situation, Ben will only obtain possession of the trust property if Dwight dies before Adam. If Adam had died first, the trust property would have been distributed to Dwight.

---

3. **Section 2033**

Section 2033 applies to reversions not included by § 2037.

Example 8.13

Donna creates an irrevocable, inter vivos trust to pay the income to Jordan for life. At Jordan's death, the trustee is to distribute the trust property to Amanda if she is living, otherwise to Donna. Donna predeceases Jordan and Amanda. Section 2037 does not apply. Amanda will obtain possession of the trust property as long as she survives Jordan. Donna's death is irrelevant.

Because it is possible that Amanda will predecease Jordan and the trust property will be distributed to Donna's estate, the value of the reversion is in her gross estate under § 2033. Donna has a property interest, *i.e.*, the reversion, immediately before her death and that reversion will transfer from her to a beneficiary either by her will or through intestacy.

---

4. **Exam Strategy**

If the decedent has retained a reversion, *i.e.*, the right to have the property return to him, start with § 2037. It is best to memorize the pattern, *i.e.*, income to A for life, then to D if living, otherwise to B. If D's reversion does not fit this pattern, determine if there is any possibility that the property will return to D's estate. If there is, then § 2033 applies.

159

G. TRANSFERS WITHIN THREE YEARS OF DEATH

1. General Principles

Section 2035 has a colorful history most of which is irrelevant today. So-called death bed gifts are not brought back into the gross estate unless they fit within the very narrow specifications of § 2035(a). The gift tax paid on any and all taxable gifts made within three years of death, however, is brought back into the gross estate. § 2035(b)

Example 8.14

Terry gave each of her five children $250,000 and died eighteen months later. Her gross estate does not include the $1,250,000 in taxable gifts because these were outright transfers to her children. The gift tax she paid on these transfers, however, will be included in her gross estate under § 2035(b).

---

2. Gifts of Life Insurance: § 2035(a)

Section 2035(a) does include in the gross estate the amount receivable by a beneficiary on the life of the decedent if the decedent owned the policy and transferred it within the three years immediately preceding his death. This rule does not apply if the beneficiary herself, or someone else, purchased the life insurance policy even if they did so within three years of death.

Example 8.15

Larry owned a life insurance policy on his own life, and his son, Silas, was the beneficiary. Larry transferred that policy to his son, Silas. Silas was then the owner as well as the beneficiary. Larry died two years after the transfer. The insurance company paid Silas $500,000. This $500,000 will be included in Larry's gross estate pursuant to § 2035(a) because the gift of the life insurance policy occurred within the three years preceding his death.

Example 8.16

Instead, Silas purchases a life insurance policy on his father's life and names himself as the beneficiary. Larry, his father, dies two years after Silas makes the purchase. As long as Larry did not own any incidents of ownership in the life insurance policy at his death or did not transfer any such incidents of ownership in the three years preceding his death, the $500,000 amount receivable by Silas will not be in Larry's gross estate under either § 2035(a) or § 2042(2).

3. Transfers of Retained Interests: § 2035(a)

Certain transfers of retained interests are also brought back into the decedent's gross estate by § 2035(a). These are the interests that would have been included in the decedent's gross estate under one of the following sections:

a. § 2036(a)(1), *i.e.*, retained life estates or right to possession of property;

b. § 2036(a)(2), *i.e.*, retained power to designate enjoyment of property;

c. § 2037, *i.e.*, certain reversions, or

d. § 2038, *i.e.*, retained power to alter, amend, revoke, or terminate.

For § 2035(a) to apply, the decedent must have (1) owned the property; (2) made a transfer and retained an interest that would trigger §§ 2036, 2037 or 2308; and (3) transferred that retained interest within three years of his death.

Example 8.17

Sophia created an irrevocable, inter vivos trust in year 1 with Friendly National Bank as trustee to pay the income to herself during her life and then to distribute the trust property to her surviving nieces and nephews. In year 10, Sophia transfers her life estate to her cousin, Craig. That transfer is, of course, a gift. Sophia dies in year 12. The entire value of the trust property will be included in Sophia's gross estate by § 2035(a) because (1) she owned property, (2) she transferred that property to the trust in year 1 and retained a right to the income for life, and (3) she gave her life estate to Craig within three years of her death. Had Sophia retained the life estate, the entire value of the trust property as of the date of her death would have been in her gross estate pursuant to § 2036(a)(1). Section 2035(a)(1) prevents her from avoiding the estate tax by making a gift of the retained interest within the three years preceding her death.

Example 8.18

Julie created a revocable, inter vivos trust in year 1 with Friendly National Bank as the trustee. In year 8, Julie released her power to revoke. Julie dies in year 10. Had she not released her right to revoke, the entire value of the trust property as of the date of her death would have been in her gross estate pursuant to § 2038. Because she released that power within three years of her death, § 2035(a) includes the trust property in her gross estate.

---

4. **Gift Tax: § 2035(b)**

   a. **General Rule**

   Section 2035(b) brings into the gross estate the gift tax paid on all gifts within three years of death. It applies to outright gifts as well as gifts of life insurance and retained interests.

Example 8.19

Assume there is a $1 million exemption amount and a maximum tax rate of 45 percent. Tanya makes gifts equal to the amount of the gift tax annual exclusion each year to her two children. In year 1, she also gives them each $500,000. No gift tax is due because of the unified credit in § 2505. In year 2, she again gives them each $500,000 in addition to the annual exclusion gifts. She pays the $435,000 gift tax due on April 15 of year 3. She dies on March 1 of year 4. Even though none of the gifts are brought back into her gross estate pursuant to § 2035(a), the $435,000 gift tax paid will be included in her gross estate pursuant to § 2035(b).

---

b. Rationale

The gift tax is **tax exclusive**. This means that the donor is liable for the gift tax over and above the amount of the gift. In example 8.19, Tanya's estate was diminished by $1,000,000 in year 1 and by $1,435,000 in year 2. The estate tax, on the other hand, is **tax inclusive**, *i.e.*, there is a tax imposed on the tax that is paid. The estate is liable for the estate tax, and it is paid from funds on which the tax was calculated. The purpose of § 2035(b) is to treat gifts made within three years of death, *i.e.*, "death-bed gifts," the same as transfers at death.

Example 8.20

In the prior example, Tanya transferred $2 million to her children and paid a gift tax of $435,000. Assume instead, that she had owned that $2,435,000 at the time of her death and, also assume a $1 million exemption amount and a maximum tax rate of 45 percent. The estate tax due would be $630,750. So her children would have received only $1,804,250 instead of $2,000,000. The difference of $195,750 is exactly equal to 45 percent of $435,000; in other words the amount of estate tax imposed on the $435,000.

Note that only gift tax paid on gifts within three years of death is included in the gross estate by § 2035(b). For the gift and estate taxes to be truly unified, the gift tax on all gifts would need to be included in the gross estate. Congress has not yet gone that far.

5. Exam Strategy

Watch out for gifts made within three years of death. Most of these gifts are not brought back into the gross estate. Only gifts of life insurance and retained interests are brought back into the gross estate if made within three years of death. On the other hand, the gift tax on any gift made within three years of death is included in the gross estate.

H. TRANSFERS FOR CONSIDERATION

1. In General

The gross estate does not include transfers that were made for adequate and full consideration in money or money's worth. Sections 2036, 2037, and 2038 explicitly exempt such transfers. The sufficiency of the consideration depends on the nature of the interest at issue.

2. Sale of a Life Estate

Section 2036(a)(1) includes in the gross estate the value of property where the decedent has retained the right to income for life. Where the decedent is entitled to all of the income, the full value of the trust principal is included in her gross estate. If the decedent decides to sell her retained life estate, the current rule is that she must receive as consideration the full value of the trust principal because that is what would have been included in her gross estate pursuant to § 2036(a)(1).

Illustrative Case

In *United States v. Allen*, 293 F.2d 916 (10th Cir. 1961), the decedent created an irrevocable, inter vivos trust and reserved 3/5th of the income for her life. When she was 78 years old, decedent was advised of the potential estate tax consequences and sold her life estate for its actuarial value to her son. She died unexpectedly a short time later. The court held that decedent had not received adequate and full consideration even though her son was a bona fide purchaser and had paid the actuarial value of the life estate. The court stated, "It does not seem plausible, however, that Congress intended to allow such an easy avoidance of the taxable incidence befalling reserved life estates. This result would allow a taxpayer to reap the benefits of property for his lifetime and, in contemplation of death, sell only the interest entitling him to the income, thereby removing all of the property which he has enjoyed from his gross estate." *Id.* at 918.

The rationale of this decision has been questioned by commentators and may no longer be viable in light of *Estate of D'Ambrosio v. Commissioner* discussed in the next section. The decision in *United States v. Allen*, however, has not been overruled either by Congress or the Tenth Circuit and it has not been confronted directly by any other court. It, therefore, continues to be the prevailing rule.

---

3. Sale of a Remainder

A taxpayer can avoid § 2036(a)(1) by selling the remainder interest for adequate and full consideration, *i.e.*, the actuarial value of the remainder interest. Initially courts refused to allow this estate planning technique, relying on the rationale of *United States v. Allen*. In *Estate of D'Ambrosio v. Commissioner*, 101 F.3d 309 (3d Cir. 1996), however, the court held that payment of the actuarial value of the remainder interest was adequate and full consideration. As a result, nothing was in the decedent's gross estate even though the decedent had retained the right to the income for life. The court in *Estate of Kelley v. Commissioner*, 63 T.C. 321 (1974), reached the same result.

The rationale of *Estate of D'Ambrosio* is simply the time value of money. The value of a remainder is the present value of the right to receive the property in the future. If the decedent receives this amount and then invests that amount without ever invading the principal or the accumulating interest, the decedent will have the full fair market value of the property in his gross estate albeit in the form of the investment rather than the property itself. The only thing missing is the appreciation in value of the original property. But there is nothing that says that a decedent cannot employ appropriate estate planning techniques to minimize his potential estate tax liability.

4. Family Limited Partnerships

The adequate and full consideration exception in § 2036 is critical in cases of family limited partnerships. The courts employ a two-step analysis. The first step is to determine if the decedent received adequate and full consideration on the creation of the family limited partnership. If the decedent receives partnership interests proportionate to her contribution of property to the partnership, this step of the analysis has been met. The second step is to determine if there has been a bona fide sale. This requires an arm's length transaction. In this context, courts require that there be a legitimate nontax business purpose for the creation of the family limited partnership. Only if this second step is also satisfied will the decedent be taxed on the value of the partnership interest, with discounts for lack of marketability and minority interests as appropriate. Failure to meet this two-part test will cause the underlying partnership assets (undiminished by any discounts) to be included in the gross estate rather than the partnership interest (which may be significantly discounted for minority status and lack of marketability).

5. Exam Strategy

Adequate and full consideration is the same for retained interests as for gifts. The consideration must be in money or money's worth. What is sufficient consideration depends on the nature of the transaction. In the context of family limited partnerships there is a two-part test. First, did the decedent receive an ownership interest equal to his contribution? Second, was there a legitimate nontax business purpose for the creation of the business entity?

CHAPTER 9

ANNUITIES AND DEATH BENEFITS

A. COMMERCIAL ANNUITIES

An annuity is the right to receive periodic payments for life or for a term of years. Annuities are sold by insurance companies as investments. Retirement benefits are often paid as annuities. So are structured settlements and lottery proceeds. Depending on the terms of the agreement, (1) nothing will be in the decedent's gross estate; (2) the value of the annuity payment following decedent's death will be in her gross estate under § 2033; or (3) the value of the annuity payments following decedent's death will be in her gross estate under § 2039.

1. Solely for Decedent's Life

If payments are made only for decedent's life, nothing will be in her gross estate. Neither § 2033 nor § 2039 will apply.

Example 9.1

Serena purchases an annuity from Metropolitan Life Insurance Company to pay her $3,500 per month from age 65 until her death. Serena dies at age 82. Payments cease at her death. Nothing is included in her gross estate. Section 2033 does not apply because nothing passes from Serena to another as a result of her death. Section 2039 does not apply because there is no other beneficiary who will receive payments under this annuity contract after Serena's death.

---

2. Refund Feature

A decedent may want to ensure that she recovers her investment in the annuity contract. She will, therefore, contract for payments for her life plus an additional payment to her estate if a stated amount has not been paid to her by the time of her death. If the payment to her estate is in fact made, the amount of that payment will be included in her gross estate pursuant to § 2033. Section 2033 applies because (1) decedent had a property interest in the annuity immediately before her death and (2) that interest passed from her to others as a result of her death either through her will or by intestacy.

Example 9.2

Serena purchases an annuity from Metropolitan Life Insurance Company to pay her $3,500 per month from age 65 until her death. If she dies before receiving $250,000 in payments, the difference between that amount and the amount she has received will be paid to her estate. Serena dies at age 75 after receiving $360,000 in annuity payments. Nothing will be in her gross estate because Metropolitan Life Insurance Company has not made any payment to her estate.

Instead, Serena dies at age 70 after receiving $180,000 in annuity payments. Metropolitan Life Insurance Company pays her estate $70,000 as required by the annuity contract. This amount will be included in her gross estate pursuant to § 2033.

---

3. Joint and Survivor Annuities

Section 2039 will apply only if:

(a) there is a contract or agreement that is not life insurance;

(b) a beneficiary will receive payments following decedent's death pursuant to this contract;

(c) the decedent was either receiving payments or had a right to payments under the same contract; and

(d) decedent's payments or right to payments were for life, for a period that did not in fact end before decedent's death, or for a period that was not ascertainable without reference to decedent's death.

Section 2039 only applies to benefits paid under contracts. It does not apply to statutory benefits such as Social Security or other statutory retirement benefits.

Example 9.3

Serena works for MNO, Inc., which has a deferred compensation and retirement plan. When Serena retires, MNO, Inc. will pay her a monthly benefit. After her death, MNO, Inc. will pay her surviving husband, Hugh, the same monthly benefit. Serena dies at age 70 while receiving retirement benefits. Hugh survives her. The value of the payments to Hugh will be included in her gross estate under § 2039. Of course, the payments will qualify for the marital deduction.

Example 9.4

Serena purchases an annuity contract from Metropolitan Life Insurance Company to pay her and her sister, Nancy, each $2,500 per month for their lives. Serena dies survived by Nancy. Assuming that Serena paid all the consideration for the annuity contract, the value of the payments to Nancy will be in Serena's gross estate pursuant to § 2039.

If Nancy had paid one-half the consideration for the contract, then only one-half of the payments would be in Serena's gross estate.

---

4. Structured Settlements

A structured settlement is simply a series of payments in satisfaction of a legal liability, usually a tort claim. If the settlement provides for payments to the decedent and to a survivor, then the value of the payments to the survivor following the decedent's death will be in his gross estate pursuant to § 2039. If the payments are for a term of years and decedent dies within that term, any amount paid to his estate will be in his gross estate pursuant to § 2033.

5. Lotteries

Lottery winners may have the option of taking a lump-sum amount or annual payments for a number of years. If the decedent dies within the term and the remaining payments are made to a beneficiary designated in the winner's will or to his heirs in intestacy, § 2033 will apply. If payments are made to a beneficiary designated in the agreement with the lottery commission, then § 2039 will apply. The only question is whether or not to value the lottery payments as annuities under the § 7520 tables. If the annuity payments are subject to transferability restrictions, they may be valued based on expert testimony rather than the tables. See section E.5.f. of chapter 2.

6. Exam Strategy

Section 2039 may apply to any arrangement that is a series of payments over time. First, determine if there is a contract or an agreement. If the benefit is paid pursuant to statute, § 2039 will not apply. Second, determine if the contract or agreement is life insurance. If it is, § 2039 will not apply. Third, determine if the decedent had a right to a payment for her life or a period that did not in fact end before her death or if she was in fact receiving payments under the contract or other arrangement. Fourth, determine if another person will receive payments under the same contract or arrangement after the decedent's death. Remember that different arrangements might be combined particularly in the employment context. Only post-employment benefits, not wages or wage substitutes will trigger § 2039. If all these conditions are met, § 2039 applies. If, on the other hand, a payment is made to the decedent's estate, then § 2033 applies.

B. PRIVATE ANNUITIES AND INSTALLMENT SALES

A private annuity is a stream of payments from an individual rather than a commercial entity. Private annuities are usually made in exchange for other property. So are installment sales. Private annuities also resemble transfers with the retained right to income. The gift and estate tax treatment may be different depending on how the arrangement is characterized.

1. Private Annuities

a. Payments Cease at Death

If decedent exchanges property for the right to payments for her life and the right to those payments ceases at her death, nothing is in her gross estate. *Estate of Bergan v. Commissioner*, 1 T.C. 543 (1943). If the value of the property exchanged is equal to the value of the annuity, there is no gift.

b. Right to a Stated Amount or Until Death

If the decedent is to receive payments until a stated amount has been paid or until her death, whichever occurs first, the arrangement might be a private annuity or it might be an installment sale. The agreement will be treated as an installment contract if the stated amount would be receivable by the decedent before the expiration of her life expectancy determined under the actuarial tables at the time of the exchange. If decedent's life expectancy is greater than the expected term, the agreement will be treated as a private annuity. If the agreement is a private annuity and no one will receive payments after decedent's death, nothing is in her gross estate. *Estate of Bergan v. Commissioner*, 1 T.C. 543.

2. Installment Sales

a. General Rule

If the decedent is to receive payments for a stated term such as 15 years, the arrangement is an installment contract. The right to payments after the decedent's death is a property interest that is transferred from decedent at death. As a result, the value of the installment contract as of decedent's death is in her gross estate pursuant to § 2033. The same rule applies if the decedent is to receive payments for a stated term or until her death, whichever occurs first, and the stated term is less than the decedent's life expectancy at the time the agreement is made.

b. Forgiveness of Debt in Will

If the decedent forgives the payments due after her death in her will, the value of the installment contract is still included in her gross estate pursuant to § 2033. The will provision forgiving the debt is treated the same as a devise in the will.

Example 9.5

Pamela transfers Wildacre to Vincent in exchange for Vincent's agreement to pay her $25,000 plus interest at the applicable federal rate for 10 years. Pamela dies in year 7. The installment contract is an asset included in her gross estate under § 2033. The value of the contract is the value of the remaining payments discounted to present value.

If Pamela forgives the debt in her will, the value of the contract is still included in her gross estate under § 2033. She has made a gratuitous transfer of that contract to Vincent in her will. It is the same as if she left him that amount of money in her will.

---

3. Self–Canceling Installment Notes (SCINS)

The parties to the agreement might include a provision in the installment contract that no payments will be due after the individual receiving the payments dies. If the cancelation term was part of the deal, *i.e.*, negotiated by the parties at arm's length, then nothing will be in the decedent's gross estate. If the cancelation feature is motivated by donative intent, it will be treated like forgiveness of the debt in a will. Courts have tended to accept SCINs at face value even in family situations.

Illustrative Case

In *Estate of Costanza v. Commissioner*, 320 F.3d 595 (6th Cir. 2003), decedent sold two parcels of real estate to his son in exchange for a self-canceling installment note that was secured by a mortgage on the property. Decedent structured the sale on advice of his attorney apparently without any discussions with his son. Decedent died unexpectedly five months after issuing the SCIN. The appellate court held that the SCIN was a bona fide transaction and remanded the case to consider the IRS's argument that the SCIN was a bargain sale and therefore a gift under § 2512.

---

4. **Retained Right to Income**

If the decedent transfers income-producing property in exchange for a private annuity or a self-canceling installment note, it is possible that the transaction will be classified as a retention of the right to income from the property. If that happens, the date of death value of the property will be included in the decedent's gross estate under § 2036(a)(1). The following factors tend to indicate a retained right to income:

(a) The decedent transfers the property to a trust.

(b) The amount due to the seller approximates the income generated by the property.

(c) The purchaser is not personally liable for the payments and the seller can only recover the property if payments are not made.

(d) There is no down-payment.

(e) The seller does not retain a security interest in the property.

(f) There is little or no relationship between the value of the property transferred and the so-called sales price.

5. **Exam Strategy**

The first step is to determine the nature of the transaction. Distinguish between (1) a private annuity; (2) a self-canceling installment note; and

(3) a transfer with the right to income. If it is not clear or you are not sure, discuss alternatives. The next step is to discuss the gift tax consequences. Compare the value of what was transferred with the value of what was received. Finally, discuss the estate tax consequences. Even if the correct answer is that nothing is in the gross estate, be sure to state that explicitly.

C. EMPLOYER–PAID DEATH BENEFITS

When an employer pays a decedent's estate, spouse, or other designated beneficiary an amount after the decedent's death, the question is whether or not that payment, often referred to as a "death benefit," will be included in the decedent's gross estate. The answer depends on whether or not the decedent had a property interest in that payment or the power to designate the recipient.

1. Contract Right to Payments: § 2033

If the decedent had a contractual right to the payment and the payment was made to the decedent's estate, the value of that payment will be included in the decedent's gross estate pursuant to § 2033. If payment will be made to a designated beneficiary, the value of that payment or series of payments will be included in the decedent's estate pursuant to either § 2033 or § 2039.

Illustrative Case

In *Goodman v. Granger*, 243 F.2d 264 (3d Cir. 1957), decedent was entitled to deferred compensation payments under an employment agreement. Decedent died before payments began, and the payments were made to his estate. The value of the payments as of the date of his death was in his gross estate under § 2033. The primary issue was how to value the payments because they were subject to a non-competition agreement. The court held that the payments were to be valued taking into account the fact that decedent's death ensured that payments would in fact be made to his estate.

---

2. Survivor Annuity: § 2039

Section 2039 will apply if (1) the decedent has a right to payments or is in fact receiving payments for life, for a period which does not in fact end before his death, or for a period that is not ascertainable without reference to his death; (2) someone else will receive payments after decedent's death under the same contract or agreement. Where an employer pays a surviving spouse or other beneficiary an amount after death, the issue will be which payments, if any, to decedent will be considered paid under the same contract. Only post-employment payments, not wages or payments similar to wages, will be combined with the post-death payment to trigger § 2039.

Illustrative Case

In *Estate of Bahen v. United States*, 305 F.2d 827, 158 Ct.Cl. 141 (1962), decedent's employer unilaterally and voluntarily adopted a plan that paid a widow or minor children 60 equal payments at employee's death, whether death occurred before or after retirement. The plan also provided for payments to the employee if he became totally incapacitated before retirement. Holding that the disability payments were post-employment benefits, the court included the payment to decedent's spouse in his gross estate under § 2039 because he had a right to the disability benefit even if he was not in fact receiving it.

---

3. Power to Designate Beneficiary: § 2038

If the decedent has made a transfer of a property interest and retained the right to designate the beneficiary, the death benefit will be in the decedent's gross estate pursuant to § 2038. For § 2038 to apply, there must be a transfer by the decedent. Some courts are reluctant to impute a transfer. The decedent must also retain the right to alter, amend, terminate, or revoke the agreement.

Illustrative Case

In *Estate of Tully v. Commissioner*, 528 F.2d 1401 (Ct. Cl. 1976), decedent was one of two equal owners. The two owners and the company entered into a contract to pay a death benefit to each of the owners' surviving spouses. The court held that decedent had made a transfer because he was married when the contract was executed, but it held that he did not possess a power to alter, amend, revoke or terminate the benefit so that nothing was in his gross estate. There was no express reservation of power to alter, amend, or revoke in the contract. The court refused to find that decedent's right to terminate his employment or divorce his spouse was a "power" within the meaning of § 2038.

> **Illustrative Case**
>
> In *Estate of Siegel v. Commissioner*, 74 T.C. 613 (1980), the decedent's employment contract provided for payment to his children at his death. The court refused to include the payments pursuant to § 2039 because decedent had no right to any post-employment benefits. The court, however, did include the payments pursuant to § 2038, because decedent reserved the power in conjunction with his employer to modify the rights of the beneficiaries. This right was greater than the decedent's rights under state law and, thus, constituted a power for purposes of § 2038.

4. Mere Promise

Nothing will be in the decedent's gross estate if the death benefit is a mere promise and not a contractual right.

> **Illustrative Case**
>
> In *Estate of Barr v. Commissioner*, 40 T.C. 227 (1963), the employer paid a salary death benefit to an employee's surviving spouse, child, parent, estate, or other beneficiary. The court held that the employee had no enforceable right to the payment because the company had to realize earnings, then declare a dividend to shareholders, then declare a wage dividend to current employees, and then exercise its discretion to pay decedent's spouse. The court held that the decedent and his spouse had no more than an expectancy. Neither § 2033 nor § 2039, therefore, applied.

5. Gift Tax

Having lost cases such as *Estate of Barr*, the IRS claimed that an employee made a gift to his spouse when he began working for an employer that paid a spousal death benefit. This argument was summarily dismissed in *Estate of DiMarco v. Commissioner*, 87 T.C. 653 (1986), because the regulations clearly state that a gift is not completed at the time of decedent's death. Regulation § 25.2511–2(f). Before death, it is impossible to determine whether or not the benefit will in fact be paid. As a result, there cannot be a completed gift before death.

6. Exam Strategy

When the decedent's employer makes a payment either to the decedent's estate or a beneficiary, start with § 2033. The first step is to determine if the payment is salary or a bonus that was earned by the decedent during his life. If so, decedent had a contractual right to the payment, and it passes to his estate or beneficiary as a result of his death. As a result, § 2033 includes the payment in the gross estate. If the payment is not salary or a bonus, determine if the decedent had a contractual right to the payment. If so, § 2033 includes it in the gross estate. Section 2039 might also be applicable if there is a contractual right. Section 2039 will apply even if there is no contract if the decedent is in fact receiving payments at the time of his death. Section 2039 will only apply if a beneficiary has a right to payments after the decedent's death under the same contract. The same contract requirement is broadly interpreted to include almost any combination of payments, as long as the decedent's payment is a post-employment benefit, *i.e.*, not wages or a replacement for wages. Finally, § 2038 will apply if decedent makes a transfer and retains the right to alter, amend, terminate or revoke the agreement, including the right to designate the beneficiary.

CHAPTER 10

POWERS OF APPOINTMENT: § 2041

A. GENERAL PRINCIPLES

1. Terminology

The **donor** is the creator of the power. The **donee** is the **power holder**, *i.e.*, the person who can exercise the power. The **objects** of the power are those individuals to whom the donee can appoint. The **appointees** are those individuals to whom the donee has actually appointed the property. The **takers in default** are those individuals who will receive the property if the donee does not exercise the power.

Example 10.1

Jesse creates an irrevocable, inter vivos trust with Friendly National Bank as trustee to pay the income to Anne for her life and then to distribute the trust property to those of Anne's issue as she appoints in her will. If Anne does not appoint to anyone, the trust property will be distributed to Anne's children in equal shares. Jesse is the donor; Anne is the donee or power holder; Anne's issue are the objects. Her children are the takers in default. Assume that Anne's will exercises her power and appoints the trust property to her two grandchildren, Mark and Megan. They are the appointees.

---

2. Creation of a Power of Appointment

No specific words are required to create a power of appointment. Any words that give someone the ability to determine beneficial enjoyment are sufficient. This includes: "to appoint," "to withdraw," "to consume," "to designate," and similar language. Powers of appointment are most often found in trusts, but may also occur in deeds or other dispositive instruments. Sometimes a deed transfers a life estate with a power to consume or sell. That language would give the life tenant a general power of appointment.

3. General Power

A **general power of appointment** is the power to appoint to (1) oneself, (2) one's creditors, (3) one's estate, or (4) the creditors of one's estate. §§ 2041(b)(1), 2514(c)(1). All other powers are special (or limited). Property subject to a general power of appointment is in the power holder's gross estate pursuant to § 2041. If a donee exercises a general power of appointment during life, that exercise is a transfer of property by that individual and is often a gift. § 2514(b).

a. Power to Appoint in Will

Example 10.2

Gwen leaves her estate in trust with Friendly National Bank as trustee to pay the income to Harriet for her life and then to distribute the trust property to whomever Harriet appoints in her will. Because Harriet can appoint to her estate or the creditors of her estate, this is a general power of appointment. The trust property is, therefore, in her gross estate under § 2041.

State law might provide otherwise. In Maryland, the language "to such person or persons as the decedent shall designate" does not include the decedent, the decedent's creditors, the decedent's estate, or the creditors of the decedent's estate. *Maryland Natl Bank v. United States*, 236 F.Supp. 532 (D. Md. 1964). This is, therefore, not a general power of appointment. To create a general power in Maryland, the donor would need to explicitly give the donee the power to appoint to the donee herself, to the donee's estate, to the donee's creditors, or to the creditors of the donee's estate.

b. Power to Appoint during Life

The donee may have a power to appoint property during his life. This can be a power to withdraw, to consume the property, or to demand property. As long as the donee can direct the property to himself or his creditors, it is a general power of appointment.

Example 10.3

Greg leaves his estate in trust with Friendly National Bank as trustee to pay the income to Owen for his life and then to distribute the trust property to Owen's issue. The trust gives Owen the right

---

> to withdraw trust principal for his own benefit during his life. Because Owen can withdraw for his own benefit, he has a general power of appointment, and the trust property will be in Owen's gross estate at his death. § 2041.

  c. Exam Strategy

  Powers of appointment are created in someone other than the grantor or settlor of the trust. Be sure to distinguish a situation involving a power of appointment, which is subject to § 2041, from an interest or power that is retained by the grantor or settlor, which is subject to § 2036 through § 2038. A general power is one where the donee/power holder can appoint to herself, her creditors, her estate, or the creditors of her estate.

4. Special or Limited Power of Appointment

Any power that is not a general power is a special or a limited power of appointment. This includes the power to appoint to one's children, one's issue, one's descendants, or any group that does not include the power holder, her creditors, her estate, or the creditors of her estate.

5. Knowledge of Power is Unnecessary

A power of appointment is valid even if the power holder is unaware that he has the power. *Estate of Freeman v. Commissioner*, 67 T.C. 202 (1976).

6. Ability to Exercise Power is Unnecessary

Property subject to a general power of appointment will be in the donee's gross estate under § 2041 even if the donee is unable to exercise the power because he is a minor or incompetent. *Boeving v. United States*, 650 F.2d 493 (8th Cir. 1981); *Estate of Alperstein v. Commissioner*, 613 F.2d 1213 (2d Cir. 1979). A minor child may be given a general power of appointment in order to qualify trust income and principal for the gift tax annual exclusion pursuant to § 2503(c). Regulation § 25.2503–4(b).

Example 10.4

Arnie creates a trust with Friendly National Bank as the trustee. The trustee has discretion to distribute trust income or principal to or for the benefit of Arnie's daughter, Debby. The trust property and any accumulated income will be distributed to Debby when she reaches age

---

21. If Debby dies before age 21, the trust property will be distributed to any person (including her estate or the creditors of her estate) that Debby designates in her will. If she does not appoint to anyone, the trust property will be distributed to Debby's cousin, Chloe. Debbie is two years old when Arnie creates the trust. He transfers an amount equal to the gift tax annual exclusion into the trust each year. Because the trust meets the requirements of § 2503(c), each transfer qualifies for the gift tax annual exclusion. It does not matter that Debby does not know about her power of appointment or that she is unable to exercise it. The power is still valid.

7. Trustee Powers

A power of appointment is the power to affect beneficial enjoyment of the property. A trustee that has discretion to distribute trust property has a power of appointment. Regulation § 20.2041–1(b)(1). Administrative, management, and investment powers are not powers of appointment. *Id.* If the trustee can appoint the trust property to herself, she will have a general power of appointment unless the trust instrument or state law restricts her ability to appoint to herself.

Example 10.5

Abby's will leaves her property in trust with her daughter, Hannah, as the trustee. The trustee has discretion to distribute income or principal to any of Abby's children as Hannah determines is in their "best interests." Hannah is a trustee and is subject to fiduciary duties of loyalty and impartiality. As a result, some courts hold that a trustee cannot appoint in favor of herself. Some jurisdictions have statutes that preclude the trustee from appointing trust property to herself. In the absence of a statute or court decision, Hannah has a general power of appointment because she can appoint to herself. Regulation § 20.2041–3(c)(2)(Ex. 3).

8. Date of Creation of Power

Property subject to powers created *on or before October 21, 1942,* is included in the donee's gross estate only if the donee exercises the power. § 2041(a)(1). The failure to exercise a power created on or before October 21, 1942, or the complete release of such a power is not considered an exercise of that power. § 2514(a). Property subject to powers created after October 21, 1942, is taxed as explained below.

9. Exam Strategy

Examine the language of the trust, deed, will, or other dispositive instrument carefully. If someone has the ability to distribute property, to appoint property, to designate who will receive property, or any similar ability, that person has a power of appointment *unless* the individual is the grantor (settlor). If the power holder can appoint to herself, her estate, her creditors, or the creditors of her estate (*i.e.*, she can benefit herself in some way), then the power is a general power of appointment. While general powers will subject the power holder to possible gift and estate tax consequences, a special or limited power may create generation-skipping transfer tax consequences.

B. ASCERTAINABLE STANDARDS

A power that is limited by an ascertainable standard is not a general power of appointment. §§ 2041(b)(1)(A); 2541(c)(1). An ascertainable standard is one that relates to health, education, maintenance, or support (hems).

1. Powers Limited by an Ascertainable Standard

An ascertainable standard is one that a court will enforce, *i.e.*, one that limits the discretion of the power holder. An ascertainable standard is one that relates to health, education, maintenance, or support. The regulations and case law provide examples. Courts will look to state law and the intent of the settlor, as detailed in the trust document, to determine if a standard is sufficiently ascertainable. Examples include:

a. support in reasonable comfort, Regulation § 20.2041–1(c)(2);

b. maintenance in health and reasonable comfort, Regulation § 20.2041–1(c)(2);

c. support in his accustomed manner of living, Regulation § 20.2041–1(c)(2);

d. to meet an emergency, Regulation § 25.2511–1(g)(2);

e. to maintain the beneficiary in his accustomed standard of living, Jennings v. Smith, 161 F.2d 74 (2d Cir. 1947);

f. in the case of prolonged illness or financial misfortune, Jennings v. Smith, 161 F.2d 74 (2d Cir. 1947);

g.   as required for the continued comfort, support, maintenance, or education of the beneficiary, Estate of Vissering v. Commissioner, 990 F.2d 578 (10th Cir. 1993);

h.   in the case of sickness or if desirable in view of changed circumstances, Old Colony Trust Co. v. United States, 423 F.2d 601 (1st Cir. 1970).

2. Powers not Limited by an Ascertainable Standard

Examples include:

a.   comfort, welfare, and happiness, Regulation § 20.2041–1(c)(2);

b.   to use the income and so much of the principal as in her sole discretion shall be necessary and desirable, Hyde v. United States, 950 F.Supp. 418 (D.N.H. 1996);

c.   the best interests of the beneficiary, Old Colony Trust Co. v. United States, 423 F.2d 601 (1st Cir. 1970);

d.   if necessary and proper, Leopold v. United States, 510 F.2d 617 (9th Cir. 1975).

3. Exam Strategy

If the person who can affect beneficial enjoyment has discretion, determine if that discretion is (1) sole or absolute or (2) limited by a standard. If there is any language qualifying the discretion, determine if that language relates to health, education, support, or maintenance. Remember the mnemonic: hems. Other terms may also qualify, but only if the standard is so definite that the beneficiary can force the distribution.

C. JOINT POWERS

1. Donor

If the donee/power holder can exercise the power only with the creator of the power, *i.e.*, the donor, the power is *not* a general power of appointment. §§ 2041(b)(1)(C)(I), 2514(c)(3)(A). The rationale is that the donee/power holder does not control the disposition of the property because the donor must agree.

2. Substantial Adverse Interest

If the donee can exercise the power only with an individual who has a substantial interest in the trust that is adverse to the donee's exercise of the power, the power is not a general power of appointment. §§ 2041(b)(1)(C)(ii), 2514(c)(3)(B). Again, the rationale is that the donee does not control the disposition of the property.

Example 10.6

Luke and John were trustees of a trust. Income was to be paid to Luke for his life, then income was to be paid to Luke's wife, Wendy, for her life, and the remainder was to be distributed to John. The two trustees, Luke and John, had discretion to distribute trust principal to Luke during his life. Because John is the remainderman, he has a substantial interest in the trust that is adverse to the exercise of the power to distribute trust principal to Luke. As a result, Luke does not have a general power of appointment. Regulation § 20.2041–3(c)(2) (Ex. 1).

D. CONDITIONAL POWERS

Section 2041 taxes powers that decedent has at the time of his death. If a power is subject to a condition that has not occurred, then the decedent does not have a general power of appointment. A delay between the exercise and the date of distribution or a requirement of giving written notice does not mean that a power is contingent. Regulation § 20.2041–3(b).

Example 10.7

Matthew's will leaves his property in trust with Friendly National Bank for the benefit of his son, Calvin. Calvin has the power to withdraw five percent of the trust principal for his own benefit each year, but only when he is married. Calvin never marries. He does not have a general power of appointment because the condition has never occurred. The trust property, therefore, will not be in his gross estate. Regulation § 20.2041–3(b).

E. PROPERTY SUBJECT TO A GENERAL POWER INCLUDED IN GROSS ESTATE

If the donee/power holder has a general power of appointment over property at the time of her death, the property subject to that power is included in her gross estate. § 2041(a)(2).

Example 10.8

Aaron's will leaves the residue of his estate to Friendly National Bank as trustee to pay the income to Darren during his life. Darren has the power to demand any amount of trust principal during his life for his own benefit or the benefit of his issue. Any trust property remaining at Darren's death will be distributed to his issue. Darren has a general power of appointment because he can demand trust property for his own benefit. Because his power exists at death and extends to the full value of the trust property, the entire value of the trust property is in his gross estate at his death.

F. EXERCISE OF A GENERAL POWER

The exercise of a power of appointment is a transfer of property. § 2514(b). If the donee exercises the power for her own benefit, there are no gift tax consequences. If the donee appoints the trust property to someone else, it will be a gift unless the donee receives adequate and full consideration in money or money's worth.

Example 10.9

Same facts as example 10.8. Darren directs the trustee to distribute $50,000 to each of his three children. Darren has exercised his general power of appointment. That exercise is a transfer of the property. Because Darren receives nothing in return from his children, the exercise of his power is a gift.

G. RELEASE OF A GENERAL POWER

A release of a power means the donee has given up the right to exercise the power. If a release occurs within nine months of the creation of the power, the release is a disclaimer. If it otherwise meets the requirements of § 2518, the donee will not be considered the transferor of the property subject to the power. If the donee fails to meet the requirements of § 2518, the release of a general power is a transfer of the property subject to the power by the donee/power holder to the other beneficiaries. It can have both gift and estate tax consequences.

Example 10.10

Same facts as example 10.8. Two years after Aaron dies, Darren releases his power of appointment by sending a letter to the trustee. Because Darren could have withdrawn all the trust property for his own benefit, his release of that power is treated as if he did in fact withdraw the property and then transferred it to the trust. Darren is, therefore, treated as the transferor. § 2514(b). He has now made a transfer—income to himself for life, remainder to his issue. The remainder is a gift to his issue. It is a future interest and does not qualify for the gift tax annual exclusion.

Darren dies ten years later. The trust property will be in his gross estate under § 2041(a)(2). Section 2041 includes not only property over which the decedent has a power at the time of death, but also property "with respect to which the decedent has at any time exercised or released [a general power of appointment] by a disposition which is of such nature that if it were a transfer of property owned by the decedent, such property would be includible in the decedent's gross estate under sections 2035 to 2038." That language applies to Darren. Had he owned the trust property initially and created the trust, § 2036(a)(1) would have included the trust in his gross estate. When he releases his general power, he is treated as the transferor of that property. As a result, the trust is in his gross estate.

H. LAPSE OF A GENERAL POWER

1. Definition of Lapse

A lapse occurs when a power can no longer be exercised. Lapse only applies if the power is limited in time and if it is non-cumulative.

Example 10.11

Donee has the right to withdraw $25,000 of trust principal each year. The power is cumulative. Donee does not withdraw any trust principal in years 1 and 2. In year 3, Donee can withdraw $75,000. If the power is non-cumulative, the donee can only withdraw $25,000 each year whether or not she has withdrawn property in prior years.

2. General Rule

The lapse of a general power of appointment is treated as a release of that power. §§ 2041(b)(2), 2514(e). A release of a power is treated as a transfer of property by the donee. §§ 2041(a)(2), 2514(b). As a result, the lapse of a general power of appointment may create gift and estate tax consequences for the donee.

3. Limited to the Greater of $5,000 or Five Percent of the Trust Property

The lapse of a general power of appointment is treated as a release of that power, but only to the extent that the property which could have been appointed by the donee exercising the power exceeds the greater of (1) $5,000 or (2) five percent of the trust principal. This limitation allows donees significant access to trust property without transfer tax consequences. It also allows donors to take advantage of the gift tax annual exclusion.

Example 10.12

Brendan creates an irrevocable, inter vivos trust by transferring $500,000 to Friendly National Bank as trustee. The trustee is to distribute income to Brendan's daughter, Martha, during her life. Martha has the right to withdraw $20,000 per year from trust principal; her right is non-cumulative and may be exercised any time during the year. Any trust property remaining at Martha's death will be distributed to Martha's issue. Martha's failure to withdraw $20,000 in year 1 is not a lapse of the power because her right to withdraw is limited to less than five percent of the trust corpus (five percent of $500,000 is $25,000). Because it is not a lapse, it is not treated as a transfer by Martha.

Example 10.13

Same facts as example 10.12 except that Martha can withdraw $40,000 each year; the right is non-cumulative. Martha does not withdraw any trust property in year 1. Her failure is now a lapse of $15,000. The entire trust property is subject to her power, and five percent of $500,000 is $25,000. Therefore, any amount over $25,000 is treated as a lapse. Because it is a lapse, it is treated as a release, which is treated as a transfer to the trust. As a result, the value of a remainder in $15,000 is a gift from Martha to her issue. In addition, the percentage of the trust property attributable to this lapse ($15,000/$500,000 or three percent) will be in Martha's gross estate at her death.

Example 10.14

Same facts as example 10.13. Assume that Brendan does not make any additional transfers to the trust and that the value of the trust property does not appreciate in value. Assume that Martha does not withdraw any trust property and dies in year 6. Her gross estate includes the amount of trust property subject to her power at the time of her death. This is the $40,000 that she can withdraw in year 6. Her gross estate also includes the percentage of the trust attributable to the lapses in years 1 through 5. Her lapse in each year was treated as a transfer of $15,000 or three percent of the trust property. As a result, she is deemed to have transferred 15 percent of the property to the trust. Because she has a right to the income, 15 percent of the trust property, *i.e.*, $75,000, will be in her gross estate. (Remember, had she been the original transferor, § 2036(a)(1) would have applied.) The total in Martha's gross estate is $115,000.

4. *Crummey* Powers

Donors create general powers of appointment in donees to ensure that property transferred to a trust qualifies for the gift tax annual exclusion. Such powers are usually referred to as *Crummey* powers because the court in *Crummey v. Commissioner*, 397 F.2d 82 (9th Cir. 1968), held that such powers were valid in minor children. If the donor gives a donee the power to withdraw the lesser of the amount contributed to the trust that year or the amount of the gift tax annual exclusion, the donor will get the full benefit of the gift tax annual exclusion. The donee, however, will have gift and estate tax consequences unless there is $260,000 in the trust (assuming a gift tax annual exclusion amount of $13,000).

Example 10.15

Paul creates an irrevocable, inter vivos trust with Friendly National Bank as trustee to pay the income to Art for his life and to distribute the trust property at Art's death to his issue. Paul gives Art the right to withdraw the lesser of the amount contributed to the trust or the amount of the gift tax annual exclusion; the right is non-cumulative. Paul transfers $13,000 to the trust each year. The power of appointment in

Art, commonly referred to as a *Crummey* power, ensures that each transfer qualifies for the gift tax annual exclusion.

If Art does not withdraw any trust property, there is a lapse to the extent that $13,000 exceeds the greater of $5,000 or five percent of the trust property. In years 1 through 7, $5,000 is greater than five percent of the trust property, so Art is treated as transferring $8,000 (the difference between the $13,000 amount he can withdraw and $5,000) to the trust. In year 8, the trust principal is $104,000 (assuming no appreciation in value) and five percent of that is $5,200. In that year, Art's failure to withdraw is treated as a lapse of $7,800.

Assume that Art dies in year 9 without every exercising his power. The amount in Art's gross estate is calculated as follows. First, include the amount subject to the power at the time of death, which is $13,000. Second, include that percentage of the trust attributable to the prior lapses because Art has a right to the income and had he been the original transferor, § 2036(a)(1) would have included the trust property in his gross estate. In year 1, Art is deemed to have contributed $8,000/$13,000 or 62 percent of the trust. In year 2, he is deemed to have contributed $8,000/$26,000 or 31 percent. In year 3, he is deemed to have contributed $8,000/$39,000 or 21 percent. And so on. The percentages are then added together and the total percentage of the trust attributable to the lapses is included in Art's gross estate under § 2041(a)(2). In this case that would be the entire value of the trust. Regulation § 20.2041–3(d)(4).

5. Exam Strategy

First, determine if the individual has a general power of appointment. Second, determine if the power must be exercised within a specific time. If there is no time limit, the power will not lapse. Third, determine if the power is cumulative, *i.e.*, if the power holder does not exercise the power in one year does the amount that can be withdrawn carry over to the next year. Only if the power is non-cumulative will there be a lapse. Fourth, if there is a lapse, then determine if the power holder had another interest in the trust, such as a life estate, that would be analogous to a retained interest in § 2035 through § 2038. If not, only the property subject to the general power is in the power holder's gross estate at death. Otherwise, determine what percentage of the trust is attributable to the lapses. Determine the percentage for each year and then add them up. There will never be more than 100 percent in the gross estate.

CHAPTER 11

LIFE INSURANCE: § 2042

A. GENERAL PRINCIPLES

1. Definition of Life Insurance

a. Section 2042

Section 2042 includes in the gross estate the amount receivable by the executor or another beneficiary as insurance on the life of the decedent. Section 2042 does not define "insurance on the life of the decedent," but the regulations provide that the section governs "life insurance of every description, including death benefits paid by fraternal beneficial societies operating under the lodge system." Regulation § 20.2042–1(a)(1).

b. Judicial Interpretation

Courts have adopted an expansive definition of the term life insurance, but that does not mean that everything is life insurance. There must be a shifting of the risk of loss from death for an agreement to be life insurance.

Illustrative Case

In *Helvering v. Le Gierse*, 312 U.S. 531 (1941), the Supreme Court defined life insurance as "a device to shift and distribute risk of loss from premature death." *Id.* at 539. The Court held that where the decedent had hedged her bets by purchasing both a life insurance contract and an annuity contract from the same company at age 80, the two policies were simply components of one agreement. Because one component neutralized the other, there was no risk and, thus, the agreement was not life insurance.

189

Illustrative Case

In *Commissioner v. Estate of Noel*, 380 U.S. 678 (1965), the Supreme Court held that flight insurance payable only if decedent died while on that particular airplane trip was life insurance for purposes of § 2042. The Court refused to distinguish between a loss that would certainly occur (death in general) from a loss that might or might not occur from a specific event (death on this particular airline flight). In both cases the risk of loss was shifted and, thus, the agreement was life insurance.

---

c.   **Section 7702**

In 1984, Congress adopted a comprehensive definition of "life insurance contract" for all sections of the Internal Revenue Code. § 7702. This definition refers to applicable law, which usually means state law, and requires that the contract meet either (1) the cash value accumulation test or (2) the guideline premium requirements and falls within the cash value corridor.

d.   **Exam Strategy**

Given the complex statutory definition in § 7702, you should be told explicitly that an agreement either is, or is not, life insurance. If an agreement is not labeled as "life insurance" but it shifts the risk of loss from death, note its similarity to life insurance but then cite § 7702. Then analyze the agreement under other sections of the estate tax. Reason by analogy and always use the facts. Note that although § 2039 applies to an annuity or other payment (which is very broad language), it explicitly excludes life insurance policies on the life of the decedent. Also note that the discussion of employer-paid death benefits (in section C of chapter 9) did not include life insurance because of the § 7702 definition.

2.   **Amount Included**

The amount included is not the value of the life insurance policy; rather it is the *amount receivable* by the designated beneficiary. The amount receivable may be more than the specified face amount of the policy. For example, the policy could be a paid-up cash value policy with dividends and interests accumulated beyond the face amount. Another example would be a provision in the policy that doubles the face amount if death occurs from certain types of accidents. In all cases, it is *the amount receivable* rather than the face amount or the value of the policy immediately before death.

B. LIFE INSURANCE PAYABLE TO THE ESTATE

1. General Rule

Section 2042(1) includes in the decedent's gross estate amounts receivable by the executor of decedent's estate in his capacity as executor from insurance policies *on the life of the decedent*.

Example 11.1

Dora owned a life insurance policy that named her sister, Nicole, as the beneficiary. Nicole was also the executor of Dora's estate. The life insurance proceeds are not included in Dora's gross estate under § 2042(1) simply because Nicole happened to be the executor of her estate. Of course, the proceeds will be included under § 2042(2) because Dora owned the policy at the time of her death.

---

2. Executor or Estate as Contingent Beneficiary

In some cases, the executor receives the insurance proceeds because the primary beneficiary has in fact predeceased the decedent or is treated as if he predeceased the decedent. If the insurance policy does not specify a secondary beneficiary, the proceeds will most likely be payable to the decedent's estate, and § 2042(1) will include the amount receivable in the decedent's gross estate.

Illustrative Case

In *Draper's Estate v. Commissioner*, 536 F.2d 944 (1st Cir. 1976), a husband owned two insurance policies on the life of his wife. He was not only the owner, but also the named beneficiary. The husband killed his wife and then committed suicide. Because he could not profit from his own crime, a constructive trust for the benefit of his wife's estate was imposed on the policy proceeds. As a result, her daughter received the policy proceeds. The court held that the amount receivable was not in the husband's gross estate although he was the owner, because nothing passed *from him* to anyone else. Instead, the amounts receivable were included in the wife's gross estate pursuant to § 2042(1) because the life insurance proceeds passed to her estate and then to the beneficiary of her will through the mechanism of the constructive trust.

191

3. Amounts Used to Pay Debts and Expenses

a. Mortgage and Credit Card Insurance

Any amount that is receivable (1) by the executor; (2) by any other beneficiary subject to a legally binding obligation to pay debts, expenses, or taxes; or (3) directly by a creditor is included in the decedent's gross estate pursuant to § 2042(1). Regulation § 20.2042–1(b)(1). It is as if the proceeds were paid to the executor who then used those proceeds to pay the designated debt. This includes mortgage insurance, credit card insurance, and similar arrangements.

b. Insurance as Collateral for a Loan

The same rule applies if the decedent purchased life insurance and used it as collateral for a loan. If the decedent dies and the proceeds are used to repay the loan, the amount receivable is included in the decedent's gross estate pursuant to § 2042(1). Regulation § 20.2042–1(b)(1). Again, it is as if the proceeds were paid to the executor who then used those proceeds to pay the designated debt.

c. Life Insurance Trusts and Arrangements to Pay Debts and Expenses

A decedent may create an irrevocable, inter vivos trust and transfer life insurance policies to it. If the trustee is required to transfer insurance proceeds to the executor to pay debts, expenses, or taxes, then the amount so transferred is in decedent's gross estate under § 2042(1). Regulation § 20.2042–1(b)(1). The same rule applies even if the trustee has the discretion to transfer proceeds to the executor for these purposes if the trustee in fact does so. *Id.* The same rule also applies to any arrangement where the recipient of the life insurance proceeds is required to pay the decedent's debts and expenses. To avoid this rule, the decedent should give the trustee (or other person) the power and discretion to purchase assets from the estate. This gives the executor the liquid assets to pay debts, claims, expenses, and taxes without subjecting the insurance proceeds to taxation in decedent's gross estate.

4. Exam Strategy

If there is life insurance on the life of the decedent, determine who received the proceeds. If the executor or administrator of the estate is the recipient, the amount receivable is included in the gross estate under § 2042(1). If someone else receives the proceeds and uses them to pay debts or expenses, that amount is included in the gross estate under § 2042(1).

C. LIFE INSURANCE PAYABLE TO OTHER BENEFICIARIES

1. General Rule

Section 2042(2) brings into the gross estate the amount receivable by a beneficiary other than the executor, but only if the decedent owned incidents of ownership in the policy at the time of his death. An **incident of ownership** is a right to the economic benefit of the life insurance policy. The decedent need only retain one incident of ownership to bring the amount receivable into his gross estate under § 2042(2). The decedent must have an actual right, not merely an illusory right, over the policy.

Illustrative Case

In *Estate of Margrave v. Commissioner*, 618 F.2d 34 (8th Cir. 1980), a wife purchased and owned a life insurance policy on the life of her husband. She designated the husband's revocable trust as the beneficiary of the policy. Although the husband could designate the ultimate beneficiary by altering, amending, or revoking the trust, the wife could prevent the insurance proceeds from reaching the trust by changing the beneficiary designation. As a result, husband's right was not sufficient to include the amount receivable by the trust on his death in his gross estate.

Illustrative Case

Compare Margrave with Estate of Karagheusian v. Commissioner, 233 F.2d 197 (2d Cir. 1956). In that case a wife owned a life insurance policy on her husband's life and made an irrevocable assignment of the policy to the trust. Because husband had the power to alter, amend, or revoke the trust, he had incidents of ownership in the policy and the proceeds were in his gross estate at death. The difference in *Karagheusian* was that the wife made an *irrevocable* assignment of the policy to the trust. By doing so, she gave up control of the policy. The husband gained control of the policy by his ability to designate where the proceeds would go through his ability to alter, amend, or revoke the trust. In essence, the husband had the right to designate the beneficiary of the life insurance policy, which is, of course, an incident of ownership.

---

2. Incidents of Ownership

Incidents of ownership refer to the right to the economic benefits of a life insurance policy. Regulation § 20.2042–1(c)(2). This includes the power to

- change the beneficiary,

- surrender the policy,

- cancel the policy,

- assign or revoke an assignment of the policy,

- borrow against the policy, or

- use the policy as collateral for a loan.

Id.

3. Reversion is an Incident of Ownership

Section 2042(2) includes a reversion, *i.e.*, the possibility that the policy might return to the decedent or be subject to disposition by the decedent, as an incident of ownership if the value of that reversionary interest exceeds five percent of the value of the policy immediately before the decedent's death. This does not include the possibility that the decedent might receive the policy or its proceeds through inheritance, a will, or by electing her spousal statutory rights. Regulation § 20.2042–1(c)(3). A reversionary interest, as a result, will occur only in very limited situations. One such context is divorce if one spouse is required to maintain a life insurance policy for a specified time period.

Example 11.2

The divorce decree requires Robin to maintain a life insurance policy on her own life payable to her ex-spouse, Sam, or their children. The primary purpose is to ensure the payment of maintenance and child support if Robin dies. Once the children reach age 18, Robin will have

---

full control over the policy. Robin dies when the children are aged 12 and 15. If the value of Robin's reversion exceeds five percent of the value of the policy, the amount receivable by Sam will be in her gross estate. Revenue Ruling 76–113, 1976–1 C.B. 276. Robin's estate might well be entitled to a deduction under § 2053(a)(4) because the proceeds were used to pay her legal obligation of support. *Id.*

4. Policy Facts Control not Decedent's Intent

In determining whether or not the decedent has incidents of ownership, the terms of the policy control. The decedent's intention is not relevant.

Illustrative Case

In *Commissioner v. Estate of Noel*, 380 U.S. 678 (1965), decedent applied for two flight insurance policies at an airport immediately before leaving. His wife paid for the policies, and the clerk gave the policies to the wife. Decedent's plane crashed and he died. The Court held that the amount receivable by the wife as beneficiary was included in decedent's gross estate under § 2042(2) because the policy gave decedent, as the insured, the right to assign the policies or change the beneficiaries. It did not matter that decedent was unable to exercise those rights immediately before his death.

Illustrative Case

The court in *United States v. Rhode Island Hospital Trust Co.*, 355 F.2d 7 (1st Cir. 1966), reached a similar result. In that case, decedent's father bought life insurance on decedent's life and that of his brother. The purpose was to provide for their mother if he and his sons died. Both decedent and his father regarded the policies as his father's, and the decedent never expected any benefit from the policy. Because the policy gave the decedent, as the insured, the right to change the beneficiary, to assign the policy, to control how the dividends were used, and other rights, the court held that the proceeds were included in his gross estate under § 2042(2).

Illustrative Case

Compare United States v. Rhode Island Hospital Trust Co. with Morton v. United States, 457 F.2d 750 (4th Cir. 1972), where the decedent obtained a life insurance policy at the behest of his father-in-law to provide financial security for decedent's wife. The premiums were paid by a corporation owned by decedent's wife, and the policy was kept in the office safe of a different corporation owned by the wife and her sister. Decedent did not consider the policy his own. The court held that the proceeds were not in his gross estate because he had executed an irrevocable beneficiary designation and mode of settlement that effectively terminated all of his power over the policy. As a result, he had no incidents of ownership in it, and § 2042(2) did not apply.

---

5. **Decedent as Fiduciary**

   a. **General Principles**

   Section 2042(2) may apply if decedent is the trustee and has the power to change the beneficial enjoyment of the policy proceeds even if he cannot do so for his own benefit. Regulation § 20.2042–1(c)(4). Courts split on whether this rule applied only if the decedent *retained* the power or if it applied whenever the decedent had the power at death no matter what the source of the power was. *Compare Estate of Skifter v. Commissioner*, 468 F.2d 699 (2d Cir. 1972) (noting that the power must be retained by decedent) *with Rose v. United States*, 511 F.2d 259 (5th Cir. 1975) (explaining that the decedent was appointed as trustee and he then purchased policies on his own life).

   b. **Revenue Ruling 84–179**

   The IRS then issued Revenue Ruling 84–179, 1984–2 C.B. 195, adopting the Second Circuit's position. That ruling creates a safe harbor for a decedent, who is serving as a trustee, if

   (1) the decedent did not transfer the policy to the trust;

   (2) the decedent did not transfer the consideration for purchasing or maintaining the policy to the trust;

   (3) the devolution of power to the decedent was not part of a prearranged plan involving the decedent; and

(4) the powers could not be exercised for the decedent's benefit.

All four conditions must be met to escape inclusion under § 2042(2).

6. Employer–Provided Life Insurance

Employers frequently purchase group term life insurance for the benefit of their employees. Such insurance is treated the same as any other life insurance policy. Most importantly, employees may transfer all the incidents of ownership in the policy to another to avoid inclusion in their gross estate under § 2042(2). The issue then is whether the decedent owned incidents of ownership in the policy because of rights associated with his employment.

a. Termination of Employment

Although the right to cancel a life insurance policy is an incident of ownership, that does not mean that an employee's right to terminate employment and thereby cancel the insurance policy is an incident of ownership. Revenue Ruling 72–307, 1972–1 C.B. 307. Collateral powers are not incidents of ownership. An employee would not terminate employment simply to cancel her insurance policy.

b. Conversion of Policy on Termination of Employment

Many group term policies give employees the right to convert the policy to individually owned policies when they terminate employment. This is not an incident of ownership. Revenue Ruling 84–130, 1984–2 C.B. 194.

c. Selection of Settlement Option

The right to choose a settlement option affects the time and manner of enjoyment. In *Estate of Lumpkin v. Commissioner*, 474 F.2d 1092 (5th Cir. 1973), the court held that this was an incident of ownership, relying heavily on the rationale of cases decided under the retained interest sections 2036 and 2038. The Third Circuit disagreed in *Estate of Connelly v. United States*, 551 F.2d 545 (3d Cir. 1977). The IRS has sided with the Fifth Circuit and treats the selection of a settlement option as an incident of ownership. The IRS will only follow *Estate of Connelly* in the Third Circuit. Revenue Ruling 81–128, 1981–1 C.B. 469.

7. Exam Strategy

If there is life insurance on the life of the decedent, determine who received the proceeds. If the recipient is the executor, the amount receivable is in the gross estate under § 2042(1). If the recipient is not the executor, then determine if the decedent owned any incident of ownership at the time of death. An incident of ownership is the right to control the economic benefits of the policy. The decedent only needs to own one incident of ownership to cause the life insurance proceeds to be included in his gross estate under § 2042(2). Remember that the provisions of the policy will control, not the decedent's belief or intention.

D. LIFE INSURANCE OWNED BY A CORPORATION

1. Benefit to the Corporation

If a decedent is the sole or a controlling shareholder of a corporation and the economic benefits of a policy on the life of the decedent flow to that corporation, the incidents of ownership in the corporation are not attributable to the decedent. Regulation § 20.2042–1(c)(6). Instead, the benefit of the insurance proceeds flows to the decedent's estate because the value of the stock will increase with the receipt of the proceeds. *Id.*

2. Proceeds Payable for Business Purpose

The same rule applies if the insurance proceeds are used for any valid business purpose, such as paying a debt of the corporation, as long as the net worth of the corporation is increased by the payment. Regulation § 20.2042–1(c)(6).

3. Proceeds Received by Beneficiary Other than the Corporation

If some or all of the insurance proceeds are receivable by a beneficiary other than the corporation, this rule does not apply. Regulation § 20.2042–1(c)(6). A split-dollar life insurance policy pays part of the proceeds to the corporation and part of the proceeds to another beneficiary. The proceeds receivable by the non-corporate beneficiary, usually the employee's spouse or children, will be in the decedent's gross estate.

4. Controlling Shareholder

Regulation § 20.2042–1(c)(6) applies not only to the sole shareholder of a corporation but also to a controlling shareholder. For purposes of this regulation, a controlling shareholder is one that owns 50 percent of the total combined voting power of the stock. *Id.*

5. Exam Strategy

If there is life insurance on the life of the decedent, determine who received the proceeds. If it is a corporation, first determine if the decedent was the sole or controlling (50 percent of the voting power) shareholder. If so, then determine if the proceeds flow to the benefit of the corporation. If so, nothing is in the decedent's gross estate. If the benefits flow to someone else, the amount of the proceeds paid to that individual will be in the decedent's gross estate under § 2042(2). The rationale is that control of the corporation gives the decedent control over the life insurance policy, *i.e.*, it gives him incidents of ownership.

E. LIFE INSURANCE ON A LIFE OF OTHER THAN DECEDENT

1. General Rule

Section 2042 only applies to proceeds from life insurance policies *on the life of the decedent*. If the decedent owns policies on the life of someone else, another section, such as § 2033 or § 2036, might apply.

2. Section 2033

If the decedent is the owner of a policy on the life of another, the value of that policy on the date of decedent's death will be included in her gross estate under § 2033.

Example 11.3

Leon and Nora are married. Leon buys a life insurance policy on his own life and the transfers the policy and all the incidents of ownership to Nora. Nora dies survived by Leon. The value of the policy is in Nora's gross estate under § 2033.

---

3. Section 2036

Section 2036 could apply if the owner will receive only payments for life under an irrevocable settlement option.

Example 11.4

Mitch and Hailey are married. Mitch buys a life insurance policy on Hailey's life and selects the settlement option that leaves the proceeds with the insurance company and only pays him the interest and

---

dividends for his life. At his death the proceeds will be paid to his children. The settlement option becomes irrevocable when Hailey dies. Hailey dies. Then Mitch dies. The value of the insurance proceeds will be in Mitch's gross estate under § 2036(a)(1). Mitch made a transfer of that policy during his life by selecting the settlement option that left the proceeds with the insurance company, and he retained the right to income from the proceeds for his life. As a result, § 2036(a)(1) applies. *In re Estate of Pyle v. Commissioner*, 313 F.2d 328 (3d Cir. 1963).

4. Exam Strategy

If the decedent owns a life insurance policy, first determine if the decedent is the insured. If so, § 2042(2) applies because the decedent has incidents of ownership. If the policy is on someone else, determine if § 2033, § 2036, or some other section applies.

F. GIFTS OF LIFE INSURANCE

1. General Principles

Life insurance is a common component of an estate plan. Because the amount receivable may be significant, a decedent will often give the policy to someone else to avoid inclusion of the proceeds in his gross estate. The decedent must survive three years from the date of the gift to avoid inclusion of the proceeds in his gross estate. § 2035(a). It is, therefore, better to have someone other than the decedent buy the life insurance in the first place.

2. Gift Tax Annual Exclusion

A gift of a life insurance policy is a gift of a present interest unless the policy is transferred into a trust. Regulation § 25.2503–3(a). An outright gift will qualify for the gift tax annual exclusion. A gift in trust will only qualify if there are mandatory payments of income or the beneficiary has a general power of appointment, *i.e.*, a *Crummey* power. See section C.4. of chapter 5.

3. Transfers Within Three Years of Death

If the decedent owns a life insurance policy on his own life and transfers that policy to another within three years of death, the amount receivable by the beneficiary will be included in the decedent's gross estate by § 2035(a). This rule applies because the value of the life insurance policy for gift tax purposes might be significantly less than the amount receivable by the beneficiary. Without § 2035(a), decedents could avoid the estate tax through death-bed transfers of life insurance.

4. Payment of Premiums

If someone other that the decedent owns a policy on the decedent's life, the payment of premiums by the decedent will be a gift. The payment of premiums will not cause the proceeds to be included in the decedent's gross estate unless the decedent is the trustee and the trust owns the policy on decedent's life. See section C.5. In all other cases, the payment of premiums does not determine whether or not the proceeds are included in the decedent's gross estate.

5. Exam Strategy

If the decedent owned a life insurance policy on his own life and gave it away, determine if the decedent lived more than three years after the gift. If not, the amount receivable is in his gross estate. § 2035(a). Remember that payment of premiums does not determine inclusion in the gross estate.

CHAPTER 12

QUALIFIED TERMINABLE INTEREST PROPERTY: § 2044

A. ESTATE TAX CONSEQUENCES

1. Included in the Surviving Spouse's Gross Estate

Section 2044 includes in the gross estate any property in which the decedent has a qualifying income interest for life. Such an interest is one that qualifies for the marital deduction under either § 2056(b)(7) or § 2523(f). See section F.6. of chapter 15 for a discussion of qualified terminable interest property (QTIP).

Example 12.1

Fred and Wilma are married. Fred dies, leaving his property to Friendly National Bank as trustee to pay the income at least annually to Wilma and, at her death, to distribute the trust property to his issue. Fred's executor elects for the trust to qualify for the marital deduction under § 2056(b)(7). Wilma dies five years after Fred. The trust property will be in her gross estate under § 2044.

---

2. Duty of Consistency

The surviving spouse cannot avoid § 2044 even if the executor's election under § 2056(b)(7) was wrong as long as the estate tax in the estate of the first to die was calculated by applying the marital deduction. Given the connection between the two estates, the courts will require the two estates to take consistent positions with respect to the trust property.

Illustrative Case

In *Estate of Letts v. Commissioner*, 109 T.C. 290 (1997), the surviving spouse's executor claimed that property left to that spouse in trust was not QTIP and therefore not included in her gross estate under § 2044. The executor of her husband's estate had checked "no" in answer to the question, "Do you elect to claim a marital deduction for [QTIP]?" Her husband's estate had, nevertheless, calculated the estate tax as if the trust qualified for the marital deduction. The survivor's executor claimed that the property could not be QTIP because the executor had not made the appropriate election. The Tax Court refused to allow the executor to whipsaw the IRS in this way. The court held that the duty of consistency required the executor to include this property in the survivor's gross estate.

In this case the court adapted the duty of consistency, an income tax doctrine, to the estate tax. In income tax cases, the duty of consistency applies if (1) the taxpayer makes a representation of fact or reports an item in one year; (2) the Commissioner acquiesces in or relies on that fact or representation; and (3) the taxpayer attempts to change the representation in a future year when the earlier year had been closed by the statute of limitations. *Id.* at 297.

In the estate tax context, the court held that there was a sufficient identity of interest between the estates of the husband and wife to apply the duty of consistency. Their estates were a single economic unit. The beneficiaries, except for the surviving spouse, were the same in both estates. One of the executors was the same in both estates.

3. **Exam Strategy**

If there is a married couple and the marital deduction shelters property in the estate of the first to die, that property must be taxed when the survivor dies. Section 2044 will apply to QTIP property. Any technical flaws in the QTIP election will be ignored, and the duty of consistency will require that the trust property be included in the gross estate of the surviving spouse. The exact reach of the duty of consistency has not yet been established. It is not clear if differing estate plans will prevent the application of that principle.

B. GIFT TAX CONSEQUENCES

Section 2519 ensures that QTIP property will be taxed if the surviving spouse gives that property away during her life. It states that "any disposition of all or part of [such property] shall be treated as a transfer of all interests in such property other than the qualifying income interest."

C. RATIONALE

1. Spouses as one Economic Unit

Transfers to spouses are not taxed by either the gift tax or the estate tax. §§ 2056, 2523. The married couple is considered one economic unit, and its wealth is not subject to tax until transferred outside that economic unit.

2. Tax Once Each Generation

A fundamental principle of the federal transfer tax system is to tax transfers once each generation. Spouses, no matter what their ages, are considered to be members of the same generation. § 2651(c).

3. *Quid Pro Quo* for the Marital Deduction

If property qualifies for the marital deduction, it is not taxed in the estate of the transferor. When property is transferred to a trust that qualifies for the marital deduction under § 2056(b)(7) or § 2523(f), the only requirement is that the spouse have the right to income payable at least annually. Congress enacted § 2044 to ensure that such property would be subject to the estate tax in the surviving spouse's gross estate.

PART IV

CALCULATION OF THE TAX

CHAPTER 13

EXPENSES, DEBTS, TAXES, AND LOSSES: §§ 2053, 2054, AND 2058

A. GENERAL PRINCIPLES

1. Type of Deductions

The estate tax is imposed on the transfer of property from the decedent to others as a result of her death. In calculating the estate tax, there are two types of deductions allowed. The first type is designed to ensure that only the *net value* of the property transferred to others is taxed. These are the deductions for: (1) expenses, debts, claims, and certain taxes (§ 2053); (2) casualty losses (§ 2054); and (3) state death taxes (§ 2058).[1] These deductions are described in this chapter and only apply to the estate tax. The second type of deduction is designed to promote specific policies. These are the deductions for: (1) charitable contributions (§§ 2055 and 2522) and (2) transfers to spouses (§§ 2056 and 2523). The second category of deductions is described in subsequent chapters and applies to both the gift and the estate tax.

2. Which Tax Return?

The executor is responsible for filing at least three different tax returns. The first is, of course, the decedent's estate tax return, *i.e.*, form 706. The second is the decedent's final income tax return, *i.e.*, form 1040. The third is the estate's income tax return. The decedent's estate is a taxable entity and must file its own income tax return, *i.e.*, form 1041. Income received by the estate, such as interest and dividends on investments, rent due after decedent's death, and salary paid after decedent's death, must be reported on this form. If the decedent made taxable gifts in the last year of her life, the executor will also be required to file a gift tax return, *i.e.*, form 709. Finally, if the state imposes an estate tax, the executor will also be required to file that tax return.

---

1. Section 2058 is scheduled for repeal on January 1, 2011, and will be replaced by the § 2011 credit for state death taxes.

209

3. No Double Deductions

Some expenses may be deductible on more than one tax return. For example, the expenses of the decedent's final illness may be deducted as a § 213 medical expense on the decedent's final income tax return. Even though other expenses must be paid before death to be deductible on this return, § 213(e) allows the executor to claim these expenses on the decedent's final income tax return. Casualty losses may be filed either on the estate tax return or the estate's income tax return. The executor must balance a number of considerations in deciding on which return to claim an expense, such as the marginal rate of tax, any monetary or percentage limitations, and who would benefit from the tax savings.

B. SECTION 2053: BASIC REQUIREMENTS

1. Source and Timing of Payments

Section 2053 permits a deduction for funeral expenses, administration expenses, claims against the estate, and debts including mortgages and certain taxes. These payments are usually made from the decedent's probate property, *i.e.*, the property that is subject to claims under local law. Sometimes the decedent's probate property is insufficient, and expenses and debts are paid with non-probate property, such as life insurance proceeds. In addition, the decedent's gross estate may include non-probate property, such as life insurance, joint tenancy property, and retained interests held in trust. There may be expenses or claims associated with these property interests that are paid by decedent's executor from either probate or non-probate funds. Section 2053 defines the parameters of the deduction for both categories of expenses.

a. Property Subject to Claims

Section 2053(c)(2) limits the deduction for expenses and claims associated with property that is subject to claims to (1) the value of the property subject to claims (probate property) in the decedent's gross estate plus (2) any amount paid from other sources (non-probate property) as long as payment occurs before the date required for filing the decedent's estate tax return. That return is due nine months after decedent's death. § 6075.

Example 13.1

Diane's gross estate includes her house valued at $300,000, bank accounts worth $25,000, life insurance proceeds of $1,000,000 payable to her daughter, a revocable trust with $5 million of assets, and joint tenancy property worth $100,000. Funeral expenses are $10,000, other administration expenses are $50,000, the mortgage is $250,000, and other debts and claims are $100,000. The value of the probate property (the property subject to claims under state law) is $325,000. The expenses and claims are $410,000. Diane's daughter contributes $85,000 of the insurance proceeds to pay those expenses and claims. If all the claims and expenses are paid within the time specified for filing the estate tax return, *i.e.*, nine months after Diane's death, the full $410,000 will be allowed as a deduction under § 2053.

---

b. Property Not Subject to Claims

Expenses and claims associated with non-probate property, such as joint tenancy property, trust property, and the like, will be deductible under § 2053 only if those expenses and claims are paid before the expiration of the statute of limitations provided in § 6501 (usually three years) regardless of the source of the funds (probate versus non-probate property). Regulation § 20.2053–1(a)(2).

Example 13.2

Donna's gross estate includes $50,000 of bank accounts, $2,500,000 in a revocable trust, and joint tenancy property worth $3,000,000. Expenses of winding up the revocable trust and filing the appropriate documents to clarify title to the joint tenancy property are $25,000. If these expenses are paid by the executor within three years of Donna's death, the amount will be allowed as a deduction under § 2053 in computing her taxable estate.

---

2. Allowable by Local Law

a. General Principles

To be deductible under § 2053, the expense or claim must be allowable by the law of the jurisdiction where the estate is being administered. This requirement presents difficulty for students and practitioners alike because they often confuse the issue of *what* is a question of local law with that of *who* decides the question. To further complicate the picture, § 2053 may involve questions of both local and federal law.

b. Federal versus State Law

The estate tax is a federal statute, *i.e.*, title 26 of the United States Code. Section 2053 allows a deduction for expenses and claims that are allowable under the law of the jurisdiction where the estate is administered. A state court allowance of a claim or an expense is not determinative. Allowability under local law is a necessary, but not a sufficient, condition for deductibility.

Example 13.3

What is, or is not, a funeral expense is a question of federal law because the Internal Revenue Code, a federal statute, uses that term. If a state enacts a statute defining what is, or is not, a funeral expense, the federal court reviewing the decedent's estate tax return need not accept that definition or a particular funeral expense approved by the state probate court if the federal court decides that such an expense is not within the meaning of the term "funeral expense" as *Congress* used that term. In this case the federal court is deciding a federal question, *i.e.*, the interpretation of a federal statute; it is not deciding the *allowable under local law* issue.

On the other hand, if a state court approves a particular *amount* for the decedent's tombstone, the federal court cannot deny the deduction because it finds that the expense is not a funeral expense. Whether or not a tombstone is a funeral expense is, of course, a question of *federal* law; but its size, shape, or cost is a question of *local* law. The federal court could deny the deduction for the tombstone only if it decided that such a tombstone was not allowable under local law.

---

c. Federal versus State Court

The decedent's will is offered for probate in state court, and the executor or administrator will submit her accountings for approval in state court. Federal law, *i.e.*, § 2053, requires that an expense be *allowable by local law*. Generally, a state court decision on the amount and allowability of such an expense will be accepted by the federal court if the state court has passed on the facts underlying the deduction. Regulation § 20.2053–1(b)(2). In cases where the state court has not decided an issue, the expense may still be deducted as long as the federal court decides that the expense is one that is allowable under local law. See section G of chapter 1.

d. Effect of Court Decree

(1) Actual Court Decree

A court decree may be relied on to establish the amount of an expense or claim if the court "passes upon the facts on which deductibility depends." Regulation § 20.2053–1(b)(3). It is presumed that the court has passed on the merits of an expense or claim if there is an active and genuine contest. *Id.*

(2) Consent Decree

A consent decree will be sufficient if there is a bona fide issue and a genuine contest. *Id.*

(3) Settlement

A settlement will establish the amount of an expense or claim only if there is a bona fide issue in a genuine contest and the settlement is the product of arm's length negotiations by parties with adverse interests. *Id.*

(4) Absence of a Court Decree

A deduction will be allowed under § 2053 in the absence of a court decree if none is required. *Id.*

3. Bona Fide Requirement

a. No Deduction Allowed if Expense or Claim is Donative in Nature

Regulations effective for decedents dying after October 20, 2009, deny a deduction for expenses or claims that are not bona fide, *i.e.*, that are donative in nature. Regulation § 20.2053–1(b)(2). The only exception is for charitable bequests.

b. Factors Applying to Claims and Expenses Involving Family Members

The regulations avoid creating a rebuttable presumption that transactions involving family members are donative in nature. Although courts often state that such transactions are subject to "close scrutiny," the regulations also avoid this phrase. Instead, they adopt a list of factors that will be considered in determining if an expense or claim is bona fide. These include:

(1)   the transaction occurs in the ordinary course of business, is negotiated at arm's length, and is free from donative intent;

(2)   the expense or claim is not related to an expectation or claim of inheritance;

(3)   there is an agreement between the decedent and family member that can be substantiated with contemporaneous evidence;

(4)   the claimant's performance of an agreement can be substantiated; and

(5)   all amounts paid are reported by each party for income and employment tax purposes if appropriate.

4.   Actually Expended

a.   In General

The amount of the deduction must be certain; it cannot be estimated. As a result, expenses and claims must be actually expended by the time of filing the estate tax return.

b.   Post–Death Events

(1)   In General

Events that occur after death may affect the amount that the estate is required to pay. This is particularly true of claims against the estate. Courts have split on whether or not to take post-death events into account and to what extent. Regulations § 20.2053–1(d) and § 20.2053–4 now provide that post-death events must be considered for decedents dying after October 20, 2009. If these events occur between the date of death and the date of filing the estate tax return, they will determine the amount claimed on that return. If events subsequent to filing the return could affect the amount of liability, the estate must file the return and pay the tax due without including that deduction. The estate must then file a protective claim for a refund and file an amended return when the liability has been established. Regulation § 20.2053–1(d)(4)(a), (b).

(2) Ascertainable Amounts

Expenses or claims that are ascertainable with reasonable certainty and that will in fact be paid are deductible on the initial estate tax return. Regulation § 20.2053–1(d)(4). Often the estate is not closed within the time required for filing the estate tax return and attorney's fees and executor's fees have not yet been paid. Regulation §§ 20.2053–1(d)(4); 20.2053–2; 20.2053–3. These fees, however, may be deducted on the estate tax return as long as the amount is reasonably ascertainable and they will in fact be paid.

(3) Claims Not Exceeding $500,000

A deduction will be allowed for claims where payment is not made before filing the estate tax return if the total of such claims does not exceed $500,000 and each claim is established by a qualified appraisal. Regulation § 20.2053–4(c).

(4) Protective Claim for Refund

If an expense or claim does not meet the requirements or exceptions described above, the estate can file a protective claim for a refund. Regulation § 20.2053–1(d)(5). Once the expense or claim has in fact been paid, the estate can then file for a refund. The IRS has indicated that it will limit its review to evidence relating to the subject of the protective claim and not open the entire estate tax return to review. Notice 2009–84, 2009–44 I.R.B. 592 (November 2, 2009).

Example 13.4

Diedre died in a car accident and the driver of the other car filed suit against her estate, claiming damages of $1 million. The case was not settled until three years after the date of Diedre's death. Her executor would need to file a protective claim for a refund and an amended return once the case was settled and payment made. The § 2053 deduction will be limited to the amount actually paid.

---

5. Necessary to Settlement of the Estate

Expenses for administration of the estate will only be deductible if they are *necessary to the proper settlement* of the decedent's estate. Regulation § 20.2053–3.

6. Exam Strategy

The first step in determining whether or not a particular cost is deductible is to determine whether or not it is enumerated in § 2053. That is, is the cost a funeral expense, an expense of administration, a claim, or a debt? The next step is to determine if that cost is allowable by the laws of the jurisdiction where the estate is being administered. This is usually state law, but may also be the law of another country. The next step is to determine if the cost is one that is for property that is subject to claims. If so, it is deductible if (1) it is paid out of the property subject to claims or (2) it is paid from other sources within nine months of the decedent's death. If the cost is one for property that is not subject to claims, it is deductible as long as it is paid within three years. In addition, the expense or claim must be (1) bona fide, (2) actually expended, and (3) necessary to the proper administration of the estate.

C. FUNERAL EXPENSES

The cost of a casket, a burial vault, the undertaker's fee, cremation, flowers, food for the mourners, and the decedent's burial clothes are all deductible as funeral expenses under § 2053. The estate may even deduct the cost of transporting the body to the place of burial and the travel costs of the person accompanying the body. Thus, if the decedent breathes her last while vacationing in New Zealand, her spouse's trip home (as long as he accompanies her body) will be deductible. Finally, the reasonable cost of a tombstone, marker, or monument as well as the perpetual care of a cemetery lot or mausoleum will be treated as funeral expenses. Regulation § 20.2053–2.

Illustrative Case

In *Davenport v. Commissioner*, 92 T.C.M. (CCH) 324 (2006), the decedent had sustained injuries at the time of her birth and died at age 12. The primary issue before the court was the inclusion of annuities payable under a settlement agreement. In addition, while the IRS allowed most of the claimed funeral expenses, it challenged the deduction of $3,639 for a "funeral luncheon." The IRS did not challenge the payments to the funeral home, the soloist, the priest, or the organist or for the cremation, the obituary notice, the cemetery niche for the urn, holy picture cards, acknowledgments, or postage. The court upheld the disallowance of the funeral luncheon because the parent's testimony did not establish either the reasonableness of the amount or the link between the luncheon and the funeral. The parents

---

testified that the luncheon was held at a different location than the funeral service because of the large number of guests and that the purpose was to "show gratitude" to those who had helped them with their daughter's care. This case demonstrates, not that the cost of a funeral luncheon will not be deductible, but that proof of the nature of the expense (*i.e.*, food and hall rental versus decorating and entertainment) as well as the purpose, (*i.e.*, to feed those who actually attended the funeral versus a party) is essential.

D. ADMINISTRATIVE EXPENSES

1. General Principles

The list of deductible administration expenses includes executor's fees, attorney's fees, and miscellaneous fees such as court costs, accountant's fees, and appraiser's fees. Regulation § 20.2053–3. The expenses must be actually expended, necessary to the settlement of the estate, and allowable by the law of the local jurisdiction.

2. Executor's Fees

The amount of the executor's fee is often set by state law or by the decedent's will. If an executor receives a bequest in lieu of a fee, that amount is not deductible. On the other hand, such a bequest will not be considered income to the executor under § 102, while the fee will be taxable compensation under § 61. Whether an amount is a bequest or a fee is not always clear. Obviously, if the executor must actually perform services to obtain the amount, the payment will be considered a fee and not a bequest.

3. Attorney's Fees

Only attorney's fees that are essential to the settlement of the estate may be deducted. Often family members or beneficiaries incur attorney's fees in litigation to settle their respective interests in the estate, and frequently these will be payable out of the estate as a matter of local law. These fees may be deducted under § 2053, but only if they are *essential to the proper settlement of the estate*. The deductibility of a beneficiary's attorney's fees will thus depend on the particular facts of the case.

Illustrative Case

In *Levine v. United States*, 10 Cl. Ct. 135 (1986), a wife sued for refund of estate taxes paid on life insurance proceeds transferred to her less than three years prior to her husband's death. The court rejected her claim, but allowed a deduction from the husband's estate taxes for the attorney's fees paid in pursuing her claim.

Illustrative Case

In *Estate of Bartberger v. Commissioner*, 54 T.C.M. (CCH) 1550 (1988), the decedent devised one ranch to O.D. Dooley, another ranch to Else Inge Sights, and the residue of her estate to Martin Petersen. After decedent's death, Dooley sued in state court, claiming that he was entitled to the ranch pursuant to an oral agreement. The state court rejected his claim. The Tax Court agreed and included the ranch in decedent's gross estate. It denied a deduction for attorney's fees incurred by Dooley because that expense was solely for his own benefit and not essential to the proper settlement of decedent's estate. In this case Dooley's interest in the litigation was directly opposed to the interest of the estate. The court did allow attorney's fees incurred by Else Inge Sights as a deduction because those fees were incurred in conferences with the IRS and in the Tax Court litigation.

---

4.   Expenses of Maintaining or Selling Property

The expenses of maintaining property are deductible. If the executor sells the property, expenses incurred in that process will be deductible if the sale is necessary in order to pay decedent's debts, other administration expenses, or taxes or to preserve the estate or to effectuate distribution of the property. Regulation § 20.2053–3(d)(2). The expenses must be incurred for the benefit of the estate, not the individual beneficiary. For example, if the estate must sell a piece of real property in order to make a proper distribution of the estate, expenses incurred in that sale will be deductible. On the other hand, if the only reason for the sale is that an individual beneficiary prefers cash to real estate, the expense will not be deductible.

218

Illustrative Case

In *Hibernia Bank v. United States*, 581 F.2d 741 (9th Cir. 1978), decedent died in May 1965, leaving an estate worth several million dollars that consisted primarily of a mansion and shares of Hibernia Bank stock. Decedent's will left her estate to four trusts for the benefit of her child and grandchildren. Although all specific bequests and the claims had been paid by December 1967, the executor, which was Hibernia Bank, decided to sell the mansion. It was not able to do so, however, until spring 1972. In the meantime, the executor (Hibernia) spent $60,000 a year to maintain the property. The court held that the cost of maintaining the mansion was not deductible under § 2053 because it was not necessary for the estate to incur that cost. The estate could have distributed the mansion to the trusts as soon as the specific bequests and claims were paid in 1967. The court held that allowability under local law was not the sole criterion for deductibility under § 2053, stating: "We cannot read section 2053(a)(2) as permitting the deduction of expenditures which simply are not expenses of administration within the meaning afforded that term by federal estate tax law." *Id.* at 745.

---

5. **Trustees' Fees**

Trustees' fees generally are not deductible because they benefit individual beneficiaries and not the estate. Such fees may be deducted against the *trust's* income tax liability, however. If a trustee performs the functions of an executor in the winding up of a trust due to the decedent's death, the fees associated with those tasks may be deducted under § 2053, subject to the general limitations already discussed.

6. **Exam Strategy**

To be deductible, expenses must first be either funeral expenses or administration expenses as defined by federal law. Second, they must be necessary to the administration of the estate. Third, they must be reasonable in amount. Fourth, they must be actually expended or reasonably ascertainable. If not, a protective claim for a refund must be filed and an amended return filed when the expense is in fact paid. The estate has the burden of proving each of these elements.

E. SECTION 2053: CLAIMS AND DEBTS

1. Personal Obligation of the Decedent

To be deductible, a claim or debt must be the personal obligation of the decedent. Regulation § 20.2053–4. If the decedent has guaranteed a debt, that amount is not deductible unless, of course, the debtor is unable to pay and the estate pays.

2. Principal and Interest

The debt or claim need not have matured at the time of death. Regulation § 20.2053–4. Remember that one function of the probate process is to pay the decedent's debts. All debts, even those that were not due at the time of death, will be paid during probate and will be deductible under § 2053. Interest is also deductible, but interest must have accrued at the time of death. This is true even if the executor elects the alternate valuation date so interest accruing in the six months after the date of death is deductible only on the estate's income tax return, if at all. Regulation § 20.2053–4.

3. Enforceable

The claim or debt must be enforceable against the decedent's estate. Regulation § 20.2053–4. If the claim or debt is barred by the statute of limitations or for any other reason, no deduction will be allowed even if the executor pays the debt and even if the state probate court approves the executor's action. *Id.* If the state's highest court has ruled on the issue following a trial on the merits, the IRS would be bound by that determination. *Estate of Bosch v. Commissioner*, 387 U.S. 456 (1967).

a. Statute of Limitations

Claims and debts must be pursued within the time established by state law, *i.e.*, within the statute of limitations. A claim or debt that would be unenforceable because it is barred by the statute of limitations or the equitable doctrine of laches is not deductible under § 2053 even if the executor pays it and even if the state court approves that payment.

b. Nonclaim Statutes

States also impose a time limit for presenting claims in the probate process, called a **nonclaim statute**. If a creditor or claimant fails to present his claim within that time limit, it is barred. As a result, that amount would not be deductible under § 2053 even if the executor paid it and even if the state court approved that payment.

4. Claims Based on a Promise or Agreement

Claims that are based on a promise or an agreement must have been contracted for adequate and full consideration in money or money's worth. § 2053(c)(1)(A). Without this limitation, decedent would be able to eliminate any estate tax liability through agreements with her heirs and beneficiaries. The same principle applies to payments to settle a will contest or to satisfy a surviving spouse's elective share. These are analogous to bequests and are not deductible under § 2053. Regulation § 20.2053–1(b)(2) now explicitly denies such claims; this regulation is effective for decedents dying after October 20, 2009.

Illustrative Case

In *Estate of Flandreau v. Commissioner*, 994 F.2d 91 (2d Cir. 1993), the decedent made gifts to family members and then immediately borrowed the exact amount of the gift from that family member. Each transaction was memorialized in a non-interest bearing promissory note. None of the notes were secured by any property interests. The court denied the claimed deduction because the transactions were "merely circular transfers of money from decedent to her children and back to decedent." *Id.* at 92. The court found that the promissory notes did not represent bona fide debts but were instead "unenforceable gratuitous promises" by the decedent. *Id.*

Illustrative Case

In *Leopold v. United States*, 510 F.2d 617 (9th Cir. 1975), on the other hand, the court allowed a deduction for a $264,000 payment to decedent's daughter. Decedent married Catherine, his second wife, on February 2, 1958, and their daughter, Beatrice Tina, was born on August 13, 1958. One year later Catherine filed for divorce and the property settlement, signed after extensive negotiations, required decedent to leave Beatrice Tina the $264,000 at issue. The court allowed the deduction because of the "exceptional circumstances" of the case, including the extensive divorce negotiations, evidence that Catherine accepted lower alimony payments in exchange for the bequest to her daughter, and decedent's preference for the children for his first marriage.

---

5. Debts

Any debt incurred by decedent before death is deductible even if the debt has not matured at the time of death. Regulation § 20.2053–4. Interest accrued as of the date of death is also deductible. *Id.* This includes both secured and unsecured debts such as car payments, credit card payments, utility payments, and the like.

6. Mortgages

If the decedent's estate includes the full value of property that is subject to a mortgage, then the full amount of the mortgage will be deductible. Regulation § 20.2053–7. If the decedent's estate is not liable for the debt because the decedent was not personally liable for the debt, then only the value of the property's equity is included in the decedent's gross estate and no deduction is allowed for the mortgage. *Id.*

7. Exam Strategy

Claims and debts must be bona fide; they cannot be disguised bequests. They must be enforceable. And they must be incurred for adequate and full consideration in money or money's worth.

F. TAXES

1. General Principles

There are two categories of taxes. The first category includes those taxes allowed as deductions by § 2053 as claims against the estate. These are decedent's income taxes, property taxes, and gift taxes. The second category is state imposed death taxes that are deductible under § 2058.

2. Taxes Deductible Under § 2053

a. Income Taxes

(1) In General

Any income tax due on income that decedent received *before* her death is deductible. Regulation § 20.2053–6(f). A decedent is a cash basis taxpayer and may only report income received before death and expenses paid before death. The only exception is the § 213(e) deduction for medical expenses paid by the estate within one year of decedent's death.

(2) Income in Respect of a Decedent

Any income received after the date of death is **income in respect of a decedent (IRD)** and must be reported by the taxpayer legally entitled to receive that income. Often that taxpayer is the decedent's estate. Remember that the estate is a separate taxpaying entity and must file its own income tax return. IRD is a property interest owned by the decedent and must be included in her gross estate under § 2033. The taxpayer reporting the IRD as income is entitled to a deduction for any estate tax that is due with respect to that property interest. § 691(c).

(3) Joint Tax Returns

If decedent is married and her surviving spouse elects to file a joint income tax return as the decedent's final income tax return, only the income tax that represents the decedent's portion of the liability is deductible.

(4) Income Tax Refund

If the decedent is entitled to a refund on her final income tax return, that amount is a property interest that must be included in the gross estate under § 2033.

b. Property Taxes

Taxes on property owned by the decedent are deductible only if those taxes accrued before the date of decedent's death. Regulation § 20.2056–6(b). The taxes must be due or have attached as a lien to the property and not merely have accrued in the accounting sense of that term. Unless the decedent had not paid her property taxes that were due before death, it is unlikely that they will be deductible as they will not have accrued within the meaning of this regulation.

c. Gift Taxes

Any gift tax due on gifts made by the decedent before death are also deductible. Regulation § 20.2056–6(d). Only the gift tax attributable to the decedent's portion of split gifts is deductible. *Id.*

3. State Death Taxes: § 2058

Prior to 2001, there was a credit rather than a deduction for state death taxes. As a result, every state imposed some form of a death tax, either an estate tax or an inheritance tax. The 2001 Tax Act replaced the § 2011 credit for death taxes with the § 2058 deduction. As long as the tax is paid by decedent's estate and paid within four years after the filing of estate tax return that amount is deductible. There are no monetary or percentage limits on this deduction.

If Congress fails to act before January 1, 2011, the § 2011 credit for state death taxes will return and the § 2058 deduction will disappear.

4. Exam Strategy

Not all taxes are deductible on the estate tax return (form 706). Gift taxes as well as some income taxes and property taxes are deductible under § 2053. State death taxes are only deductible under § 2058. Other taxes, such as property taxes due and payable after decedent's death, may be deductible on the estate's income tax return.

G. LOSSES: § 2054

1. Deduction for Casualty Losses

Section 2054 allows the executor to claim a deduction for certain losses incurred during the settlement of decedent's estate. Only losses arising from theft, or from fire, storm, shipwreck, or other casualty are allowed and then only to the extent such losses are not compensated for by insurance or otherwise. This deduction is analogous to the casualty loss deduction allowed by § 165(h).

2. No Double Deduction Allowed

The decedent's estate is itself an entity subject to the income tax. It is the owner of property during settlement of the estate. If a casualty loss occurs with respect to property owned by the estate, the executor must decide whether or not to claim the deduction on the estate's income tax return or on the estate tax return. Usually, it is better to claim the deduction on the estate tax return because there are no monetary limits on the deduction on that return and because the estate is subject to a 45 percent tax rate while the marginal rate of the income tax is much lower.

CHAPTER 14

THE CHARITABLE DEDUCTION

A. GENERAL PRINCIPLES

Both the gift tax (§ 2522) and the estate tax (§ 2055) allow a deduction for transfers to charitable organizations. These provisions permit an unlimited deduction and are, at least with respect to outright gifts and bequests, simple and straightforward. Because of the possibility of manipulation and abuse, the provisions governing transfers of split interests and transfers in trust are detailed and complex.

1. Similarity to the Income Tax

The gift and estate tax charitable deductions are nearly identical. They are similar to, but not always identical to, the income tax deduction in § 170. Section 170 permits some deductions that §§ 2055 and 2522 do not, and it imposes monetary and percentage limitations on the amount of the deduction. In addition, § 501(c) exempts certain organizations from the income tax and its rules are similar to, but not always identical to, the rules in §§ 170, 2055, and 2522.

2. Rationale

The deduction for transfers to charities reflects a policy of promoting private support for governmental-type services and other charitable purposes.

3. Charitable Defined

a. In General

As the titles to §§ 2055 and 2522 suggest, only transfers for public, charitable, and religious uses qualify for the deduction. Gifts to governmental entities must be exclusively for public purposes. §§ 2055(a)(1); 2522(a)(1). Gifts to corporations must be for religious, charitable, scientific, literary, or educational purposes or the encouragement of art or amateur sports or the prevention of cruelty to children or animals. §§ 2055(a)(2); 2522(a)(2).

b. No Private Benefit

Transfers must be exclusively for charitable purposes and not for the benefit of a particular person. Moreover, a corporation must ensure that none of its earnings benefit a private shareholder or individual. A bequest to a college to provide scholarships for the decedent's grandchildren would not qualify, nor would a bequest to that college to provide scholarships for individuals with a certain name.

Illustrative Case

In *Griffin v. United States*, 400 F.2d 612 (6th Cir. 1968), the decedent created a trust for the education of his grandchildren in the first instance and then other deserving parties. The court held that the trust was not charitable because the grandchildren were not required to establish their need for scholarship assistance and they received a larger amount than non-relatives.

Illustrative Case

In *Commonwealth Trust Co. v. Grander*, 57 F.Supp. 502 (W.D. Pa. 1944), the decedent created a scholarship fund and expressed a preference in favor of individuals bearing his last name. He did not, however, limit distributions to these individuals. The court allowed a charitable deduction. *Compare* Technical Advice Memorandum 9631004, where the decedent limited the scholarship recipients to those of a specified name. In that situation, the IRS disallowed the deduction.

---

4. Limits

There are no percentage or monetary limits on the gift tax or the estate tax charitable deduction. §§ 2055, 2522. The amount of the estate tax deduction cannot exceed the value of the property transferred to charity that is included in the gross estate. § 2055(d).

5. Exam Strategy

If there is a gift, bequest, or devise to an organization, determine if the purpose of the gift, bequest, or devise is charitable or public. If so, a deduction will be allowed. Remember that there are no monetary limitations on the gift tax or the estate tax charitable deduction. A lifetime gift may qualify for both the gift tax deduction and the income tax deduction.

B. QUALIFYING ORGANIZATIONS

1. Governmental Entities

Transfers to governmental entities, *i.e.*, the United States, a state, a political subdivision of a state, or the District of Columbia, will qualify if the transfer is exclusively for public purposes. §§ 2055(a)(1), 2522(a)(1).

2. Public Charities and Private Foundations

Transfers to non-governmental organizations qualify if those organizations are organized and operated *exclusively* for religious, charitable, scientific, literary or educational purposes. §§ 2055(a)(2), 2522(a)(2). This includes encouragement of art, fostering amateur sports, and the prevention of cruelty to children and animals. *Id.*

Example 14.1

Brent bequeaths $50,000 to the Parkwood Cemetery Association. This bequest will not be deductible under § 2055 because cemetery associations are not operated *exclusively* for charitable purposes. Because a cemetery association's principal purpose is to receive full value for its products, a transfer to it does not qualify under § 2055 even if it accepts indigents or has a sliding scale based on income. Revenue Ruling 67–170, 1967–1 C.B. 272. It does not matter that the cemetery association might be a non-profit organization and exempt from tax under § 501(c)(13) or that contributions are deductible for purposes of the income tax under § 170(c)(5).

---

3. Other Organizations

Transfers to a society or association operating under the lodge system will be deductible as long as the donations are to be used exclusively for religious, charitable, scientific, literary or educational purposes. §§ 2055(a)(3); 2522(a)(3). Transfers to veterans' organizations are also deductible. §§ 2055(a)(4); 2522(a)(4).

4. Choice of Organization by Executor or Trustee

For the transfer to qualify for the estate tax charitable deduction, the decedent himself must indicate an intention to make a charitable contribution in his will. His failure to do so cannot be remedied by the agreement of his beneficiaries or heirs. The decedent can, however, leave to his executor or other designated individual the choice of which charities will receive contributions, but only if state law will uphold the validity of the donation and restrict the executor to organizations that qualify under § 2055. *Compare* Revenue Ruling 69–285, 1969–1 C.B. 222 (stating that Massachusetts law was at least as restrictive as § 2055) *with* Revenue Ruling 71–441, 1971–2 C.B. 335 (explaining that Alabama law would not enforce the provision as a charitable trust and that the doctrine of *cy pres* would not apply because decedent had not designated a specific charitable purpose).

Illustrative Case

In *Estate of Pickard v. Commissioner*, 60 T.C. 618 (1973), decedent left her estate in trust to pay an annuity of $3,000 to her mother and then the property was to be distributed in fee simple to her stepfather. Decedent's stepfather died seven weeks *before* decedent, leaving his property in trust for his wife (decedent's mother) and the remainder to two specific charitable organizations. The court held that decedent's estate was not entitled to a charitable deduction even though her property would pass to the designated charities because the decedent herself did not manifest an intent in her will to benefit those (or any) charities.

---

5. **Prohibition Against Lobbying**

Transfers to an organization will not qualify for the charitable deduction if that organization engages in lobbying or other attempts to influence legislation or participates or intervenes in political campaigns on behalf of candidates. §§ 2055(a)(2); 2522(a)(2).

6. **No Violation of Public Policy**

The organization cannot engage in behavior that violates established public policy. *See Bob Jones University v. Simon*, 416 U.S. 725 (1974) (revoking tax exempt status); and *Green v. Connally*, 330 F.Supp. 1150 (D.D.C. 1971), *aff'd without opinion sub nom. Coit v. Green*, 404 U.S. 997 (1971) (denying tax exempt status and income tax deduction).

7. **Exam Strategy**

When it comes to determining if an organization is a *qualified organization*, the rules are the same for the income tax, the gift tax, and the estate tax. Donations must be to an organization, not an individual. The organization must be charitable or governmental. There can be no private benefit, no lobbying, and no violation of public policy.

C. OUTRIGHT GIFTS

1. General Principles

Outright transfers (*i.e.*, transfers other than in trust or of split interests) that are to qualifying organizations will be deducted in computing either the gift tax or the estate tax. There are no monetary or percentage limitations.

2. Conditional Gifts

Often a donor or a decedent will designate a donation for a specific purpose. If that donation is conditional, the possibility that the condition will not take effect must be *so remote as to be negligible*. Regulation § 20.2055–2(b)(1). If the probability that the condition will occur *does not exceed five percent*, then it will be so remote as to be negligible, and the deduction will be allowed. Revenue Ruling 70–452, 1970–2 C.B. 199.

Example 14.2

Brent bequeaths $100,000 to Law School to endow a professorship in the name of his tax professor. Law School requires an endowment of $2.5 million to create an endowed professorship. Law School's development office determines that it will not be able to raise the required funds. Brent's estate will not be entitled to a charitable deduction if the likelihood that the professorship will be created was less than five percent on the date of his death.

D. TRANSFERS IN TRUST AND SPLIT–INTERESTS

1. General Principles

The amount of a deduction must be ascertainable at the date of death. When a decedent creates a trust and gives the remainder to a charity, it is not always clear that the charity will receive any property, let alone the value that was claimed as a charitable deduction. In the days when the interest rates used for valuing life estates, remainders, and similar interests were fixed by regulation, it was possible that the value of the estate tax deduction would far exceed the actual benefit to the charity. In 1969,

Congress enacted significant changes to the charitable interest rules to prevent this type of manipulation. The rules are detailed and complex and only the highlights are presented here.

2. Charitable Remainder Trusts

A charitable remainder trust is one in which the decedent bequeaths a life estate or term of years to an individual or individuals and the remainder to a charitable organization. A charitable deduction will be allowed for the remainder interest only if the remainder is in (1) a charitable remainder annuity trust, (2) a charitable remainder unitrust, or (3) a pooled income fund. § 2055(e)(2). The same rules apply to the gift tax. § 2522(c)(2).

a. Charitable Remainder Annuity Trusts (CRATs)

To qualify as a charitable remainder annuity trust, the trust must pay a sum certain at least annually to one or more persons who are living at the time of the creation of the trust. The annuity must be paid for the life of the individual(s) or for a term of years not in excess of 20 years. The annuity amount must be at least 5 percent and not more than 50 percent of the initial fair market value of all the property placed into the trust, and it can be expressed either as a dollar amount or as a percentage or fractional share. The remainder, of course, must be paid to a qualified charitable organization, and the value of the remainder must be at least 10 percent of the initial fair market value of the property contributed to the trust. § 664(d)(1).

Example 14.3

Marcia's will leaves $500,000 to Friendly National Bank as trustee, to pay $40,000 a year to her niece, Nisha, for her life and, at Nisha's death, to distribute the remainder to Law School, a § 501(c)(3) organization. The income must be distributed quarterly. If the remainder interest, valued under the § 7520 tables, is equal to at least $50,000, this trust will qualify as a charitable remainder annuity trust, and Marcia's estate will be entitled to a charitable deduction for the value of the remainder interest.

---

b. Charitable Remainder Unitrusts (CRUTs)

To qualify as a charitable remainder unitrust, the trust must pay a fixed percentage of the net fair market value of the trust assets to one or more persons who are living at the time of the creation of the trust. The annuity must be paid for the life of the individual(s) or for a term of years not in excess of 20 years. The amount must be at least 5 percent and not more than 50 percent of the fair market value of the trust property, valued annually. The remainder, of course, must be paid to a qualified charitable organization and the value of the remainder must be at least 10 percent of the initial fair market value of the property contributed to the trust. § 664(d)(1).

Example 14.4

Chloe's will leaves $800,000 to Friendly National Bank as trustee, to pay eight percent of the fair market value of the trust assets valued annually to her nephew, Owen, for 15 years, and then to distribute the trust property to Church, a § 501(c)(3) organization. The income must be distributed quarterly. If the remainder interest, valued under the § 7520 tables, is equal to at least $80,000, this trust will qualify as a charitable remainder annuity trust, and Chloe's estate will be entitled to a charitable deduction for the value of the remainder interest.

---

c. Pooled Income Funds

A pooled income fund is a trust maintained by a public charity (defined in § 170(b)(1)(A) as other than charities in clauses (vii) and (viii)) to which any number of individuals have made contributions. The charity is the remainder beneficiary, and the income interest is paid to one or more individuals designated by the donor or decedent. The life interest can only be paid to individuals living at the time of the donation, and the amount is determined by the rate of return on the investments in the pooled income fund. The value of the charitable deduction will be based on the highest rate of return earned by the fund for any of the three tax years preceding the year of the transfer. § 642(c)(5).

3. Income Interest to a Charitable Organization

Sections 2055 and 2522 allow a deduction for a trust where the income interest benefits a qualified charity and the remainder interest is distributed to one or more individuals. The amount distributed to the charity must be either a guaranteed annuity or a fixed percentage of the trust funds, and the amount must be distributed on an annual basis. §§ 2055(e)(2)(B); 2522(c)(2)(B).

4. Split–Interest Gifts

The same concern that the donor or decedent will manipulate property interests and their valuation has led Congress to limit charitable deductions for donations of the use of property or donations of less than the donor's or decedent's entire interest in property. §§ 2055(e)(2); 2522(c)(2). The only deductions that are allowed are for donations of (1) an undivided interest in property; (2) a remainder interest in a personal residence or a farm; or (3) a conservation easement as defined in § 170(f)(3)(B).

a. Undivided Portion

An undivided portion must be a fractional, *e.g.,* one-half or one-third, or percentage, *e.g.,* 20 percent or 45 percent, share of the donor's or decedent's interest in the property. The charitable organization will then be a tenant in common with the other owners.

b. Remainder Interest in a Personal Residence or Farm

A donor or a decedent's estate will receive a charitable deduction for a remainder interest in the donor's or decedent's personal residence or farm if that interest is given to a qualified charitable organization. This is not a gift in trust, but instead is a remainder interest in a deed.

c. Conservation Easements

(1) General Principles

Section 2031(c) excludes from the gross estate a portion of the value of real property subject to a qualified conservation easement. The easement must meet the requirements in § 170(h). That is, the deduction must be of a qualified real property interest to a qualified organization and exclusively for conservation purposes.

(2) Amount Excluded

The amount excluded is the lesser of (1) $500,000 or (2) the applicable percentage of the value of the land subject to the easement reduced by the amount of any § 2055(f) charitable deduction with respect to the land. The applicable percentage is 40 percent as long as the value of the easement is at least 30 percent of the value of the land, determined without regard to the easement. If the value of the easement is less than 30 percent of the value of the land, then the applicable percentage (40 percent) is reduced by 2 percentage points for every percentage point that the value of the easement is less than the value of the land.

(3) Contribution Need Not Be Made by Decedent

Under § 2031(c), the decision to contribute a qualified conservation easement does not need to be made by the decedent. If the decedent does not include the donation in her will, her executor can make the election on the estate tax return. § 2031(c)(6). This allows the decedent's family to decide after her death to make the qualified conservation easement donation.

5. Reformation

Because the rules for charitable remainder trusts and other split interests are detailed and complex, it is easy for estate planners to make inadvertent mistakes. Sections 2055 and 2522 recognize this and allow a deduction when the trust document or other governing instrument is reformed, amended, or construed to conform to the statutory requirements as long as the reformation meets the requirements of § 2055(e)(3), which again are detailed and complex. The difference between the actuarial value of the charitable interest without reformation and the actuarial value of the charitable interest with the reformation cannot exceed five percent of the reformable interest. The interest of the non-charitable beneficiary must be expressed either as a specified dollar amount or a fixed percentage of the fair market value of the property.

6. Exam Strategy

The rules applicable to donations of split interests in property or transfers in trust are complex. If confronted with this issue on an exam, do not generalize or guess. Refer to the applicable IRC provisions.

CHAPTER 15

THE MARITAL DEDUCTION

A. GENERAL PRINCIPLES

1. Historical Perspective

a. Origins of the Marital Deduction

During the first three decades of its existence, the federal estate tax treated each individual as a separate taxpayer. The transfer of property was taxed based on who held title to the property. The same was true of the income tax; whoever earned the income had to pay the tax. Then the Supreme Court held that income earned in a community property jurisdiction was taxed one-half to each spouse. *Poe v. Seaborn*, 282 U.S. 101 (1930). The same principle applied in the estate tax context; only one-half of the community property was included in the gross estate of the first spouse to die. Taxpayers in common law property jurisdictions quickly realized the advantages of community property, and states began to change from common law to community property. Congress responded by enacting a deduction for transfers between spouses as well as a joint filing system for the income tax.

b. Pre–1981 Marital Deduction

The original estate marital deduction provision reflected its roots in community property law. The deduction was limited to one-half the value of the property in the decedent's gross estate. If the decedent left the property in trust, the survivor had to be entitled to all the income payable at least annually and have the ability to appoint the trust property to herself or her estate. In 1976, Congress amended the marital deduction to allow a deduction for the greater of $250,000 or 50 percent of the adjusted gross estate. (The adjusted gross estate was the gross estate minus the § 2053 and the § 2054 deductions.)

c. 1981 Economic Recovery Tax Act

In 1981, Congress lifted all monetary and percentage limits on the marital deduction. It also enacted a provision that allowed the decedent to leave the surviving spouse only an income interest as long as no one had the ability to appoint to anyone other than the surviving spouse during her life. This new provision, § 2056(b)(7), is referred to as the QTIP trust provision.

2. Rationale

As this brief history demonstrates, the rationale for the marital deduction has changed over time.

a. Treat Common Law Property the Same as Community Property

The initial rationale for the marital deduction was to provide equality between common law and community property jurisdictions. The initial form of the deduction mimicked community property as closely as possible. Although the remnants of this rationale remain in § 2056(b)(5), this is no longer the primary purpose of the marital deduction.

b. Married Couple as One Economic Unit

The 1981 amendments to the marital deduction reflected a shift in theory and a recognition that a married couple usually functions as a single economic unit or partnership.

c. Taxing Property Once Each Generation

The adoption of a generation-skipping transfer tax (see chapter 17) reflects a policy of taxing property once at each generation. A husband and wife are treated as belonging to the same generation no matter what their ages might be. As noted below, the *quid pro quo* for the marital deduction is that any property not consumed or given away by the surviving spouse will be taxed in the estate of the surviving spouse.

B. TRANSFEROR AND RECIPIENT ELIGIBILITY REQUIREMENTS

1. Transferor Must Be Subject to Tax

The marital deduction is only available to a decedent who is subject to the federal estate tax. This means that the decedent must be a citizen or resident of the United States or must own property located in the United States.

2. Property Received by Spouse Must Be Subject to Tax

The *quid pro quo* for the marital deduction is that the property received by the surviving spouse will be subject to the federal estate tax when she dies. The following requirements ensure that this will happen.

a. Citizen

In most cases, the surviving spouse is a citizen and, therefore, subject to the federal estate tax. In these cases, the property can be left outright or in a trust.

b. Qualified Domestic Trusts

If the surviving spouse is not a citizen, the decedent's estate will be entitled to the marital deduction only if the property passes to a **qualified domestic trust (QDOT)**. § 2056(d); § 2056A(a). A QDOT is one where at least one trustee is either a citizen of the United States or a domestic corporation and has the right to withhold tax on a distribution, other than a distribution of income. Section 2056A(b) imposes an estate tax on any property distributed from the trust at the death of the surviving spouse as well as an estate tax on any property remaining in the trust.

3. Transferor and Recipient Must Be Married

a. Impact of State Law

The decedent and the surviving spouse must, of course, be married. This includes common law marriage if the state recognizes it, but it does not necessarily include same-sex married couples or couples in civil unions or other relationships recognized by state law as the equivalent of marriage. The Defense of Marriage Act (DOMA), 1 U.S.C. § 7, provides that federal law does not need to recognize such relationships.

b. Divorce

If the decedent dies while a divorce action is pending, the decedent is still married, and the marital deduction will apply to any property devised to the surviving spouse. Before no-fault divorce became available, there were often issues concerning the marital status of the decedent or the survivor if one had obtained a divorce in a jurisdiction, such as Nevada or Mexico, where the individual did not reside. Those confusing days have passed, and now the issue is whether or not the divorce is final.

4. Recipient Must Survive

The recipient must in fact survive the decedent. This may seem obvious, but it can be an issue if the couple dies simultaneously or in circumstances where the order of death cannot be determined.

a. Simultaneous Deaths

Where both spouses die simultaneously or in circumstances where the order of death cannot be determined, state law will determine survivorship. The Uniform Simultaneous Death Act, or similar legislation, will usually provide that each individual is deemed to survive with respect to his or her own property and that jointly owned property is treated as if each survived with respect to one-half of it. This will often mean that no property passes to the other spouse so there will be no marital deduction.

b. Survivorship Clause in Spouse's Will

The application of the Uniform Simultaneous Death Act or similar laws can cause unnecessary taxation where a couple's estate plan is structured so that property passed from the richer to the poorer spouse so that both can claim the benefit of the unified credit. To ensure that such estate planning is not wasted, a couple may include a clause in their wills that determines the order of death. The clauses must be *mirror images* not identical or the desired effect will be lost. Such clauses will only affect the marital deduction when the spouses in fact die in circumstances when the order of death cannot be determined. See discussion of *Estate of Lee v. Commissioner*, section F.3.

Example 15.1

Henry and Willow are married. Henry owns $7 million worth of property, and Willow owns very little property. Henry's will provides that one-half his property goes into a credit-shelter trust and one-half goes into a marital deduction trust. To ensure that this occurs in the event of a simultaneous death, Henry's will provides: "If my wife, Willow, and I die in circumstances where the order of death cannot be determined, then my wife, Willow, shall be deemed to survive me."

For this plan to work Willow needs a corresponding provision in her will. It should read: "If my husband, Henry, and I died in circumstances where the order of death cannot be determined, then I will be deemed to survive Henry." Notice that this is not exactly the same as the clause in Henry's will. Estate planners often make

---

> that mistake. If each clause reads exactly the same, *i.e.*, that the other spouse survives, the clause does nothing. Both wills must state that one of the parties (in this example Willow) is deemed the survivor.

5. Exam Strategy

Watch for status and survivorship issues. If the surviving spouse is not a citizen, the property must pass to a qualified domestic trust. If the order of deaths is not clear, first determine if the wills state a presumption of survivorship. If not, treat each spouse as if he or she survived with respect to his or her own property. Remember that a will beneficiary must in fact survive the testator, so a provision in the will leaving "all my property to my spouse" will not pass property to a spouse who predeceases or is treated as predeceasing the decedent.

C. PROPERTY MUST BE IN THE GROSS ESTATE

1. General Principles

To qualify for the marital deduction, the property must be included in the decedent's gross estate. § 2056(a). Without this rule, property passing to someone other than the surviving spouse might be sheltered from tax.

Example 15.2

At the time of his death, Tad owned $5 million in investments. In addition, Tad had the power to appoint trust property worth $4 million to his surviving spouse or his children. Tad's will exercised the power of appointment in favor of his spouse, Sonia, and devised the rest of his property in equal shares to his children. The trust property would not be in his gross estate because Tad had only a special power of appointment over it. (Only property subject to a general power is included in the gross estate. § 2041. See chapter 10, section A.3.) Without the requirement that the property transferred to the surviving spouse be in the decedent's gross estate, Tad would have a gross estate of $5 million and a taxable estate of $1 million. As it is, Tad's gross estate and his taxable estate are both $5 million.

---

2. Net Value Rule

Only the net value of the property passing to the surviving spouse qualifies for the marital deduction. § 2056(b)(4). This rule applies when the property is subject to a lien or mortgage or an estate or inheritance tax is imposed on the property. In both situations, the amount actually received by the surviving spouse is reduced and the marital deduction is limited to this reduced value.

Example 15.3

Tad owned Greenacre that had a fair market value of $2.5 million and a $1 million mortgage on it. Tad devised Greenacre to his spouse, Sonia, and the mortgage was not discharged at Tad's death. Only the net value of the property that passes to Sonia, $1.5 million, qualifies for the marital deduction.

If, on the other hand, the mortgage is paid by the executor, then the amount of the mortgage is allowed as a deduction under § 2053 and that amount is treated as an additional bequest from Tad to Sonia. Regulation § 20.2056(b)–4(b). If the $1 million mortgage in this example is discharged in the probate process, then the full value of the property, $2.5 million, will qualify for the marital deduction. Whether or not a mortgage is discharged during probate depends on the decedent's will as well as state law.

D. PASSING REQUIREMENT

To qualify for the marital deduction, the property must not only be in the decedent's gross estate, but it must also **pass** from the decedent to the surviving spouse. § 2056(a). Most transfers from the decedent to the surviving spouse meet this requirement. § 2056(c).

1. Probate Property

Property that the decedent bequeaths or devises to the surviving spouse passes from decedent to that spouse. § 2056(c)(1). If the decedent dies intestate, any property that the surviving spouse inherits also passes from decedent to that spouse. § 2056(c)(2).

2. Joint Tenancy/Tenancy by the Entirety

If decedent and the surviving spouse own property as joint tenants with the right of survivorship or as tenants by the entirety, the decedent's interest that transfers to the survivor by operation of law at the moment of death is considered as passing for purposes of the marital deduction. § 2056(c)(5).

3. Life Insurance

Any proceeds of insurance on the life of the decedent receivable by the surviving spouse also pass from the decedent to that spouse for purposes of the marital deduction. § 2056(c)(7).

4. Powers of Appointment

If the decedent exercises a power to appoint property to the surviving spouse, that property passes from the decedent to the surviving spouse. § 2056(c)(6).

5. Elective Share

If the surviving spouse exercises her statutory elective share, that property passes from the decedent to the surviving spouse. § 2056(c)(3). The payment must be a "bona fide recognition of enforceable rights of the surviving spouse in the decedent's estate." Regulation § 20.2056(c)–2(d). Any interest surrendered by the surviving spouse is not considered as passing from decedent to her. *Id.*

6. Passing at Any Time

Any property interest transferred by the decedent to the surviving spouse at any time, even during life, will qualify as passing. § 2056(c)(4). Remember that the property interest must be included in the decedent's gross estate at death.

Example 15.4

Tad created an irrevocable, inter vivos trust to pay the income to himself during life and the remainder to his spouse, Sonia. The creation of the trust is a completed gift of the remainder interest. The trust property, however, will be in Tad's gross estate at death because he retained the right to the income for his life. § 2036(a)(1). That property will qualify for the estate tax marital deduction because the property was in Tad's gross estate and he transferred it to his surviving spouse, Sonia, during his life. § 2056(c)(4).

---

7. Annuities and Similar Payments

If the surviving spouse is entitled to an annuity payment because she survived the decedent and if the value of the annuity is included in decedent's gross estate pursuant to § 2039, then the spouse's interest is deemed to have passed to her from the decedent. Regulation § 20.2056(c)–1(a)(6).

8. Disclaimers

A person who disclaims is not considered the transferor for purposes of the federal transfer taxes. § 2518. Thus, if decedent leaves property to a person other than the surviving spouse and that other person disclaims, the disclaimant is not the transferor. If the surviving spouse is then entitled to the property, the property is deemed to have passed from the decedent to the survivor. Regulation § 20.2056(d)–2(b). On the other hand, if the surviving spouse disclaims an interest in property devised by decedent, that property will not qualify for the marital deduction. Because of the disclaimer, the spouse is treated as if she predeceased the decedent and, thus, the marital deduction would not apply. Regulation § 20.205(d)–2(a).

Example 15.5

Oren's will leaves all of his property to his son, Chris, but provides that if Chris disclaims any or all of the property or predeceases him, the property will pass to his (Oren's) wife, Naomi. When Oren dies, he owns property valued at $10 million. Chris disclaims his interest in $6 million and that property is distributed to Naomi. Chris is not treated as the transferor (§ 2518) so the $6 million passes from Oren to Naomi and qualifies for the marital deduction. Regulation § 20.2056(d)–4(b).

---

9. Will Contests and Family Settlements

Property acquired by the surviving spouse as a result of a will contest or family settlement will only qualify as passing from the decedent if the payment is a "bona fide recognition of enforceable rights of the surviving spouse in the decedent's estate." Regulation § 20.2056(c)–2(d). A court decree will be presumed to meet this standard, but only if there has been an adversary proceeding and a genuine and active contest. *Id.* The court must decide the facts upon which the deduction depends. A consent decree or a settlement before trial will not necessarily qualify for the marital deduction. *Id.* Like all intra-family transfers, such agreements are closely scrutinized.

Example 15.6

Assume the same basic facts as in example 15.5 except that Oren's will does not provide for a gift to Naomi if Chris disclaims or predeceases him. After Oren's death, Chris and Naomi agree that Naomi will receive $4 million of Oren's property. Assume that Naomi would be entitled

---

under state law to one-half, *i.e.*, $5 million, of Oren's estate as her statutory share. In this situation, it is highly likely that the $4 million will qualify for the marital deduction. The agreement between Chris and Naomi provides her with less than she would have been entitled to under local law. It is, therefore, most likely a bona fide recognition of her enforceable rights.

Example 15.7

Assume the same basic facts as in example 15.6 except that Oren and Naomi had a valid pre-nuptial agreement. Naomi waived her rights to her statutory share in that agreement, and she received substantial property from Oren upon their marriage. Assume that she and Chris sign an agreement giving her $2 million from Oren's estate. Chris signs the agreement because he believes "it is the right thing to do." The $2 million will not qualify for the marital deduction because Naomi had no enforceable legal right to any of Oren's property. Instead, the $2 million will be treated as a gift from Chris to Naomi.

---

10. Exam Strategy

Property that the decedent transfers to his surviving spouse will meet the *passing* requirement of § 2056(c) if the decedent is the transferor. Be alert for special situations such as disclaimers and family settlements. While some post-mortem estate planning, such as disclaimers, will be recognized, other arrangements will not qualify for the marital deduction. The arrangement must be a bona fide recognition of the surviving spouse's enforceable rights.

E. THE TERMINABLE INTEREST RULE

1. General Principles

A terminable interest is one that will terminate or fail on the lapse of time, the occurrence of an event or contingency, or the failure of an event or contingency to occur. § 2056(b)(1). A terminable interest is non-deductible, *i.e.*, it will not qualify for the marital deduction, if the terminable interest passes to the surviving spouse and an interest in the same property passes from the decedent to another person (without adequate and full consideration). *Id.*

2. Rationale

The transfer of property will be taxed at least once each generation and when it passes to someone outside the marital unit. The *quid pro quo* for the marital deduction is that the property will be taxed in the estate of the surviving spouse. If the surviving spouse has only a terminable interest, this will not happen. Life estates, terms of years, and similar arrangements are not included in the gross estate.

3. Deductible Terminable Interests

Some terminable interests are deductible because no one, other than the surviving spouse receives an interest in the property. Examples include a patent, a copyright, a license of limited duration, or an annuity. Each of these interests will fail on the lapse of time, but no one other than the surviving spouse receives an interest in the property. As a result, the value of each of these property interests qualifies for the marital deduction.

4. Non–Deductible Terminable Interests

a. Life Estate or Term of Years

The classic terminable interest is a life estate or a term of years. These interests will cease to exist at the death of the life tenant or at the end of the specified term. When that interest terminates, the remainderman is entitled to the property. Unless the remainderman paid adequate and full consideration, the interest is non-deductible. (A life estate may qualify as an exception to the terminable interest rule if the executor elects QTIP treatment. See section F.6.)

b. Support Allowance

The support allowance given to a surviving spouse may be a non-deductible terminable interest. Such allowances are usually paid only during probate or for a specific time period. If the property that generates the income used for the allowance passes to someone other than the surviving spouse, the support allowance will be a non-deductible terminable interest.

Illustrative Case

In *Jackson v. United States*, 376 U.S. 503 (1964), the Supreme Court held that the allowance paid to a surviving spouse under California law was a non-deductible terminable interest. In California,

---

the right to such an allowance is not a vested right; the allowance is within the discretion of the court. In addition, the right is lost if the surviving spouse dies or remarries. Because the right is not fixed as of the date of the decedent's death and could terminate, it is non-deductible.

If the right to the allowance is fixed and the amount is certain as of the date of the decedent's death and if the surviving spouse is the only beneficiary of the estate, the amount of the allowance will qualify for the marital deduction. If either condition is missing (as it is in most jurisdictions), the amount of the allowance is not deductible.

5. Exam Strategy

Watch out for successive interests in property if the decedent is the transferor of those multiple interests. If a property interest will terminate or fail and the surviving spouse is the only person with an interest in that property, it is deductible. If someone besides the surviving spouse receives an interest in the property from the decedent, the spouse's interest is not deductible unless it qualifies for one of the exceptions described in the next section.

F. EXCEPTIONS TO THE TERMINABLE INTEREST RULE

1. General Principles

A terminable interest will be deductible if it qualifies for one of the exceptions described below. In each case, the property will be taxed to the surviving spouse when she dies or when she gives it away.

2. The Estate Trust

If the decedent leaves property in trust for the benefit of the surviving spouse and at the spouse's death the property passes to her estate, the value of the property will qualify for the marital deduction. Section 2056(b)(1) denies the deduction if "an interest in such property passes . . . from the decedent to any person other than such surviving spouse *(or the estate of such spouse)*." (Emphasis added.) This type of trust, called an **estate trust**, is not common. One advantage of such a trust is that the trustee can have discretion to distribute income to the surviving spouse or to accumulate it; the income need not be distributed annually as in a power of appointment or QTIP trust. Another advantage is that the trust property need not produce income, and the trustee need not make the trust property productive. An estate trust, therefore, is used when a decedent has stock in a closely-held company that he wants to keep in the family or when a surviving spouse has sufficient resources of her own and does not need the income from the trust.

Example 15.8

Stuart leaves $10 million in trust for the benefit of his wife, Melanie. The trustee has discretion to distribute income to, or for the benefit of, Melanie or to accumulate the income. When Melanie dies, the trust property is to be distributed to her estate; she can then devise the property to whomever she wants. The $10 million will qualify for the marital deduction. The property is in Stuart's gross estate; the property passes from Stuart to Melanie; and the property is not a non-deductible terminable interest because it is an estate trust.

---

3. Survivorship Condition for Limited Time

A decedent often wants to avoid the cost, delay, and complexity of two probate proceedings in a relatively short period of time. He may, therefore, require that his spouse must survive him by a specified number of days or months. Such a survivorship clause will not prevent qualification for the marital deduction, but only if the following conditions are met. This is a different survivorship issue than that discussed at section B.4.

a. Spouse Must Survive

The spouse must in fact survive the decedent by the requisite period of time. If she does so, she will then receive the property. As a result, the property will *pass* to her from the decedent as required by § 2056.

Illustrative Case

In *Estate of Lee v. Commissioner*, 94 T.C.M. (CCH) 604 (2007), the decedent and his wife drafted their wills to ensure the maximum tax benefit to both their estates. Decedent's wife in fact predeceased him by four months. Her will provided that "any person who shall die within six (6) months after my death shall be

---

deemed to have predeceased me." Decedent's will provided that any person *other than his wife* who died within six months of his death would be deemed to have predeceased him and that if he and his wife died simultaneously, his wife would be deemed to survive him. Property passed to decedent's wife's estate under his will. Decedent's estate claimed the marital deduction for this property, asserting that § 2056(b)(3) allowed the deduction. The court rejected this argument and held that the wife must actually survive the decedent.

b. Time Period Cannot Exceed Six Months

The required period of survivorship cannot exceed six months. The only exception to the six-month rule is if the decedent provides that the property will not pass to the surviving spouse if both decedent and his spouse die as a result of a common disaster. This limitation ensures that the condition will be met before the due date for the decedent's estate tax return. That return is due within nine months of the decedent's death. § 6075(a).

Example 15.9

Jack's will provides: "All the rest and residue of my estate I bequeath to my wife, Jill, but only if she survives me by three months." Jill survives Jack by the requisite three months, and the property is distributed to her. Jack's estate will be entitled to a marital deduction equal to the value of the property passing to Jill even though, as of the date of Jack's death, it was not certain that Jill would in fact survive.

Example 15.10

Henry's will provides: "All the rest and residue of my estate I bequeath to my wife, Wanda. . . . If my wife Wanda and I die as a result of a common disaster, then I bequeath this property to my brother, Ben." Henry dies of a heart attack, and Wanda survives him. She will receive the property, and Henry's estate will be entitled to a martial deduction equal to the value of the property passing to her.

4. Power of Appointment Trust

Before 1981, property left in trust for the surviving spouse had to meet the requirements of § 2056(b)(5) as a life estate with power of appointment trust in order for the property to qualify for the marital deduction. The § 2056(b)(5) requirements were designed to mimic community property. There are two basic requirements of a § 2056(b)(5) trust. First, the surviving spouse must be entitled to distributions of all the income (or a specific portion of it) at least annually. Second, the surviving spouse must have a power to appoint the property (or the same specific portion of it) to herself during life or to her estate at her death. Property in a trust that qualifies under § 2056(b)(5) will be included in the surviving spouse's gross estate at her death pursuant to § 2041 because she has a general power of appointment, *i.e.*, the power to appoint to herself during life or to her estate at her death.

a. Right to Income

The surviving spouse must be entitled to all of the income from the trust or to a specific portion of the income. The spouse must have the same degree of beneficial enjoyment as the life beneficiary of a trust would have. Regulation § 20.2056(b)–5(f)(1).

(1) Property Must Produce Income

The trust property must in fact produce income. If non-income producing property is transferred to the trust from decedent's estate, the trustee must have the power to dispose of that property and invest in income-producing assets. Regulation § 20.2056(b)–5(f)(5).

(2) Payable Annually or at More Frequent Intervals

The income must be paid to the spouse at least annually. If the trust does not specify how often the income must be distributed, state law will usually imply that income must be paid at reasonable intervals. If state law interprets this to mean at least annually, the trust will meet this condition. Regulation §§ 20.2056(b)–5(e); 20.2056(b)–5(f)(2).

(3) Trustee Cannot Accumulate Income

The trustee must be required to distribute the income. The trustee cannot have discretion to distribute or accumulate income unless the surviving spouse has the power to compel distributions, for example, through a demand provision or power to appoint the income to herself. Regulation §§ 20.2056(b)–

5(f)(5); 20.2056(b)–5(f)(8). Administrative powers in the trustee are permitted as long as the overall effect of those powers does not deprive the surviving spouse of the beneficial enjoyment of the trust income. Regulation § 20.2056(b)–5(f)(4).

(4) Distributions Subject to a Standard

(a) Ascertainable Standard

The trustee must be required to distribute the income; the trustee cannot have discretion to withhold income. If income may be distributed only for the spouse's health, education, maintenance, or support, the trust will not qualify for the marital deduction. This is an ascertainable standard and although the spouse could require the trustee to distribute income to her for those purposes, she cannot require distributions beyond that needed for those purposes. She would not be treated as the *owner* of the trust income, and the trust will not qualify for the marital deduction. Regulation §§ 20.2056(b)–5(f)(5); 20.2056(b)–5(f)(7).

(b) Other Standard

If the trustee can distribute income for the spouse's welfare, comfort, and happiness, the standard is not an ascertainable one. Nonetheless, it is not clear that the trust will qualify for the marital deduction because such a provision might allow the trustee to withhold income. If so, the trust will not qualify for the marital deduction. The court will look to the totality of the circumstances to determine if the surviving spouse is entitled to all of the income.

Illustrative Case

In *Estate of Ellingson v. Commissioner*, 964 F.2d 959 (9th Cir. 1992), decedent gave the trustee discretion to accumulate income if the trust income exceeded the amount necessary for the spouse's "needs, best interests, and welfare." The trust included a **tax saving clause** that provided that the trust should be interpreted to qualify for the marital deduction. The

---

court held that this clause by itself was not sufficient to save the trust. Instead, the court relied on the "best interests" language, holding that it would not be in the spouse's "best interests" to be required to sell estate assets to pay the resulting estate tax bill.

Illustrative Case

Compare Ellingson with Estate of Walsh v. Commissioner, 110 T.C. 393 (1998). That trust also included a tax saving clause, but the trust was to terminate and the property be distributed to the decedent's children if the spouse became incompetent. The court found that one purpose of the trust was to ensure that the spouse qualified for medical assistance if she became incapacitated. Because the trust would terminate in the event of the spouse's incompetency, the court held that it was a non-deductible terminable interest and that it failed to qualify for the marital deduction.

---

b. Power of Appointment

The surviving spouse must also have the power to appoint the trust property to herself during life or to her estate at her death. § 2056(b)(5).

(1) Alone and in All Events

The surviving spouse and *only* the surviving spouse must have the power to appoint the trust property. She must be able to do so without the consent of any other person. And there must be no conditions or contingencies on her ability to appoint. The "all events" language of § 2056(b)(5), however, does not require that the spouse have the power to appoint both during life and at death. Either one is sufficient.

(2) May Appoint to Other than the Surviving Spouse

If the surviving spouse has the power to appoint to herself during life or to her estate at her death, she may also have the power to appoint to others. In a QTIP trust, on the other hand, no one, including the surviving spouse can have the power to appoint to anyone other than that spouse during her life.

(3) Surviving Spouse as Trustee

The surviving spouse may serve as the trustee of a § 2056(b)(5) trust. Her fiduciary responsibilities do not preclude her from invading the trust property for her own benefit or from appointing the trust property in her will.

(4) Power Limited by a Standard

If the spouse's power is limited by a standard, the trust will not qualify. The spouse must be able to appoint the trust property "in all events." Regulation § 20.2056(b)–5(g)(3).

Example 15.10

Bonnie leaves $3.5 million to her children and the residue of her estate ($5 million) to Friendly National Bank as trustee for the benefit of her husband, Clyde. The trustee is required to distribute all of the trust income at least annually to Clyde. At Clyde's death, the trust property is to be distributed to whomever Clyde appoints in his will, including his estate. This trust will qualify for the marital deduction under § 2056(b)(5).

Example 15.11

Kayla leaves $3.5 million to her children and the residue of her estate ($10 million) to Friendly National Bank as trustee for the benefit of her husband, Jeremy. The trustee is required to distribute all of the trust income at least annually to Jeremy. At Jeremy's death, the trust property will be distributed to those of Kayla's descendants as Jeremy appoints in his will. The trust will not qualify for the marital deduction under § 2056(b)(5) because Jeremy does not have the power to appoint to himself during life or his estate at his death. The trust might qualify for the marital deduction under § 2056(b)(7) (see section F.6.) if Kayla's executor makes the required QTIP election.

---

5. Life Insurance With Power of Appointment

Section 2056(b)(6) provides that proceeds of a life insurance contract that are held by the insurer pursuant to an agreement to pay the interest earned on those proceeds to the surviving spouse will qualify for the marital deduction under certain conditions. The interest payments must be made annually or more frequently, and the surviving spouse has the power to appoint the proceeds to herself during her life or to her estate at her death. The power must be exercisable alone and in all events. This provision has been interpreted in the same way as § 2056(b)(5).

6. Qualified Terminable Interest Property

In 1981, Congress added a new exception to the terminable interest rule known as qualified terminable interest property (QTIP). § 2056(b)(7). This provision requires (1) that the surviving spouse be entitled to all the income (or a specific portion of it) payable annually or at more frequent intervals; (2) that no person have a power to appoint any part of the trust property to anyone other than the surviving spouse during her life; and (3) that the executor elect QTIP treatment. If the trust property qualifies for the marital deduction under § 2056(b)(7), it will be in the surviving spouse's gross estate pursuant to § 2044. (See chapter 12.)

a. Right to Income

With the exception of the stub income requirement noted below, the income requirements of a QTIP trust are the same as those of a power of appointment trust. That is, the property must be income producing; the income must be distributed at least annually; and the surviving spouse must be the virtual owner of the trust income.

b. Power to Appoint during Spouse's Life

In contrast to a § 2056(b)(5) trust, no one needs to have a power to appoint in a QTIP trust. If there is a power to appoint during the surviving spouse's life, that power must be exercisable only in favor of the surviving spouse. It cannot be exercised in favor of anyone else. The surviving spouse herself can have the power; the trustee can have the power; or a third person can have the power.

c. Power to Appoint at or after Spouse's Death

There does not need to be a power to appoint the trust property at or after the spouse's death. If there is, that power can be in anyone. The spouse can have a testamentary special (or limited) power to appoint. The trustee can have the right to distribute trust property. Or a third person can have the power to appoint. As long as the appointment occurs at or after the surviving spouse's death, the power can be limited. In most cases, the decedent will have provided that the trust property be distributed to his children, his issue, or other family members.

> **Example 15.12**
>
> Same facts as example 15.11, except that Kayla's executor makes the QTIP election on her estate tax return. Because no one has the power to appoint to anyone during Jeremy's life, the trust will qualify for the marital deduction under § 2056(b)(7).

7. Specific Portion

Both § 2056(b)(5) and § 2056(b)(7) allow a deduction for the entire trust or a specific portion of it. Section 2056(b)(10) defines a **specific portion** as a fractional or percentage share. One-half or 50 percent will qualify as a specific portion. An amount, such as $150,000, will not. In a § 2056(b)(5) trust, the right to income and the right to appoint a specific portion must be over the same property.

8. Stub Income

Stub income is the income earned between the last distribution date preceding the surviving spouse's death and the date of her death. Because income is only distributed periodically, *e.g.*, monthly or quarterly, there will always be some income that was earned but undistributed at the spouse's death. The stub income must be subject to the surviving spouse's power to appoint in a § 2056(b)(5) trust. Regulation § 20.2056(b)–5(f)(8). There is no such requirement in a § 2056(b)(7) trust. *See, e.g., Estate of Shelfer v. Commissioner*, 86 F.3d 1045 (11th Cir. 1996), where the court held that the stub income requirement was mandated by the power of appointment provision of § 2056(b)(5) not be the income requirement of that section. Regulation § 20.2056(b)–7(d)(4) now explicitly provides that the stub income need not be subject to a spouse's power of appointment in a QTIP trust.

9. Duty of Consistency

If the decedent's estate claims the marital deduction for property left in trust, the surviving spouse's estate cannot avoid including that trust property in her gross estate even if the trust did not actually qualify under § 2056(b)(5) or § 2056(b)(7). Because of the identity of interest between the two estates, courts have held that the duty of consistency requires that the trust be treated the same way in both estates.

Illustrative Case

In *Estate of Letts v. Commissioner,* 109 T.C. 290 (1997) *aff'd without published opinion,* 212 F.3d 600 (11th Cir. 2000), a husband left his property in trust for his surviving spouse, and his executor checked the box "no" following the question: "Do you elect to claim a marital deduction for qualified terminable interest property (QTIP) under § 2056(b)(7)?" *Id.* at 293. The executor listed no property on Schedule M as QTIP property but calculated the decedent's estate tax as if the trust property qualified for the marital deduction. The surviving spouse died after the statute of limitations had expired with respect to decedent's estate. The spouse's estate did not include the trust property in her gross estate, arguing that the trust was not subject to § 2044 because decedent's executor had failed to make the appropriate QTIP election. The court rejected the argument and held that the duty of consistency applied. Although that doctrine usually is invoked in an income tax context when the same taxpayer takes different positions with respect to an item of income or deduction, the court held that the doctrine applied because the two estates were so closely aligned in interest that the surviving spouse's estate was estopped from taking a differing position.

The duty of consistency only applies to representations of fact. If there is a mutual mistake of law by the IRS and an estate, the surviving spouse's estate will not be bound by that mistake. *Estate of Posner v. Commissioner,* 87 T.C.M. (CCH) 1288 (2004).

---

10. Exam Strategy

Make a chart of the exceptions to the terminable interest rule so that you can compare and contrast them if necessary. Factors relating to income are: annual distributions of income; productivity of property; trustee discretion to distribute or accumulate; trustee discretion limited by ascertainable standard; trustee discretion limited by other standard; and stub income. Factors relating to power to appoint to include are: power required; who can be the power holder; and to whom (and when) can property be distributed.

G. PLANNING

1. General Principles

a. Minimize Total Tax

There is little need to engage in sophisticated estate planning for most married couples. The estate tax is imposed on less than two percent of all decedents. So only those couples who together own more than the applicable exemption amount (*i.e.*, the amount sheltered by the unified credit in § 2010) need to consider marital deduction planning. For most couples, the basic philosophy is to minimize the total tax paid and to defer all estate tax until the death of the surviving spouse.

b. The Unified Credit

The unified credit ensures that a donor or decedent's estate pays no tax on an amount usually referred to as the "exemption amount." §§ 2010, 2505. The unified credit is explained in chapter 16, section B. When a married couple owns more than the exemption amount, it is important to structure their estate plans so that property is sheltered in each estate by the unified credit. Failure to take advantage of the unified credit in the estates of both members of a married couple could be legal malpractice.

c. NonTax Considerations

While avoiding the estate tax is a basic tenet of most estate plans, it is not the only consideration. Often it is not the most important consideration. There are a myriad of nontax issues that will impact an estate plan, such as stepchildren, children from a prior marriage, a family business, or descendants with special needs.

2. Illustrations

The following situations avoid using specific dollar amounts because it is not certain what the exemption amount will be in the future. Additional examples using specific dollar amounts are included in Appendix D.

a. Combined Estates Less Than the Applicable Exemption Amount

If the married couple owns less than the amount sheltered by the unified credit, there is no need for sophisticated estate planning. The first to die can leave all the property to the survivor, and there will be no estate tax in either estate. If the decedent wants to ensure that his children will ultimately receive the property, he can leave the property in trust for the benefit of his spouse. Because the trust need not qualify for the marital deduction, the trustee can have discretion to accumulate income, to retain non-productive property, or to distribute property to the surviving spouse only for health, maintenance, and support.

b. Combined Estates Exceed the Applicable Exemption Amount

When the combined estates exceed the applicable exemption amount, it is important to consider the impact of the estate tax. It is critical to fully utilize the § 2010 unified credit in both estates. Exactly how to accomplish this will depend on who owns the property, the size of the estate, and nontax considerations. The couple should also use other techniques, such as annual exclusion gifts, qualified payments of tuition and medical expenses, and family limited partnerships to minimize the impact of the estate tax.

(1) Equal Ownership

When the married couple each owns approximately the same amount of property, their estate plans can be the same. Each should leave an amount equal to the exemption amount in a trust for the benefit of the survivor, but that trust should *not* qualify for the marital deduction. That trust, referred to as a credit-shelter or by-pass trust, will be in the decedent's taxable estate. Because it is funded with an amount equal to the exemption equivalent, no tax will be due because of the unified credit, § 2010. The remainder of the property should be left to the surviving spouse in a manner that qualifies for the marital deduction. Nontax considerations will influence whether the property is left outright or in trust and, if in trust, whether a power of appointment trust or a QTIP trust.

Example 15.13

George and Martha are married. Each owns approximately $5 million worth of property. George's will leaves an amount equal to the exemption amount in trust for the benefit of Martha. That trust will *not* qualify for the marital deduction. The purpose of the trust should be to use the unified credit in George's estate. The remaining property can be left to Martha outright or in a marital deduction trust. No tax will be due

---

when George dies and the property in the credit-shelter trust will not be taxed in Martha's gross estate when she dies.

If Martha owns more than the exemption amount when she dies, her estate will pay an estate tax. Martha could avoid some or all of this tax by making gifts to her descendants that qualify for the gift tax annual exclusion or by making qualified payments of tuition or medical expenses.

Martha's estate plan should be the same as George's in case she predeceases him. The result will be the same regardless of who dies first because their estates are equal.

(2) The Rich Spouse/Poor Spouse Conundrum

Planning becomes more complex when one spouse owns most or all of the assets. It is impossible to know which spouse will die first. If the poorer spouse dies first, the benefit of the unified credit is lost to his estate. This can be remedied by giving the poorer spouse an amount equal to the exemption amount during his life. Once that happens, the estate plan is much like that of George and Martha in example 15.13.

In many situations, the rich spouse will not want to cede control over her property to her spouse. She can give him the property in trust. The gift will qualify for the marital deduction as long as he has the right to the income for his life and the trust is either a power of appointment trust or a QTIP trust. § 2523(e), (f).

If the rich spouse does not want to lose the benefit of the trust property, she can retain a secondary life estate. Doing so will not cause the property to be in her gross estate because her spouse will be treated as the transferor. Regulation § 25.2523(f)–1(f)(Ex. 10 and 11).

Example 15.14

Sally owns $10 million worth of property. Her spouse, David, owns nothing. They want to minimize their estate taxes, but Sally also wants to ensure that her property will pass to her children from a prior marriage. So Sally creates an irrevocable, inter vivos trust to pay the income to David during his life. At David's death, the trust will continue if Sally survives and pay her the income for her life. After the death of both Sally and David, the trust property will be distributed to Sally's issue. Sally transfers an amount equal to the exemption amount to this trust.

The creation of the trust will be a nontaxable transfer if Sally elects to treat the transfer as QTIP under § 2523(f). Assume David dies before Sally. The trust property will be in his gross estate under § 2044. He is, therefore, considered the transferor. The property in this trust will be sheltered from the estate tax by the unified credit. When Sally dies, the trust property will not be in her gross estate. Regulation § 25.2512(f)–1(f)(Ex. 10).

If Sally dies before David, the trust will not be in her gross estate even though she retained the right to the income after David's death. Once again, David is treated as the transferor. Regulation § 25.2512(f)–1(f)(Ex. 11).

(3) Joint Tenancy Property

Many married couples own all, or almost all, of their property as joint tenants with the right of survivorship or as tenants by the entirety. This is a very simple estate plan. It avoids the costs and delays of probate, and it ensures that the property will pass to the survivor. Joint tenancy ownership also reflects the partnership theory of marriage. The problem, however, is that all the property passes automatically to the survivor. None of it will be sheltered by the unified credit in the estate of the first to die. As a result, the couple will pay estate tax that they could have avoided.

Example 15.15

John and Betty are married and own $12 million as joint tenants with the right of survivorship. John dies. His estate will pay no tax as one-half of the property will be in his gross estate (§ 2040(b)), and it will qualify for the marital deduction (§ 2056). When Betty dies, her taxable estate (assuming no deductions) will be $12 million.

If John and Betty had owned some portion of the $12 million in their individual names or as tenants in common, they could have avoided at least some of the estate tax. John's will could have left an amount of his property equal to the exemption amount in a credit-shelter trust to pay the income to Betty for her life. On her death, the property would pass to their children. The remainder of John's property will pass to Betty either outright or in a trust that qualifies for the marital deduction. No estate tax will be due because of the unified credit. § 2010.

When Betty dies, her estate will not include the property in the credit-shelter trust. The amount of estate tax due at her death will depend on the exemption amount in effect at that time. Converting some of the joint tenancy property into individual ownership or tenancy in common will save John and Betty estate tax equal to the amount of the unified credit in the estate of the first to die.

(4) Portability of the Unified Credit

Estate planning for a couple where one owns substantially more property than the other can be complicated. One solution is to allow a married couple to share the amount of their unified credit. Any amount of unified credit that is not used in the estate of the first person to die would transfer to the surviving spouse. In other words, the unified credit would be portable between spouses. Although proposed in The Taxpayer Certainty and Relief Act of 2009, S. 722 (111th Cong., 1st Sess. 2009), a portability provision has not yet been enacted. Examples in Appendix D demonstrate how it might operate.

CHAPTER 16

CREDITS AND CALCULATION OF THE GIFT AND ESTATE TAXES

A. GENERAL PRINCIPLES

1. Unified Rate Structure

The gift tax and the estate tax are transfer taxes imposed on the transfer of property from the donor or the decedent to others. Since 1976, the gift and estate taxes have been calculated under the same rate structure. §§ 2001, 2502. The unified tax rate schedule is designed to impose an increasingly higher rate of tax on each successive taxable transfer.

The 2001 Tax Act lowered the top marginal tax rate and increased the estate tax exemption amount but retained the existing tax tables in § 2001. As a result, the estate tax has become a flat tax, and the gift tax had only slight progressivity. The 2001 amendments are scheduled to be repealed as of January 1, 2011, and the future of the gift and estate tax, the exemption amounts, and the rate structure is uncertain. See Appendix A for calculation examples.

2. Role of Credits in the Calculation of the Tax

A credit is the final step in calculating the tax. The amount of a credit is subtracted from the tentative amount of tax to determine the tax that is actually due and payable.

3. Deduction Versus a Credit

A deduction reduces the size of the taxable estate. A deduction, thus, saves the taxpayer the amount of the deduction multiplied by the marginal rate of tax. A credit reduces the amount of tax due. A credit saves $1 of tax for every $1 of credit. For this reason, credits are often limited in amount or to a certain percentage. A credit treats all taxpayers equally while a deduction saves more tax for a higher bracket taxpayer than for a lower

261

bracket taxpayer. When the estate tax was a flat tax at 45 percent, the distinction between a deduction and a credit had little, if any, relevance in the estate tax.

Example 16.1

Assume the estate is allowed a deduction of $100,000, and the marginal tax rate is 45 percent. A deduction would save the estate $45,000 of estate taxes. If the estate is entitled to a $100,000 credit, the estate will save $100,000 of tax.

B. THE UNIFIED CREDIT: §§ 2010 AND 2505

1. General Principles

Many tax systems have a **zero bracket amount**, *i.e.*, an amount that is not subject to tax. In the transfer tax system, the zero bracket amount is created by the unified credit in §§ 2010 and 2505. There is also a generation-skipping transfer tax exemption in § 2631 that is equal to the estate tax exemption amount.

2. Rationale

The primary justifications are administrative feasibility and taxpayer compliance. The cost of enforcement cannot exceed the revenue generated. Imposing even a very low rate of tax on the smallest estates would be outweighed by the cost of collecting that tax. Moreover, the populist movement of the early 20th century, which contributed to the passage of the estate tax, has all but disappeared. Concern with the "evils of inherited wealth" has also diminished. The current political climate supports the accumulation of wealth, particularly through hard work, wise investment, and savings. As a result, taxpayers will only support the imposition of the transfer tax on the extremely wealthy. Without public support for the tax, compliance would plummet. As a result, the cost of enforcement and collection would begin to exceed the taxes collected even at moderate rates on high levels of wealth.

3. Unification

Prior to 1976 the gift tax and the estate tax each had its own separate exemption (zero bracket) amount. In 1976, Congress unified the taxes and converted the exemption to a credit. The unified credit is simply the amount of tax on the **applicable exemption amount**. Reference is almost always to the exemption amount (sometimes called the "exemption equivalent amount") rather than the amount of the credit.

4. Amount

The exemption amount has increased steadily since 1976. Prior to 2001, the amount was $1,000,000 for both the gift tax and the estate tax. The 2001 Tax Act left the exemption amount for the gift tax at $1,000,000, but increased it to $3,500,000 in 2009 for the estate tax. The estate tax was repealed as of January 1, 2010, but only for one year. The estate tax is scheduled to return on January 1, 2011, with an exemption amount of $1,000,000. It is not certain if that will happen. If Congress raises the estate tax exemption amount above that, it is not certain what that amount will be or whether the gift tax exemption amount will also increase. Appendix A demonstrates the operation of the unified credit using three different models.

5. Coordination of the Gift and Estate Tax Credits

There is only one unified exemption amount. Even though in 2009 the exemption amount for the gift tax was $1,000,000 and the exemption amount for the estate tax was $3,500,000, a taxpayer could not transfer more than a *total* of $3,500,000 without paying any tax. Section 2001 accomplishes this by including all taxable gifts in the calculation of the estate tax. Gifts are either included in that calculation as part of the gross estate or as **adjusted taxable gifts** (*i.e.*, taxable gifts that are not included in the gross estate). A tentative tax is then calculated on the sum of the taxable estate and the adjusted taxable gifts, *i.e.*, the **tax base**. Then the gift tax actually paid as well as the full amount of the unified credit is subtracted.

Example 16.2

Tamara has made no taxable gifts during her life and died in 2009 with a taxable estate of $2,750,000. Her estate will not owe any federal estate tax because the amount of her taxable estate ($2,750,000) plus her adjusted taxable gifts ($0) did not exceed the applicable exemption amount ($3,500,000).

> **Example 16.3**
>
> Instead, Tamara made taxable gifts during her life of $500,000. She paid no gift tax because of the § 2505 credit. Tamara died in 2009 with a taxable estate of $3,000,000. Her estate will not owe any federal estate tax because the amount of her taxable estate ($3,000,000) plus her adjusted taxable gifts ($500,000) did not exceed the applicable exemption amount for that year ($3,500,000).
>
> If Tamara had a taxable estate of $3,500,000, her estate would owe an estate tax of $225,000 (*i.e.*, 45 percent times $500,000).

C. THE CREDIT FOR STATE DEATH TAXES: § 2011

1. General Principles

Prior to 2001, an estate was allowed a credit, subject to certain limitations, for the amount of any state estate or inheritance tax. That credit was phased out and replaced with the § 2058 deduction for state death taxes. The § 2058 deduction is not worth as much to the estate as the § 2011 credit. The deduction only reduces the size of the taxable estate and, thus, saves the estate 45 percent of the amount of the state tax. The § 2011 credit will return on January 1, 2011 if the sunset provisions of the 2001 Tax Act become effective.

2. State Death Taxes

When the § 2011credit existed, all states had some form of estate or inheritance tax. Many had an estate tax equal to the amount of the § 2011 credit. In these jurisdictions, the decedent's estate paid exactly the same amount of tax it would have paid if the state had no estate tax; the § 2011 credit simply allowed states to collect a portion of that tax. The repeal of the credit has changed the political landscape for states, and many repealed their estate and inheritance taxes in the wake of the 2001 Tax Act. What will happen if § 2011 reappears is uncertain.

3. Limitations

The § 2011 credit has three basic limitations. First, it cannot exceed the amount of the state estate, inheritance, legacy or succession tax actually paid. § 2011(a). Second, it cannot exceed the amount specified in § 2011(b), which is equal to 80 percent of the federal estate tax imposed in 1926. Third, it cannot exceed the amount of the federal estate tax imposed by § 2001 reduced by the § 2010 credit.

The § 2011 credit is also limited to amounts paid within 4 years of filing the federal estate tax return unless (1) a petition for redetermination has been filed; (2) an extension of time for payment has been granted; or (3) a claim for refund has been filed. § 2011(c).

Example 16.4

Assume that Ted's taxable estate is $5,100,000, his federal estate tax liability is $560,000, and the state imposes an estate tax of $500,000. The § 2011 credit is limited to $402,800. § 2011(b).

The § 2011(b) limitation is based on the **adjusted taxable estate**, which is the taxable estate minus $60,000. (In 1926, the federal estate tax allowed an exemption for $60,000.)

Example 16.5

Same facts as example 16.4, except that the state imposes an estate tax of $250,000. The § 2011 credit is limited to $250,000, the amount of the state estate tax actually imposed. § 2011(a).

Example 16.6

Same facts as example 16.5, except that the federal estate tax liability is $350,000 and the state estate tax is $500,000. The § 2011 credit is limited to $350,000. § 2011(e).

D. CREDIT FOR PRIOR TRANSFERS: § 2013

1. Rationale

The § 2013 credit for prior transfers is designed to mitigate the impact of the federal estate tax when there are successive deaths within a short time period.

Example 16.7

Mother (the original transferor) dies in year 1, leaving her entire estate to her Daughter. Daughter (the decedent) dies in year 2, leaving her entire estate to her Son (Mother's grandson). As a result, Mother's property is taxed twice within two years: (1) once when Mother dies and (2) once when Daughter dies. Section 2013 mitigates this by providing a credit in *Daughter's* estate for the tax attributable to the transfer of property to her from Mother.

---

2. Limitations on the Credit

a. Percentage Limitation

The § 2013 credit, subject to the other limitations discussed below, will be 100 percent for decedents dying within the two years before or the two years after the original transferor (Mother in example 16.7). If the decedent (Daughter in example 16.7) dies more than two years after the original transferor, the credit is decreased as follows:

- to 80 percent if death occurs in the third or fourth year,

- to 60 percent if death occurs in the fifth or sixth year,

- to 40 percent if death occurs in the seventh or eighth year,

- to 20 percent if death occurs in the ninth or tenth year.

No credit is allowed if the decedent dies more than ten years after the original transferor.

b. First Limitation

The § 2013 credit cannot exceed the federal estate tax in the transferor's estate. § 2013(b); Regulation § 20.2013–2. In example 16.7, if Mother's estate paid no estate tax, Daughter's estate will not be entitled to a § 2013 credit.

c. Second Limitation

The § 2013 credit cannot exceed the amount of the federal estate tax attributable to the inclusion of the transferred property in the decedent's gross estate. § 2013(c); Regulation § 20.2013–3.

Appendix B includes examples of the calculation of the § 2013 credit.

E. CREDIT FOR FOREIGN DEATH TAXES: § 2014

Section 2014 allows a credit for any estate, inheritance, legacy, or succession taxes paid to a foreign country that are imposed on property located in that country when that property is also included in the gross estate of the decedent. This can occur when a United States citizen owns property in a foreign country because § 2031 provides that the gross estate includes property "wherever situated." The United States has tax treaties with a number of countries that coordinate the taxation of property at death. If a tax treaty applies, the § 2014 credit may or may not apply depending on the terms of the treaty.

F. CREDIT FOR GIFT TAXES BEFORE 1977: § 2012

Once the gift and estate taxes were unified in 1976, credit for gift taxes paid was incorporated into the estate tax calculation under § 2001. The credit in § 2012 is necessary only for gift taxes paid on gifts before unification and only to the extent that those gifts are included in the decedent's gross estate.

G. CREDIT FOR DEATH TAXES ON REMAINDERS: § 2015

This is not a separate credit. Section 2015 simply provides for the allocation of any § 2014 credit for foreign death taxes to ensure the proper timing of the credit.

H. EXAM STRATEGY

The most important credit is the unified credit because it establishes the amount that each individual can transfer free of tax. Remember that the gift tax and estate tax credits are unified by the calculation in § 2001 so that an individual cannot transfer the full amount sheltered by the gift tax unified credit *and* the full amount sheltered by the estate tax unified credit.

PART V

THE GENERATION–SKIPPING TRANSFER TAX

CHAPTER **17**

THE GENERATION–SKIPPING TRANSFER TAX

A. GENERAL PRINCIPLES

1. Rationale

Since 1976, a fundamental principle of the transfer tax system is to tax the transfer of wealth once at each generation. The failure to tax wealth at each generation allows those with greater wealth to avoid tax by transfers that skip generations or that skip the tax at a particular generation.

Example 17.1

Grandmother bequeaths $10 million to Granddaughter. There is no tax at the parent's generation. Assuming a flat rate of tax of 50 percent and no exemption amount, the tax would be $5,000,000, and the net to Granddaughter would be $5,000,000.

Instead, assume that Grandmother bequeathed the $10 million to Daughter who then bequeathed to Granddaughter. The net to Daughter would be $5,000,000 and the tax on the transfer of that to Granddaughter would be $2,500,000. So the net to Granddaughter would be $2,500,000.

Example 17.2

Compare two different families—the Smiths and the Browns. Again assume a flat rate of tax of 50 percent and no exemption amount. The Smiths and the Browns each have $20 million. The Smiths bequeath

---

that money outright to each generation. The Browns leave the property in trust, income to each succeeding generation. By the fifth generation, the wealth disparity is significant.

The Smith Family pays a tax of $10 million on the transfer to the first generation, a tax of $5 million on the transfer to the second generation, a tax of $2.5 million on the transfer to the third generation, a tax of $1.25 million on the transfer to the fourth generation, and a tax of $625,000 on the transfer to the fifth generation, leaving $625,000 in that generation. The Brown Family pays a tax of $10 million on the transfer to the first generation and no further tax as each generation has only a life interest in the trust. The fifth generation has $10 million.

Only the very wealthy could afford to skip generations or leave property in trust for each generation with only a life estate. To equalize the transfer tax treatment of the very wealthy with the moderately wealthy, Congress enacted the generation-skipping transfer tax.

2. History

Congress enacted a generation-skipping transfer tax in 1976. Because of its complexity, it was repealed and all taxes paid under it were refunded. Congress enacted a much different generation-skipping transfer tax in 1986.

B. TERMINOLOGY

1. Transferor

The most important concept in the generation-skipping transfer tax is that of the transferor. The **transferor** is the individual subject to the estate tax (the decedent) or the gift tax (the donor). § 2642(a). Generation-skipping transfers are measured by reference to the transferor. The identity of the transferor can change in certain situations, such as disclaimers, powers of appointment, and marital deduction trusts. See section D.5. below.

2. Skip Person

A **skip person** is an individual assigned to a generation which is two or more generations below that of the transferor. § 2613(a)(1). A trust is a **skip person** if all the interests in the trust are held by skip persons. A trust is also a **skip person** if there is no person holding an interest in the trust and no distributions can be made from the trust to a non-skip person. § 2613(a)(2).

3. Interest

A person has an **interest** in property held in trust if the individual (1) has a current right to receive income or corpus from the trust or (2) is a permissible current recipient of income or corpus from the trust (if the trustee has discretion to distribute income or corpus but is not required to do so). It is possible that no person has an interest in the trust. This concept of interest differs significantly from the property concept of an interest. A remainder is a future interest for purposes of classifying property rights, but a remainder-person does not have an "interest" for purposes of the generation-skipping transfer tax.

Example 17.3

David creates an irrevocable, inter vivos trust with Friendly National Bank as trustee to pay the income to his grandchildren, Aaron and Rachel, for their lives, and then to distribute the trust property to his great-granddaughter, Leah. Aaron and Rachel each has an interest in the trust because they have the current right to receive income from the trust. Leah does not have an interest in the trust because her right to trust principal is a future interest.

Example 17.4

Dawn creates an irrevocable, inter vivos trust with Friendly National Bank as trustee. The trustee has the discretion to distribute income or corpus to Dawn's grandnieces, Nancy and Nesha, during their lives. At their death, the trust corpus will be distributed to her great-grandnephew, Max. Nancy and Nesha each has an interest in the trust because they are permissible current recipients of income or corpus. Max does not have an interest in the trust because his right to trust principal is a future interest.

Example 17.5

Ellen creates an irrevocable, inter vivos trust with Friendly National Bank as trustee. The trustee is to accumulate income until Ellen's oldest grandchild, who is seven when the trust is created, reaches the age of 30. At that time, the trustee has discretion to distribute income or corpus to any of Ellen's grandchildren. Upon creation no one has an interest in this trust because no one has a *right* to income or corpus and no one is a *permissible recipient* of income or corpus. Once the eldest grandchild reaches 30, then each of Ellen's grandchildren will have an interest in the trust.

4. Trust

The term **trust** is defined broadly to include any arrangement (other than an estate) that has substantially the same effect as a trust. § 2652(b)(1). This includes (1) a life estate or a term of years coupled with a remainder; (2) life insurance; and (3) annuity contracts. Regulation § 26.2652–1(b)(1). The regulation does not mention a joint tenancy. A joint tenancy could have the same effect as a life estate and a remainder when the interests are held by individuals in different generations.

Example 17.6

Gwen transfers Whiteacre, valued at $2 million, to her daughter, Diane, and her grandson, Silas, as joint tenants with the right of survivorship. In most cases such an arrangement has the same effect as a transfer to Diane for life and remainder to Silas or a trust with similar terms. Although the regulation does not mention this situation, the IRS could claim that it was a generation-skipping transfer if Diane dies before Silas.

---

5. Exam Strategy

If you suspect that there is a generation-skipping transfer tax issue, first determine who the *transferor* is. Remember that the transferor can change over time. The transferor will be subject to either the gift tax or the estate tax. Then determine who has *an interest* in the trust. Once you have identified these two elements, you can determine if there are any *skip persons*.

C. GENERATION ASSIGNMENTS

Generation assignments are crucial to an understanding of the generation-skipping transfer tax. Because most gifts, bequests, and devises are to family members, it is usually easy to determine generation assignments.

1. Spouses

Spouses are assigned to the same generation as the transferor or other individual. § 2651(c). As a result, the spouse of the transferor is always in the transferor's generation no matter what his or her age might be. An individual who is married to a lineal descendant of the grandparent of the transferor or who is married to a lineal descendant of the grandparent of the transferor's spouse or former spouse is always in the same generation as his or her spouse.

2. Lineal Descendants

An individual who is a lineal descendant of a grandparent of the transferor is assigned to a generation based on the number of generations between that individual and the grandparent of the transferor compared to the number of generations between the transferor and the grandparent of the transferor. § 2651(b)(1). (If this is confusing, find or create a table of consanguinity.) All others are assigned to generations based on their age.

a. Lineal Descendants of the Transferor

A grandchild is two generations below the transferor (her grandparent) and a great-great-grandchild is four generations below the transferor (her great-great-grandparent).

b. Lineal Descendants of the Transferor's Siblings

A niece is one generation below the generation of the transferor (her aunt). A grandniece is two generations below that of her great-aunt. A great-grandniece is three generations below that of the transferor (her great-great-aunt.)

c. Cousins of the Transferor and Their Descendants

Only first cousins of the transferor and their descendants are included in the generation assignment rule of § 2651(b)(1). The transferor's first cousin is in the same generation as the transferor. That cousin's child is the transferor's first cousin once removed and is in the first generation below that of the transferor. That cousin's grandchild is the transferor's first cousin twice removed and is in the second generation below that of the transferor.

d. Lineal Descendants of the Grandparent of the Transferor's Spouse or Former Spouse

The same rules apply to lineal descendants of the grandparent of the transferor's spouse or former spouse. § 2651(b)(2). That is, the generation assignment is based on a comparison of generations not ages.

3. **Adoption**

a. **General Rule**

An individual who is adopted is treated the same as a blood relative. § 2651(b)(3)(A).

b. **Adoption After Death of Parent**

As discussed below at section E, if the recipient's parent is dead, the recipient moves up a generation so that transfers from the grandparent are not treated as generation-skipping transfers. § 2651(e). If a child is adopted by an aunt or uncle following the death of his parent, the child does not lose the generation assignment created by the deceased parent exception. *Id.*

Example 17.7

Greg has two children, Paul and Renee. Paul dies leaving a child, Carol. Renee, who has two children of her own, adopts Carol. Greg dies, leaving his property to his grandchildren equally. The transfers to Renee's two biological children will be direct skips, § 2612(c). The transfer to Carol will not. She does not lose the benefit of the deceased parent exception when she is adopted by her aunt. Private Letter Rulings 199907015, 9709015, 9310005.

---

4. **Half–Blood Relatives**

A relative of the half-blood is treated the same as a relative of the whole-blood. § 2651(b)(3)(B).

5. **Persons Who Are Not Lineal Descendants**

Individuals who are not assigned to generations based on the rules in § 2651(b), *i.e.*, those who are not lineal descendants of the transferor's grandparent or the grandparent of the transferor's spouse or former spouse, are assigned to generations based on ages. Those individuals born not more than 12.5 years after the transferor are in the transferor's generation. Thereafter each generation is 25 years.

Example 17.8

Melanie devises property to the daughter of her housekeeper. Melanie is 83 years old. Her housekeeper, Hilda, is 50 years old. Hilda's daughter, Lisa, is 30 years old. Hilda is not in Melanie's generation because she is 33 years younger than Melanie. Hilda is in the next generation below Melanie because she is not more than 37.5 years younger than Melanie. Lisa is in the second generation below Melanie because she is 53 years younger than Melanie. If Lisa was 18 years old, she would be in the third generation below Melanie because she would be 65 years younger than Melanie. Remember, Melanie's generation includes those who are 70.5 and older; the next generation extends to those who are 45.5 and older, and the following generation extends to those who are 20.5 years and older.

6. Exam Strategy

Add a table of consanguinity to your notes. This will allow you to see at a glance who is subject to generation assignment based on relationship and who is subject to generation assignment based on age.

D. TAXABLE EVENTS

1. General Principles

There are three generation-skipping transfer taxable events: (1) a direct skip, (2) a taxable distribution, and (3) a taxable termination. A direct skip will incur a gift tax or an estate tax in addition to the generation-skipping transfer tax. The creation of a trust will incur a gift tax or an estate tax and then distributions from that trust or the termination of an interest in that trust will incur the generation-skipping transfer tax.

2. Direct Skip

A **direct skip** is a transfer that skips a generation. It is a transfer to a skip person that is subject to the gift tax or the estate tax. § 2612(c). A skip person can be either a natural person or a trust. § 2613(a).

Example 17.9

Grandparent gives Grandchild $5 million. This is a direct skip. Grandparent will pay both a gift tax and a generation-skipping transfer tax. The amount of the generation-skipping transfer tax is considered to be a gift by Grandparent. § 2515.

Example 17.10

Grandparent bequeaths $10 million to Grandchild. This is also a direct skip. Grandparent's estate will pay both an estate tax and a generation-skipping transfer tax. The estate tax is tax inclusive, *i.e.*, it is calculated on the amount that is eventually paid as the estate tax. This is also true of the generation-skipping transfer tax imposed at death. There is no additional "gift" when the estate pays the generation-skipping transfer tax because the property has already been subject to both the estate tax and the generation-skipping transfer tax.

Example 17.11

Grandparent creates a trust to pay the income to her Grandchildren for their lives and the remainder to her Great–Grandchildren. The creation of the trust is a direct skip because all interests in the trust are held by skip persons. § 2613(a)(2). Grandparent will pay both a gift tax and a generation-skipping transfer tax on the creation of the trust. The payment of the generation-skipping transfer tax in this case will again be treated as a gift by grandparent. § 2515.

Example 17.12

Grandparent gives Great–Grandchild $5 million. Although this transfer skips two generations, there is only one generation-skipping transfer tax due in addition to the gift tax. To impose two generation-skipping transfer taxes on such a transfer creates significant complexity. The cost of enforcement outweighs the potential revenue to be collected in the rare cases where this occurs.

3.   **Taxable Distribution**

A **taxable distribution** is a distribution of income or corpus to a skip person that is not a taxable termination or direct skip. § 2612(b).

Example 17.13

Glen creates a trust with Friendly National Bank as trustee. The trustee has discretion to distribute income or corpus to any of Glen's children or grandchildren. At the death of the last grandchild, the trust property is to be distributed to Glen's descendants. A distribution of income or corpus to a child is not a taxable distribution. Glen's children are not skip persons because they are only one generation below Glen. A distribution of income or corpus to a grandchild during the lives of the children is a taxable distribution because the grandchild is a skip person.

---

4. Taxable Termination

A **taxable termination** is the termination by death, lapse of time, release of a power, or otherwise of an interest in property held in trust unless (1) after such termination a non-skip person has an interest in the property or (2) after such termination no distribution may be made to a skip person. § 2612(a).

Example 17.14

Teresa creates a trust with Friendly National Bank as trustee to pay the income to her daughter, Chloe, for her life, then to pay the income to her granddaughter, Debra, for her life, and then to distribute the trust property to Debra's issue. The creation of the trust is a taxable gift. Distributions of income to Chloe are not taxable distributions because Chloe is only one generation below the transferor, Teresa. Chloe's death is a taxable termination because immediately after her death the only person with an interest in the trust is Debra, who is a skip person.

Distributions of income to Debra will not be taxable distributions because of the rule of multiple skips. See section F. Debra's death will also be a taxable termination because immediately after her death, the only persons with interests in the trust are her issue who are skip persons.

---

5. Special Situations

a. Disclaimers

A disclaimer is an unqualified refusal to accept property. If the requirements of § 2518 are met, the person disclaiming (the disclaimant) is treated as if he predeceased the transferor. As a result, the disclaimant is not treated as the transferor. See section K.2. of chapter 3 for a discussion of the § 2518 requirements. Because the disclaimant is treated as predeceasing the transferor, the property often passes to the disclaimant's children. This might create a generation-skipping transfer.

Example 17.15

Gabe bequeaths $5 million to his son, Sean. Sean disclaims. Because Gabe's will does not designate an alternate taker, the state anti-lapse statute applies. As a result, Chad (Sean's son) receives the $5 million. This creates a direct skip because Chad is two generations below Gabe who is the transferor. Sean is not the transferor because of the application of § 2518.

Although Sean is treated *as if* he predeceased Gabe because he disclaimed, the deceased parent exception (see section E below) does not apply. The parent must in fact be dead, not treated as predeceased under state law, for that exception to apply. Regulation § 26.2651–1(a)(2)(iv).

---

b.   Powers of Appointment

(1)   General Power of Appointment

A general power of appointment is the ability to appoint to oneself, one's creditors, one's estate, or the creditors of one's estate. §§ 2041(b)(1), 2514(c)(1). An individual who has a general power of appointment will be the transferor of any property subject to that power. Section 2652(a)(1) defines transferor as the donor, *i.e.*, the person subject to the gift tax, or the decedent, *i.e.*, the person who must include the property in her gross estate. Section 2514(b) provides that the exercise of a general power of appointment is a transfer of property that will incur the gift tax. Section 2041(a)(2) provides that property subject to a general power of appointment is included in the power holder's gross estate.

Example 17.16

Gail creates a trust that provides income to her daughter, Diane, for her life. At Diane's death, the trust property will be distributed to whomever Diane appoints in her will, including her estate. Diane has a general power of appointment and the property will be included in her gross estate. Assume Diane appoints the trust property to her children, Carl and Caryn. This is not a generation-skipping transfer. Although Gail created the trust and was originally the transferor, Diane became the transferor for purposes of the estate tax and the generation-skipping transfer tax at her death. As a result, the trust property will be included in Diane's gross estate, and it will not be subject to the generation-skipping transfer tax.

---

(2) Special Power of Appointment

A special (or limited) power of appointment is the ability to appoint to anyone other than oneself, one's creditors, one's estate, or the creditors of one's estate. The holder of a special power of appointment is treated as the agent of the initial transferor and is not herself considered to be a transferor. Because she is not the transferor, the holder of a special power of appointment will not be subject to either the gift tax or the estate tax. As a result, there might be a generation-skipping transfer tax.

Example 17.17

Gail creates a trust that provides income to her daughter, Diane, for her life. At Diane's death, the trust property will be distributed "to those of Diane's issue as she appoints in her will." Diane cannot appoint to her estate or the creditors of her estate; she can only appoint to her issue. This is a special power of appointment, and the property will not be in Diane's gross estate. As a result, Gail remains the transferor. When Diane dies, there will be a taxable termination, which is a generation-skipping transfer.

---

c. Marital Deduction Trusts

(1) Both Spouses are Transferors

Marital deduction trusts have two transferors. Initially, the spouse who creates the trust is treated as the transferor because the property is included in his gross estate. § 2652(a)(1). When the surviving spouse dies, the property will be in her gross estate either because she has a general power of appointment (§ 2041(a)(2)), or because the trust is qualified terminable interest property (QTIP) (§ 2044). As a result, the surviving spouse becomes the transferor at her death. § 2652(a)(1). There will be a generation-skipping transfer only if the property passes to skip persons (*i.e.*, grandchildren, great-grandchildren, or anyone who is two generations below the surviving spouse).

Example 17.18

Grant leaves $10 million in trust for the benefit of Sierra, his surviving spouse. She is entitled to all of the income from the trust, payable at least annually. When Sierra dies, the trust property is to be distributed to Grant's and Sierra's grandchildren. The executor makes the appropriate election and the trust qualifies for the marital deduction under § 2056(b)(7) as QTIP. When Sierra dies, the trust property will be in her gross estate under § 2044. Because the trust property goes to Grant's grandchildren, who are two generations below her, there is a taxable termination and a generation-skipping transfer.

Example 17.19

Same facts as example 17.18. Assume that Grant and Sierra have one daughter, Marta, and three grandchildren. Marta survives Grant, but predeceases Sierra. The transfer occurs when Sierra dies, because the trust property is in her gross estate. In this situation, the deceased parent exception in § 2651(e) will apply and there will not be a generation-skipping transfer.

---

(2) The Reverse QTIP Election

Because the surviving spouse becomes the transferor of a QTIP trust, the initial transferor would lose the ability to allocate his generation-skipping transfer tax exemption to that trust. Section 2652(a)(3) provides a remedy by allowing the initial transferor (Grant in examples 17.18 and 17.19) to treat the trust as if the QTIP election has not been made. This is called the **reverse QTIP election** and applies only for purposes of the generation-skipping transfer tax, not the estate tax. This allows a married couple to establish one trust for the benefit of their descendants that is exempt from the generation-skipping transfer tax.

6.   Exam Strategy

When there is a multi-generational transfer, determine who the transferor is. Remember that there can be more than one transferor. The identity of the transferor will determine whether or not there is a generation-skipping transfer. Then determine who receives the property and calculate their generation assignment in relation to that of the transferor. Pay particular attention to unusual situations, such as disclaimers and powers of appointment.

E.   THE DECEASED PARENT EXCEPTION

It does not make sense to impose a generation-skipping transfer tax when a transfer skips a generation if there is no one in that generation to receive the property. Section 2651(e), therefore, provides that if a recipient's parent dies before the transfer that is subject to the gift tax or the estate tax, then the recipient is *moved up* to the parent's generation. This exception only applies if the recipient is a descendant of a parent of the transferor, *i.e.*, it is limited to intra-family transfers.

Example 17.20

Rhonda bequeaths $5 million to her grandson, Devon. Devon's mother, Megan, is Rhonda's daughter. Megan predeceases Rhonda. The deceased parent exception will apply to move Devon up to Megan's generation. The bequest is, therefore, not a generation-skipping transfer. § 2651(e).

Example 17.21

Roger leaves the residue of his estate, $10 million, in trust with Friendly National Bank as trustee, to pay the income to his daughter, Julie for her life, then to pay the income to his grandson, Lester, for his life, and at Lester's

---

death to distribute the trust property to Lester's issue. Julie is alive when Roger dies. When Julie dies there will be a taxable termination and a generation-skipping transfer tax. Distributions of income to Lester will not be subject to the generation-skipping transfer tax because of the rule of multiple skips. The deceased parent exception will not apply because Julie was alive when the trust was created.

F. THE RULE OF MULTIPLE SKIPS

The **rule of multiple skips** prevents imposition of a second generation-skipping transfer at the same generation. § 2653. It *moves the transferor down* to the generation immediately above that of highest generation of any person with an interest in the trust following imposition of the generation-skipping transfer tax.

Example 17.22

Same facts as example 17.14. Teresa creates a trust with Friendly National Bank as trustee to pay the income to her daughter, Chloe, for her life, then to pay the income to her granddaughter, Debra, for her life, and then to distribute the trust property to Debra's issue. The creation of the trust is a taxable gift. Chloe's death is a taxable termination, and a generation-skipping transfer tax is imposed. The rule of multiple skips will then move Teresa down to the generation immediately above Debra. Now Debra is no longer a skip person, because she is only one generation below that of the transferor (Teresa). As a result, distributions of income to Debra will not be taxable distributions. There is no need to impose a generation-skipping transfer tax on those distributions because the property was subject to tax at Teresa's generation when she created the trust and at Chloe's generation when she died.

When Debra dies, the rule of multiple skips will again apply and this time move Teresa down to Debra's generation. Now the distribution of trust property to Debra's children will not be a taxable distribution because they are only one generation below that of the transferor (Teresa). Because the trust property was subject to the generation-skipping transfer tax on Debra's death, there is no need to impose it again.

Example 17.23

Timothy creates a trust with Friendly National Bank as trustee to pay the income to his grandson, Simon for his life and the remainder to Simon's children. Simon's parent, who is Timothy's child, is alive at the creation of the trust. The creation of the trust is a direct skip because only skip persons have an interest in the trust. As a result, Timothy will pay both a gift tax and a generation-skipping transfer tax. The rule of multiple skips will then apply to move Timothy down to the generation immediately above Simon. Distributions of income to Simon will not be taxable distributions because he is only one generation below the transferor, Timothy.

When Simon dies, there will be a taxable termination and the generation-skipping transfer tax imposed. The rule of multiple skips will again apply to move Timothy down to Simon's generation. As a result, the distribution of trust property to Simon's children will not be a taxable distribution.

G. EXCLUSIONS AND EXEMPTIONS

There are a number of exclusions and exemptions that shield transfers from the generation-skipping transfer tax. The rules are not identical to the gift tax so some transfers may escape the gift tax but not the generation-skipping transfer tax.

1. Generation–Skipping Transfer Exemption

a. Amount

Each transferor is allowed a generation-skipping transfer exemption in an amount equal to the applicable exemption amount for the estate tax. § 2631. This exemption allows a transferor to create a trust that is totally exempt from the generation-skipping transfer tax as long as the transferor transfers no more than the amount of the exemption to the trust and allocates the entire exemption amount to the trust. Thus are born dynasty trusts, *i.e.*, a trust that will not be subject to tax no matter how long it continues. Remember, though, that the Rule Against Perpetuities might prevent a trust from continuing forever. (The Rule has been abolished in some jurisdictions.)

b. Allocation of the Exemption Amount

The transferor may allocate the generation-skipping exemption amount in any manner that he wants. § 2631(a). If the transferor does not make the allocation, the default rules in § 2632 will apply.

c. The Reverse QTIP Election

A married couple needs to plan carefully to ensure appropriate allocation of their respective generation-skipping transfer tax exemption amounts. When property is left to a surviving spouse in a QTIP trust, the surviving spouse becomes the transferor at her death because that property is in her gross estate. See section D.5.c. Section 2652(a)(3) allows the initial transferor to treat the trust as if the QTIP election has not been made. This is called the **reverse QTIP election** and applies only for purposes of the generation-skipping transfer tax, not the estate tax. The estate plan of a wealthy individual might well involve as least three trusts: (1) a credit-shelter trust to take advantage of his estate tax unified credit; (2) a reverse QTIP trust that will qualify for the marital deduction and the generation-skipping transfer tax exemption; and (3) a QTIP trust that will qualify for the marital deduction but not the generation-skipping transfer tax exemption.

2. Nontaxable Gifts

Nontaxable gifts, *i.e.*, gifts of present interests that qualify for the gift tax annual exclusion and qualified transfers for tuition and medical expenses have an inclusion ratio of zero. § 2642(c). With an inclusion ratio of zero, the tax rate is also zero. The transferor need not allocate any of her generation-skipping transfer exemption amount to such transfers.

Example 17.24

Travis sends each of his grandchildren a check for the amount of the gift tax annual exclusion on January 5 of each year. These are outright transfers, and they qualify for the gift tax annual exclusion because the grandchildren have the right to the immediate use of the money. There will not be any generation-skipping transfer tax because of § 2642(c). These gifts do not use up any of the gift tax life-time exemption amount, § 2505, or the generation-skipping transfer tax exemption, § 2631.

---

3. Nontaxable Gifts in Trust

A gift in trust that is a nontaxable gift, *i.e.*, one that qualifies for the gift tax annual exclusion, has an inclusion ratio of zero only if two conditions are met. § 2642(c)(2). First, during the life of the beneficiary no portion of the income or corpus can be distributed to anyone other than that beneficiary. Second, if the trust does not terminate during the beneficiary's lifetime, the trust assets will be in that beneficiary's gross estate. In other words, transfers to trusts for the benefit of grandchildren, great-grandchildren, and the like that qualify for the gift tax annual exclusion, for example, because each grandchild or great-grandchild has a *Crummey* power, will be subject to the generation-skipping transfer tax unless the trust is only for the benefit of that one grandchild or great-grandchild. Trusts with multiple beneficiaries will not meet both conditions of § 2642(c)(2).

Example 17.25

Thelma creates a trust for her grandchild, James. She transfers an amount equal to the gift tax annual exclusion to Friendly National Bank as trustee. The trustee has discretion to distribute income or corpus to James. When James is 21 years old, the trust will terminate and any accumulated income and corpus will be distributed to James. If James dies before age 21, the trust property will be distributed to any person, including James's estate, that he designates in his will. Because no one other than James has an interest in the trust, the inclusion ratio will be zero and there will be no generation-skipping transfer tax. Because the trust qualifies under § 2503(c), transfers to it will qualify for the gift tax annual exclusion.

H. CALCULATION OF THE GENERATION–SKIPPING TRANSFER TAX

Understanding how the generation-skipping transfer tax is calculated helps you understand its structure. The tax is imposed on the taxable amount multiplied by the applicable rate.

1. Taxable Amount

The taxable amount depends on the nature of the generation-skipping transfer.

a. Direct Skip

The **taxable amount** in the case of a direct skip is the value of the property received by the transferee. § 2623. The transferor—either the donor in the case of a gift or the decedent's estate in the case of a bequest—is liable for the tax. § 2603(a)(3).

b. Taxable Distribution

The **taxable amount** in the case of a taxable distribution is the value of the property received by the transferee reduced by any expense incurred by that transferee in connection with the determination, collection or refund of the generation-skipping transfer tax paid with respect to that distribution. § 2621. The transferee is liable for the generation-skipping transfer tax on a taxable distribution. § 2603(a)(1).

c. Taxable Termination

The **taxable amount** in the case of a taxable termination is the value of the property with respect to which the termination has occurred reduced by any deduction under § 2053 attributable to that property. § 2622. The trustee is liable for the generation-skipping transfer tax on a taxable termination. § 2603(a)(2).

2. Applicable Rate

The **applicable rate** is (1) the maximum federal estate tax rate multiplied by (2) the inclusion ratio. § 2641.

a. Rate of Tax

The maximum federal estate tax rate has changed over time. At one point it was 70 percent. Prior to the 2001 Tax Act it was 55 percent. The exemption amount in those years was significantly less. As a result, there was a graduated rate of tax. In those days, it made no sense to incur the generation-skipping transfer tax. In 2007, the estate tax applicable exemption of $2 million and the maximum tax rate of 45 percent resulted in a flat rate of tax on all estates over $2 million. In that year, the difference between paying the generation-skipping transfer tax and the estate tax disappeared, except for allocation of the respective exemption amounts.

b. Inclusion Ratio

The inclusion ratio depends on the allocation of the generation-skipping transfer exemption amount as well as the value of the property transferred. The inclusion ratio is 1 minus the applicable fraction. § 2642(a). The **applicable fraction** is the generation-skipping transfer exemption amount allocated to the trust (or in the case of a direct skip to the property) divided by the value of the property transferred. The value of the property is reduced by any federal and state death taxes recovered from the trust that are attributable to the property as well as any charitable deduction allowed with respect to the property.

$$1 - \frac{\text{generation-skipping transfer exemption amount for this transfer}}{\text{value of property transferred minus certain taxes and deductions}}$$

Example 17.26

Assume that the exemption amount is $3.5 million and the maximum estate tax rate is 45 percent. Tom transfers $3.5 million to a trust for the benefit of his grandchildren and allocates his entire generation-skipping transfer tax exemption to the trust. The inclusion ratio will be zero and so will the rate of tax. (Zero times any other number is always zero.)

$$1 - \frac{\$3,500,000 \text{ (the amount of the exemption allocated to this transfer)}}{\$3,500,000 \text{ (the value of the property transferred to the trust)}}$$

$$1 - 1 = 0$$

Because the inclusion ratio is zero, the rate of tax is also zero. (.45 x 0 = 0).

Example 17.27

Assume that the exemption amount is $3.5 million and the maximum estate tax rate is 45 percent. Tom transfers $3.5 million to a trust for the benefit of his grandchildren and does not allocate any of his entire generation-skipping transfer tax exemption to the trust. The inclusion ratio will be one and the rate of tax 45 percent.

$$1 - \frac{\$0 \text{ (the amount of the exemption allocated to this transfer)}}{\$3,500,000 \text{ (the value of the property transferred to the trust)}}$$

$$1 - 0 = 1$$

Because the inclusion ratio is one, the rate of tax is 45 percent. (.45 x 1 = .45).

---

3. **Calculation Examples**

See Appendix C.

Appendix A

CALCULATION OF THE GIFT AND ESTATE TAXES

A. INTRODUCTION

1. Overview

There is one rate structure that applies to both the gift and estate taxes. §§ 2001, 2502. The gift tax exemption amount is coordinated with the estate tax exemption amount. §§ 2010, 2505. There is no "double-tax" when a transfer is both a completed gift and included in the gross estate. § 2001.

2. Exemption Amount

Each individual is allowed to transfer a certain amount of property without paying any tax. This amount is in addition to the gift tax annual exclusion, the gift tax exclusion of qualified transfers for tuition and medical expenses, the charitable deduction, and the marital deduction. Since 1976, this exemption amount has been expressed as a credit against tax. §§ 2010, 2505. Prior to 2001, the exemption amount was $1 million for both the gift and estate taxes. In the 2001 Tax Act, Congress increased the estate tax exemption amount to $3.5 million but left the gift tax exemption amount at $1 million. The estate tax exemption amount is scheduled to return to $1 million on January 1, 2011. Congress continues to debate the issue of the appropriate level for the exemption amounts.

3. Rate of Tax

Prior to 1981, the tax rates were progressive, beginning at 18 percent and extending to 70 percent. In 1981, Congress lowered the top rate to 55 percent but phased out the benefit of the graduated rates and unified credit for estates greater than $10 million. In 2001, Congress lowered the top tax rate to 45 percent. If an individual made taxable gifts over the $1 million exemption amount, the tax rates were graduated from 41 to 45 percent. Estates over $3.5 million were taxed at a flat rate of 45 percent.

4. Sample Calculations

Congress has been unable to reach agreement on the appropriate exemption amount and tax rate, and the future remains uncertain. This appendix includes sample calculations using three different models: (1) pre–2001 Tax Act exemption amounts and rates; (2) the 2009 exemption amounts and rates; and (3) a $5 million exemption amount for both the gift and the estate taxes and a flat rate of tax of 35 percent.

B. STEPS IN THE CALCULATION OF THE GIFT TAX

1. Transfer of Property Without Adequate and Full Consideration

Determine if there has been a transfer of property. § 2501. Is this particular transfer excluded from this definition by § 2501(a)(4) (political contribution) or § 2503(e) (qualified transfer for tuition or medical expense)? Then determine if the transfer of property was without adequate and full consideration in money or money's worth. § 2512(b). A transfer may be a part-sale/part-gift.

2. Complete

Determine if the transfer was complete. Has the donor given up dominion and control? Regulation § 25.2511–2. Only completed transfers are subject to the tax.

3. Value

Determine the fair market value of the property transferred.

4. Annual Exclusion

Is the transfer a present interest? Only present interests qualify for the gift tax annual exclusion. § 2503(b). If the transfer qualifies, subtract the amount of the exclusion from the value of the gift. Remember that only the first $13,000 (in 2010) of gifts are excluded. So review the gifts in chronological order.

5. Deductions

Determine if the transfer qualifies for other deductions, *e.g.*, transfers to charity or transfers to spouses, and subtract the appropriate amount. §§ 2522, 2523.

6. Current Year Taxable Gifts

The result will be the amount of the current year's taxable gifts. § 2503.

7. Prior Year Taxable Gifts

Add the current year's taxable gifts to the amount of taxable gifts from all prior years. § 2502.

8. Aggregate Amount of Taxable Gifts

The result is the aggregate amount of taxable gifts. § 2502.

9. Tentative Tax on Aggregate Amount of Taxable Gifts

Determine the tentative tax on the aggregate amount of taxable gifts. § 2502. Be sure to use the tax table in § 2001(c).

10. Less Tentative Tax on Prior Taxable Gifts

Subtract the tentative tax on the amount of the prior taxable gifts. § 2502.

11. Tentative Tax on Current Year Taxable Gifts

The result is the tentative tax on the current year's taxable gifts. § 2502.

12. Unified Credit

Determine if the unified credit will apply. § 2505. Subtract the amount of credit used in prior years to determine the amount of credit available in the current year. Then subtract the amount of credit available for the current year from the tentative tax on the current year's taxable gifts.

13. Gift Tax Due

The result is the gift tax due for that year.

14. Repeat Steps 1 Through 13 For Each Tax Year

The gift tax is imposed on an annual basis. Steps 1 through 13 apply in each year.

C. STEPS IN THE CALCULATION OF THE ESTATE TAX

1. Gross Estate

When decedent dies, calculate the amount of the gross estate. § 2033 through § 2044. Remember to include the amount of any gift tax paid on gifts made within three years of death. § 2035(b).

2. Deductions

Subtract any applicable deductions in § 2053 through § 2058.

3. Taxable Estate

The result is the taxable estate.

4. Adjusted Taxable Gifts

Add the amount of adjusted taxable gifts. § 2001(b)(1)(B). **Adjusted taxable gifts** are the taxable gifts that are *not* included in the gross estate. Some completed gifts are brought into the gross estate at their date of death value. These are excluded from adjusted taxable gifts because they are already in the taxable estate. Annual exclusion gifts are also excluded because they are not *taxable* gifts.

5. Tax Base

The result is the "tax base."

6. Tentative Tax

Determine the tentative tax on the tax base.

7. Less Gift Taxes Paid

Subtract the amount of gift taxes actually paid.

8. Unified Credit

Subtract the unified credit. § 2010. Do not decrease this amount even if the decedent had made taxable gifts during life and used the § 2505 unified credit. Remember that all taxable gifts are in the tax base.

9. Credits

Subtract any other credits, such as the credit for prior transfers in § 2013, if appropriate.

10. Estate Tax Due

The result is the estate tax due.

D. EXAMPLES

The same example is used for each model. For simplicity, it is assumed that the donor or decedent makes gifts in the amount of the gift tax annual exclusion to each donee each year. These transfers are excluded from the calculations. The example also assumes that there is no state estate tax.

Donald is a widower and has no children. Assume that Donald gives Ellen and Fred, the children of his neighbor, Ned, cash gifts equal to the gift tax annual exclusion amount on January 2 of each year. In year 1, Donald established an irrevocable trust to pay the income to himself for his life and the remainder to Ellen. (The value of the remainder interest is $500,000 at the time of the gift.) In year 2, Donald purchased Blackacre by paying the full purchase price of $500,000 in cash and taking title as joint tenants with the right of survivorship with Fred. (The value of Fred's interest is 50 percent.) In year 3, Donald gave Ellen $500,000 cash. In year 4, Donald gave Fred $750,000 cash. Donald dies in year 5. At that time the joint tenancy property has a fair market value of $800,000. The trust principal has a value of $1,500,000. Donald also owns other property valued at $2,765,000. His estate has expenses of $250,000. There is no state estate or inheritance tax.

1. $1,000,000 Exemption Amount and Top Rate of 55 Percent

This model assumes that the gift tax and estate tax exemption amounts are both $1,000,000 and that the top tax rate is 55 percent. These are the pre–2001 Tax Act amounts and may be the amounts as of January 1, 2011.

Year 1

taxable gifts	§ 2503		$ 500,000
plus prior taxable gifts			0
aggregate taxable gifts			$ 500,000
tentative tax on aggregate taxable gifts	§ 2502		$ 155,800
less tentative tax on prior taxable gifts			0
tentative tax on current gifts			$ 155,800
unified credit	§ 2505	$345,800	
less credit used in prior years		0	
credit available in current year		$345,800	345,800
gift tax due			$ 0

Year 2

taxable gifts	§ 2503		$ 250,000
plus prior taxable gifts			500,000
aggregate taxable gifts			$ 750,000
tentative tax on aggregate taxable gifts	§ 502		$ 248,300
less tentative tax on prior taxable gifts			155,800
tentative tax on current gifts			$ 92,500
unified credit	§ 2505	$345,800	
less amount used already		$155,800	
amount available		$190,000	190,000
gift tax due			$ 0

295

Year 3

taxable gifts	§ 2503		$ 500,000
plus prior taxable gifts			750,000
aggregate taxable gifts			$ 1,250,000
tentative tax on aggregate taxable gifts	§ 2502		$ 448,300
less tentative tax on prior taxable gifts			248,300
tentative tax on current gifts			$ 200,000
unified credit	§ 2505	$345,800	
less amount used already		248,300	
amount available		$ 97,500	97,500
gift tax payable			$ 102,500

Year 4

taxable gifts	§ 2503		$ 750,000
plus prior taxable gifts			1,250,000
aggregate taxable gifts			$ 2,000,000
tentative tax on aggregate taxable gifts	§ 2502		$ 780,800
less tentative tax on prior taxable gifts			448,300
tentative tax on current gifts			$ 332,500
unified credit	§ 2505	$345,800	
less amount used already		345,800	
amount available		$ 0	0
gift tax due			$ 332,500

Year 5

gross estate	§ 2033	$ 2,765,000
	§ 2035(b)	435,000
	§ 2036(a)(1)	1,500,000
	§ 2040(a)	800,000
		$ 5,500,000
less deductions	§ 2053	$ 250,000
taxable estate		$ 5,250,000
plus adjusted taxable gifts		1,250,000
tax base		$ 6,500,000

tentative tax § 2001	$1,290,800	+ $6,500,000	
		$3,000,000	
		$3,500,000	
		x .55	
		$1,925,000 =	$ 3,215,800
less gift tax paid			$ 435,000
less unified credit	§ 2010		345,800
estate tax due			$ 2,435,000

2. **$3,500,000 Estate Tax Exemption Amount, $1,000,000 Gift Tax Exemption Amount, and Top Rate of 45 Percent**

This model reflects the amounts and rates in effect in 2009.

Year 1

taxable gifts	§ 2503		$ 500,000
plus prior taxable gifts			0
aggregate taxable gifts			$ 500,000
tentative tax on aggregate taxable gifts	§ 2502		$ 155,800
less tentative tax on prior taxable gifts			0
tentative tax on current gifts			$ 155,800
unified credit	§ 2505	$345,800	
less credit used in prior years		0	
credit available in current year		$345,800	345,800
gift tax due			$ 0

Year 2

taxable gifts	§ 2503		$ 250,000
plus prior taxable gifts			500,000
aggregate taxable gifts			$ 750,000
tentative tax on aggregate taxable gifts	§ 502		$ 248,300
less tentative tax on prior taxable gifts			155,800
tentative tax on current gifts			$ 92,500
unified credit	§ 2505	$345,800	
less amount used already		$155,800	
amount available		$190,000	190,000
gift tax due			$ 0

Year 3

taxable gifts	§ 2503		$ 500,000
plus prior taxable gifts			750,000
aggregate taxable gifts			$ 1,250,000
tentative tax on aggregate taxable gifts	§ 2502		$ 448,300
less tentative tax on prior taxable gifts			248,300
tentative tax on current gifts			$ 200,000
unified credit	§ 2505	$345,800	
less amount used already		248,300	
amount available		$ 97,500	97,500
gift tax payable (*i.e.*, $200,000 tentative tax minus $97,500 credit)			$ 102,500

Year 4

taxable gifts	§ 2503		$ 750,000
plus prior taxable gifts			1,250,000
aggregate taxable gifts			$ 2,000,000
tentative tax on aggregate taxable gifts	2502		$ 780,800
less tentative tax on prior taxable gifts			448,300
tentative tax on current gifts			$ 332,500
unified credit	§ 2505	$345,800	
less amount used already		345,800	
amount available		$ 0	0
gift tax due			$ 332,500

Year 5

gross estate	§ 2033	$ 2,765,000
	§ 2035(b)	435,000
	§ 2036(a)(1)	1,500,000
	§ 2040(a)	800,000
		$ 5,500,000
less deductions	§ 2053	$ 250,000
taxable estate		$ 5,250,000
plus adjusted taxable gifts		1,250,000
tax base		$ 6,500,000

tentative tax § 2001 $555,800	+	$6,500,000	
		$1,500,000	
		$5,000,000	
		x .45	
		$2,250,000 =	$ 2,805,800
less gift tax paid			$ 435,000
less unified credit	§ 2010		1,455,800
estate tax due			$ 915,000

3. **$5,000,000 Gift and Estate Tax Exemption Amounts and Top Rate of 35 Percent**

This model reflects one of the many proposals for permanent revision of the federal transfer taxes. It assumes that the rate schedule in § 2001(c) is replaced with a flat rate of tax of 35 percent. The §§ 2010 and 2505 unified credits would be $1,750,000.

Year 1

taxable gifts	§ 2503		$ 500,000
plus prior taxable gifts			0
aggregate taxable gifts			$ 500,000
tentative tax on aggregate taxable gifts § 2502			$ 175,000
less tentative tax on prior taxable gifts			0
tentative tax on current gifts			$ 175,000
unified credit	§ 2505	$1,750,000	
less credit used in prior years		0	
credit available in current year		$1,750,000	1,750,000
gift tax due			$ 0

Year 2

taxable gifts	§ 2503		$ 250,000
plus prior taxable gifts			500,000
aggregate taxable gifts			$ 750,000
tentative tax on aggregate taxable gifts § 502			$ 262,500
less tentative tax on prior taxable gifts			175,000
tentative tax on current gifts			$ 87,500
unified credit	§ 2505	$1,750,000	
less amount used already		$ 175,000	
amount available		$1,575,000	1,575,000
gift tax due			$ 0

Year 3
taxable gifts	§ 2503		$ 500,000
plus prior taxable gifts			750,000
aggregate taxable gifts			$ 1,250,000

tentative tax on aggregate taxable gifts	§ 2502		$ 437,500
less tentative tax on prior taxable gifts			262,500
tentative tax on current gifts			$ 175,000

unified credit	§ 2505	$1,750,000	
less amount used already		$ 262,500	
amount available		$1,487,500	1,487,500
gift tax payable			$ 0

Year 4
taxable gifts	§ 2503		$ 750,000
plus prior taxable gifts			1,250,000
aggregate taxable gifts			$ 2,000,000

tentative tax on aggregate taxable gifts	§ 2502		$ 700,000
less tentative tax on prior taxable gifts			437,500
tentative tax on current gifts			$ 262,500

unified credit	§ 2505	$1,750,000	
less amount used already		437,500	
amount available		$1,321,500	1,312,500
gift tax due			$ 0

Year 5
gross estate	§ 2033		$ 2,765,000
	§ 2036(a)(1)		1,500,000
	§ 2040(a)		800,000
			$ 5,065,000

less deductions	§ 2053		$ 250,000
taxable estate			$ 4,815,000
plus adjusted taxable gifts			1,250,000
tax base			$ 5,065,000

tentative tax	§ 2001		$ 2,122,750
less unified credit	§ 2010		1,750,000
estate tax due			$ 372,750

E. OBSERVATIONS

1. The Unified Credit

The exemption amounts for the gift and estate taxes are expressed as credits against the tax. Prior to the 2001 Tax Act, the amounts were the same. The 2001 Tax Act increased the exemption amount for the estate tax but not for the gift tax. If Congress enacts an estate tax exemption amount of $3.5 million or $5 million, it may not increase the gift tax exemption to the same level.

Even when the exemption amounts are different, they are unified. This means that a taxpayer cannot increase the amount sheltered from tax by making taxable gifts during life. In model #1, the taxpayer can transfer $1 million during life free of tax or he can transfer $1 million at death free of tax. He cannot do both. In model #2, the taxpayer can only transfer a total of $3,500,000 without paying a transfer tax. In model #3, the taxpayer can transfer $5 million during life or $5 million at death or a combination without paying any tax.

2. There is no Double Tax

Section 2001 includes all taxable gifts in the calculation of the estate tax, either because the gift is brought back into the gross estate or because the gift is an adjusted taxable gift. Because all gifts are in the tax base, the full amount of the § 2010 unified credit is subtracted in calculating the estate tax due. This prevents taxpayers from transferring more than the amount sheltered by the § 2010 credit without paying tax.

Although all gifts are included in the tax base when calculating the estate tax, these transfers are not taxed twice. Section 2001 provides that both the gift tax paid and the full amount of the § 201 unified credit are subtracted from the tentative tax to reach the estate tax due.

APPENDIX B

CALCULATION OF THE § 2013 CREDIT

A. INTRODUCTION

The calculation of the § 2013 credit may appear complex and confusing. Remember that there are two decedents: (1) the original transferor (Toby in the examples below) and (2) the "recipient" decedent (Dean in the examples below). The § 2013 credit is allowed in calculating the "recipient" decedent's estate tax. It does not eliminate the impact of acquiring property from a transferor who dies within two years of the decedent's death. It does, however, give the recipient (Dean) a credit equal to the estate tax paid by Toby's estate.

B. EXAMPLES

The same basic example is used for all three models. The amounts, however, are different.

1. $1,000,000 Exemption Amount and Top Rate of 55 Percent

This model assumes that the gift tax and estate tax exemption amounts are both $1,000,000 and that there is a progressive rate of tax with a top rate of 55 percent. These are the pre–2001 Tax Act amounts and may be the amounts as of January 1, 2011.

Example B.1

Toby (the transferor) dies with a will that leaves all of his property to Dean. Toby has a taxable estate of $2,000,000. His estate pays a federal estate tax of $435,000. As a result, Dean receives $1,565,000 from Toby's estate. Dean (the decedent) dies within two years of Toby's death. Dean owns other property worth $2,000,000 so his taxable estate is $3,565,000. His estate tax will be calculated as follows:

Dean's taxable estate without Toby's property	$ 2,000,000
plus property Dean received from Toby's estate	1,565,000
Dean's total taxable estate	$ 3,565,000

tentative tax on $3,565,000

$$
\begin{array}{ll}
\$1,290,800 \quad + & \$\,3,565,000 \\
& -\,\underline{3,000,000} \\
& \$\quad 565,000 \\
& \underline{x \quad .55} \\
& \$\quad 310,750 \quad = \qquad \$\,1,601,550
\end{array}
$$

less § 2010 unified credit   345,800

less § 2013 credit for prior transfers   435,000

estate tax due $ 820,750

The § 2013 credit is calculated as follows. The first limitation is in § 2013(b). It limits the § 2013 credit to the amount of the federal estate tax paid by the transferor's estate that is attributable to the property transferred to the decedent.

$$
\text{transferor's estate tax} \quad x \quad \frac{\text{value of property transferred to decedent}}{\text{transferor's taxable estate less death taxes}}
$$

$$
\$435,000 \quad x \quad \frac{\$\,1,565,000}{\$\,2,000,000 \;-\; \$435,000}
$$

$$
\$435,000 \quad x \quad \frac{\$\,1,565,000}{\$\,1,565,000}
$$

$$
\$435,000 \quad x \quad 1 \quad = \qquad\qquad\qquad \$\;435,000
$$

So the first limitation on the amount of the § 2013 credit is the $435,000.

The second limitation is in § 2013(c). This limits the § 2013 credit to the amount of the federal estate tax that is attributable to including the transferor's property in the decedent's gross estate. In other words, it is the amount of the tentative tax on the decedent's taxable estate without regard to the § 2013 credit minus the amount of tax that would have been due had the transferor not given the property to the decedent. In Dean's estate, this limitation is calculated as follows:

the estate tax on Dean's taxable estate *with* Toby's property but *without* the § 2013 credit

tentative tax on Dean's estate of $3,565,000	$1,601,500
less § 2010 unified credit	345,800
	$1,255,750

minus

the estate tax on Dean's taxable estate *without* Toby's property or the § 2013 credit

taxable estate of $ 2,000,000

tentative tax =	$ 780,800
less § 2010 unified credit	345,800
	$ 435,000

So the second limitation on the amount of the § 2013 credit is $820,750 (*i.e.,* $1,255,250 minus $435,000).

The § 2013 credit is the lesser of the two limitations, which is $435,000.

Notice that the estate tax due on Dean's death is $820,750. Without the § 2013 credit, it would have been $1,255,750. The difference, $435,000, is the estate tax paid by Toby's estate.

2. **$3,500,000 Estate Tax Exemption Amount, $1,000,000 Gift Tax Exemption Amount, and Top Rate of 45 Percent**

This model assumes that the gift tax exemption amount is $1,000,000, the estate tax exemption amount is $3,500,000, and the maximum rate of tax is 45 percent. These assumptions are the same as the 2009 amounts.

Example B.2

Toby (the transferor) dies with a will that leaves all of his property to Dean. Toby has a taxable estate of $5,000,000. His estate pays a federal estate tax of $675,000. As a result, Dean receives $4,325,000 from Toby's estate. Dean (the decedent) dies within two years of Toby's death. Dean owns other property worth $5,000,000 so his taxable estate is $9,325,000. His estate tax will be calculated as follows:

Dean's taxable estate without Toby's property	$5,000,000
plus property Dean received from Toby's estate	4,325,000
Dean's total taxable estate	$9,325,000

tentative tax on	$9,325,000			
	$555,800	+	$9,325,000	
			−1,500,000	
			$7,825,000	
			x .45	
			$3,521,250	= $4,077,050

less § 2010 unified credit	1,455,800
less § 2013 credit for prior transfers	675,000
estate tax due	$1,946,250

The § 2013 credit is calculated as follows. The first limitation is in § 2013(b). It limits the § 2013 credit to the amount of the federal estate tax paid by the transferor's estate that is attributable to the property transferred to the decedent.

$$\text{transferor's estate tax} \quad x \quad \frac{\text{value of property transferred to decedent}}{\text{transferor's taxable estate less death taxes}}$$

$$\$675,000 \quad x \quad \frac{\$\,4,325,000}{\$\,5,000,000 - \$675,000}$$

$$\$675,000 \quad x \quad \frac{\$\,4,325,000}{\$\,4,325,000}$$

$$\$675,000 \quad x \quad 1 \quad = \quad \$\,675,000$$

So the first limitation on the amount of the § 2013 credit is the $675,000.

The second limitation is in § 2013(c). This limits the § 2013 credit to the amount of the federal estate tax that is attributable to including the transferor's property in the decedent's gross estate. In other words, it is the amount of the tentative tax on the decedent's taxable estate without regard to the § 2013 credit minus the amount of tax that would have been due had the transferor not given the property to the decedent. In Dean's estate, this limitation is calculated as follows:

the estate tax on Dean's taxable estate *with* Toby's property but without the § 2013 credit

tentative tax on Dean's estate of $9,325,000	$4,077,050
less § 2010 unified credit	1,455,800
	$2,621,250

minus

the estate tax on Dean's taxable estate *without* Toby's property or the § 2013 credit

taxable estate of $ 5,000,000

tentative tax	=	$555,800	+	$5,000,000			
			−	1,500,000			
				$3,500,000			
				x .45			
				$1,575,000	=	$2,130,800	
less § 2010 unified credit						1,455,800	
						$ 675,000	

So the second limitation on the amount of the § 2013 credit is $1,946,250 (*i.e.*, $2,621,250 minus $675,000).

The § 2013 credit is the lesser of the two limitations, which is $675,000.

Notice that the estate tax due on Dean's death is $1,946,250. Without the § 2013 credit, it would have been $2,621,250. The difference, $675,000, is the estate tax paid by Toby's estate.

3. **$5,000,000 Gift and Estate Tax Exemption Amounts and Top Rate of 35 Percent**

This model reflects one of the many proposals for permanent revision of the federal transfer taxes. It assumes that the rate schedule in § 2001(c) is replaced with a flat rate of tax of 35 percent. The §§ 2010 and 2505 unified credits would be $1,750,000.

Example B.3

Toby (the transferor) dies with a will that leaves all of his property to Dean. Toby has a taxable estate of $6,000,000. His estate pays a federal estate tax of $350,000. As a result, Dean receives $5,650,000 from Toby's estate. Dean (the decedent) dies within two years of Toby's death. Dean owns other property worth $6,000,000 so his taxable estate is $11,650,000. His estate tax will be calculated as follows:

Dean's taxable estate without Toby's property	$ 6,000,000
plus property Dean received from Toby's estate	5,650,000
Dean's total taxable estate	$11,650,000

tentative tax on $11,650,000	$ 4,077,050
less § 2010 unified credit	1,750,000
less § 2013 credit for prior transfers	350,000
estate tax due	$ 1,977,050

The § 2013 credit is calculated as follows. The first limitation is in § 2013(b). It limits the § 2013 credit to the amount of the federal estate tax paid by the transferor's estate that is attributable to the property transferred to the decedent.

$$\text{transferor's estate tax} \quad \times \quad \frac{\text{value of property transferred to decedent}}{\text{transferor's taxable estate less death taxes}}$$

$$\$350,000 \quad \times \quad \frac{\$5,650,000}{\$6,000,000 - \$350,000}$$

$$\$350,000 \quad \times \quad \frac{\$5,650,000}{\$5,650,000}$$

$$\$350,000 \quad \times \quad 1 \quad = \qquad \qquad \$350,000$$

So the first limitation on the amount of the § 2013 credit is the $350,000.

The second limitation is in § 2013(c). This limits the § 2013 credit to the amount of the federal estate tax that is attributable to including the transferor's property in the decedent's gross estate. In other words, it is the amount of the tentative tax on the decedent's taxable estate without regard to the § 2013 credit minus the amount of tax that would have been due had the transferor not given the property to the decedent. In Dean's estate, this limitation is calculated as follows.

the estate tax on Dean's taxable estate *with* Toby's property but without the § 2013 credit

tentative tax on Dean's estate of $9,325,000	$4,077,050
less § 2010 unified credit	1,750,000
	$2,327,500

minus

the estate tax on Dean's taxable estate *without* Toby's property or the § 2013 credit

taxable estate of $6,000,000

tentative tax =	$2,100,000
less § 2010 unified credit	1,750,000
	$ 350,000

So the second limitation on the amount of the § 2013 credit is $1,977,500 (i.e., $2,327,500 minus $350,000).

The § 2013 credit is the lesser of the two limitations, which is $350,000.

Notice that the estate tax due on Dean's death is $1,977,050. Without the § 2013 credit, it would have been $2,327,500. The difference, $350,000, is the estate tax paid by Toby's estate.

APPENDIX C

CALCULATION OF THE GENERATION–SKIPPING TRANSFER TAX

A. INTRODUCTION

The generation-skipping transfer (GST) tax is imposed on the taxable amount multiplied by the applicable rate. The examples are direct skips so the taxable amount is the value of the property received by the transferee. The applicable rate is the maximum federal estate tax rate multiplied by the inclusion ratio.

B. EXAMPLES

The examples are simplified to highlight the nature of the GST tax. Each transfer is a direct skip and an outright gift. As a result, the amount of the GST tax is an additional gift by the transferor. § 2515. In the examples, the transferor has already used his gift tax unified credit on prior gifts to his children and has already made gifts that year to this particular donee that qualify for the gift tax annual exclusion.

There are three models. The first uses a maximum estate tax rate of 55 percent and an exemption amount of $1 million. The second uses a maximum estate tax rate of 45 percent and an exemption amount of $3.5 million. The third uses a maximum estate tax rate of 35 percent and an exemption amount of $5 million. Each models includes two examples. In the first, the transferor allocates all of his GST exemption amount to the transfer. In the second example, the transferor allocates none of his GST exemption amount to the transfer.

1. $1,000,000 Exemption Amount and Top Rate of 55 Percent

This model assumes that the gift, estate, and GST tax exemption amounts are $1 million and that the tax rate schedule has a maximum rate of 55 percent. These assumptions mirror the pre–2001 Tax Act provisions that are scheduled to reappear on January 1, 2011.

Example C.1

Troy gives his grandson, Rex, $1,000,000. Troy allocates his entire GST exemption amount to this transfer. This is a direct skip. Because § 2515 treats the GST tax as a gift from Troy to Rex, the GST tax is calculated first.

The taxable amount is the value of the property received by Rex, *i.e.*, $1,000,000.

The tax rate is the maximum federal estate tax rate of 55 percent multiplied by the inclusion ratio.

The inclusion ratio is:

$$1 - \frac{\text{GST exemption allocated to the transfer}}{\text{value of property transferred}}$$

The tax rate is: .55   x   1 $- \dfrac{\$1,000,000}{\$1,000,000}$

.55   x   1 $-$ 1

.55   x   0

0

Because the tax rate is 0, there is no GST tax imposed on this gift.

The gift tax is calculated as follows:

value of property transferred	$1,000,000
plus GST tax paid	0
plus prior taxable gifts	1,000,000
aggregate taxable gifts	$2,000,000
tentative tax on aggregate taxable gifts	$ 780,800
minus tentative tax on prior taxable gifts	345,800
tentative tax on current taxable gifts	$ 435,000

§ 2505 credit	$345,800	
used on prior transfers	345,800	
available for this transfer	$ 0	
gift tax due		$ 435,000

The total tax paid on this transfer is $435,000, and the effective tax rate is 43.5 percent.

Example C.2

Troy gives his grandson, Rex, $1,000,000. Troy allocates none of his GST exemption to this transfer. This is a direct skip. Because § 2515 treats the GST tax as a gift from Troy to Rex, the GST tax is calculated first.

The taxable amount is the value of the property received by Rex, *i.e.*, $1,000,000.

The tax rate is the maximum federal estate tax rate of 55 percent multiplied by the inclusion ratio.

The inclusion ratio is:

$$1 - \frac{\text{GST exemption allocated to the transfer}}{\text{value of property transferred}}$$

The tax rate is: $.55 \quad \text{x} \quad 1 \quad - \dfrac{\$ \qquad 0}{\$1,000,000}$

$.55 \quad \text{x} \quad 1 \quad - 0$

$.55 \quad \text{x} \quad 1$

$.55$

The GST tax is, therefore, $550,000.

The gift tax is calculated as follows:

value of property transferred	$1,000,000
plus GST tax paid	550,000
plus prior taxable gifts	1,000,000
aggregate taxable gifts	$2,550,000

313

tentative tax on aggregate taxable gifts

$$
\begin{array}{rlr}
\$1,025,800 \quad + & \$2,550,000 & \\
& \underline{-2,500,000} & \\
& \$ \quad 50,000 & \\
& \underline{\text{x} \quad .53} & \\
& \$ \quad 26,500 \quad = & \$ \ 1,052,300
\end{array}
$$

minus tentative tax on prior taxable gifts   <u>345,800</u>

tentative tax on current taxable gifts $ 706,500

§ 2505 credit	$ 345,800	
used on prior transfers	<u>345,800</u>	
available for this transfer	$ 0	<u>0</u>
gift tax due		$ 706,500

The total tax paid on this transfer is $1,256,500 (the $550,000 GST tax plus $706,500 gift tax), and the effective tax rate is 125 percent.

The tax rate exceeds 100 percent in this example because (1) there are two taxes—the gift tax and the GST tax—imposed on the same transfer; (2) the GST tax is a flat 55 percent while the gift tax marginal rate is 53 percent; (3) the GST tax is treated as an additional gift; and (4) neither the gift tax nor the GST tax exemption amounts are allocable to this transfer.

2. **$3,500,000 Estate Tax Exemption Amount, $1,000,000 Gift Tax Exemption Amount, and Top Rate of 45 Percent**

This model assumes that the gift tax exemption amount is $1 million, that the estate tax exemption amount is $3.5 million, and that the tax rate schedule has a maximum rate of 45 percent. These assumptions reflects the amounts and rates in effect in 2009.

Example C.3

Troy gives his grandson, Rex, $3,500,000. Troy allocates his entire GST exemption to this transfer. This is a direct skip. Because § 2515 treats the GST tax as a gift from Troy to Rex, that tax is calculated first.

The taxable amount is the value of the property received by Rex, *i.e.*, $3,500,000.

The tax rate is the maximum federal estate tax rate of 45 percent multiplied by the inclusion ratio.

The inclusion ratio is:

$$1 \quad - \quad \frac{\text{GST exemption allocated to the transfer}}{\text{value of property transferred}}$$

The tax rate is: $.45 \quad \text{x} \quad 1 \quad - \dfrac{\$3,500,000}{\$3,500,000}$

$$.45 \quad \text{x} \quad 1 \quad - 1$$

$$.45 \quad \text{x} \quad 0$$

$$0$$

Because the tax rate is 0, there is no GST tax imposed on this gift.

The gift tax is calculated as follows:

value of property transferred	$3,500,000
plus GST tax paid	0
plus prior taxable gifts	1,000,000
aggregate taxable gifts	$4,500,000

tentative tax on aggregate taxable gifts

$555,800	+	$4,500,000	
		−1,500,000	
		$3,000,000	
		x .45	
		$1,350,000 =	$1,905,800
minus tentative tax on prior taxable gifts			345,800
tentative tax on current taxable gifts			$ 1,560,000

§ 2505 credit	$ 345,800		
used on prior transfers	345,800		
available for this transfer	$ 0		0
gift tax due			$ 1,560,000

The total tax paid on this transfer is $1,560,000, and the effective tax rate is 44.57 percent.

Example C.4

Same facts as example C.3, except that Troy does not allocate his GST exemption to this transfer. Troy gives his grandson, Rex, $3,5000,000.

APPENDIX C

This is a direct skip. Because § 2515 treats the GST tax as a gift from Troy to Rex, that tax is calculated first.

The taxable amount is the value of the property received by Rex, *i.e.*, $3,500,000.

The tax rate is the maximum federal estate tax rate of 45 percent multiplied by the inclusion ratio.

The inclusion ratio is:

$$1 - \frac{\text{GST exemption allocated to the transfer}}{\text{value of property transferred}}$$

The tax rate is: .45   x   1   – $\dfrac{\$\ \ \ \ \ 0}{\$\ 3,500,000}$

                 .45   x   1   –   0

                 .45   x   1

                 .45

The GST tax is, therefore, $1,575,000.

The gift tax is calculated as follows:

value of property transferred	$3,500,000
plus GST tax paid	1,575,000
plus prior taxable gifts	1,000,000
aggregate taxable gifts	$6,075,000

tentative tax on aggregate taxable gifts

$555,800	+	$6,075,000		
		−1,500,000		
		$4,575,000		
		x .45		
		$2,058,750	=	$ 2,614,550
minus tentative tax on prior taxable gifts				$ 345,800
tentative tax on current taxable gifts				$ 2,268,750

§ 2505 credit	$ 345,800	
used on prior transfers	345,800	
available for this transfer	$ 0	0
gift tax due		$2,268,750

The total tax paid on this transfer is $3,843,750 ($1575,000 GST tax plus $2,268,750 gift tax), and the effective tax rate is 110 percent.

The tax rate exceeds 100 percent in this example because (1) there are two taxes—the gift tax and the GST tax—imposed on the same transfer; (2) both taxes are at the maximum rate of 45 percent; (3) the amount of the GST tax is treated as a gift; and (4) none of the gift tax or the GST tax exemption amounts are allocable to this transfer.

3. **$5,000,000 Gift and Estate Tax Exemption Amounts and Top Rate of 35 Percent**

This model reflects one of the many proposals for permanent revision of the federal transfer taxes. It assumes that the rate schedule in § 2001(c) is replaced with a flat rate of tax of 35 percent, the §§ 2010 and 2505 unified credits would be $1,750,000, and the § 2631 GST exemption amount would be $5,000,000.

Example C.5

Troy gives his grandson, Rex, $5,000,000. Troy allocates his entire GST exemption to this transfer. This is a direct skip. Because § 2515 treats the GST tax as a gift from Troy to Rex, the GST tax is calculated first.

The taxable amount is the value of the property received by Rex, *i.e.*, $5,000,000.

The tax rate is the maximum federal estate tax rate of 35 percent multiplied by the inclusion ratio.

The inclusion ratio is:

$$1 \quad - \quad \frac{\text{GST exemption allocated to the transfer}}{\text{value of property transferred}}$$

The tax rate is: $.35 \quad \times \quad 1 \quad - \quad \dfrac{\$5,000,000}{\$5,000,000}$

.35   x   1   –   1

.35   x   0

0

Because the tax rate is 0, there is no GST tax imposed on this gift.

The gift tax is calculated as follows:

value of property transferred	$ 5,000,000
plus GST tax paid	0
plus prior taxable gifts	5,000,000
aggregate taxable gifts	$10,000,000
tentative tax on aggregate taxable gifts	$ 3,500,000
minus tentative tax on prior taxable gifts	1.750,000
tentative tax on current taxable gifts	$ 1,750,000

§ 2505 credit	$1,750,000	
used on prior transfers	1,750,000	
available for this transfer	$ 0	0
gift tax due		$ 1,750,000

The total tax paid on this transfer is $1,560,000, and the effective tax rate is 35 percent.

Example C.6

Same facts as example C.5, except that Troy does not allocate his GST exemption to this transfer. Troy gives his grandson, Rex, $5,000,000. This is a direct skip. Because § 2515 treats the GST tax as a gift from Troy to Rex, the GST tax is calculated first.

The taxable amount is the value of the property received by Rex, *i.e.*, $5,000,000.

The tax rate is the maximum federal estate tax rate of 35 percent multiplied by the inclusion ratio.

The inclusion ratio is:

$$1 - \frac{\text{GST exemption allocated to the transfer}}{\text{value of property transferred}}$$

The tax rate is: .35   x   1   – $ \dfrac{0}{\$5,000,000}$

.35   x   1   –   0

.35   x   1

.35

The GST tax is, therefore, $1,750,000.
The gift tax is calculated as follows:

value of property transferred	$ 5,000,000
plus GST tax paid	1,750,000
plus prior taxable gifts	5,000,000
aggregate taxable gifts	$11,750,000
tentative tax on aggregate taxable gifts	$ 4,112,500
minus tentative tax on prior taxable gifts	1,750,000
tentative tax on current taxable gifts	$ 2,362,500

§ 2505 credit	$1,750,000	
used on prior transfers	1,750,000	
available for this transfer	$ 0	0
gift tax due		$ 2,362,500

The total tax paid on this transfer is $4,112,500 ($1,750,000 GST tax plus $2,362,500 gift tax), and the effective tax rate is 82.25 percent.

The tax rate does not exceed 100 percent in this example because both the gift and the GST taxes are 35 percent.

APPENDIX D

ESTATE PLANNING FOR THE
MARRIED COUPLE

A. GENERAL PRINCIPLES

Although many other factors will influence estate plans, it is assumed that all couples want to minimize their total transfer tax burden. Most estate plans will include techniques other than those described in this appendix. These include, but of course are not limited to, gifts equal to the amount of the gift tax annual exclusion, qualified transfers for tuition and medical expenses, charitable contributions, grantor-retained interest trusts, personal residence trusts, private annuities, and family limited partnerships. Nontax factors also play an important role.

Most estate plans defer payment of the estate tax until the death of the surviving spouse, and the examples reflect this. Most estate plans also are designed to utilize the unified credit in both estates.

Congress has been unable to reach agreement on the appropriate exemption amount and the future remains uncertain. This appendix includes examples using three different models: (1) the pre–2001 Tax Act estate tax exemption amount of $1 million and a maximum rate of 55 percent; (2) the 2009 estate tax exemption amount of $3.5 million and maximum rate of 45 percent; and (3) a $5 million estate tax exemption amount and a flat rate of tax of 35 percent.

B. PORTABILITY OF THE UNIFIED CREDIT

Estate planning can be complicated when one spouse owns substantially more property than the other. A solution would be to allow any amount of the unified credit that is not used in the estate of the first to die to transfer to the surviving spouse. In other words, the unified credit would be "portable" between spouses. Such a provision has been proposed, but not yet enacted. The following examples demonstrate how such a provision might operate based on The Taxpayer Certainty and Relief Act of 2009, S. 722 (111th Cong., 1st Sess.

2009). Under that act, the applicable exemption amount in § 2010 would be the sum of (1) the basic exemption amount and (2) the deceased spouse's unused exemption amount.

C. EXAMPLES

The examples are greatly simplified to demonstrate the impact of the unified credit on planning for a married couple. The examples are not the same for each model, but demonstrate variations of the same issue.

1. $1,000,000 Exemption Amount and Top Rate of 55 Percent

This model assumes that the gift tax and estate tax exemption amounts are both $1,000,000 and that the top tax rate is 55 percent. These are the pre–2001 Tax Act amounts and may be the amounts as of January 1, 2011.

Example D.1

Hugh and Wendy are married and have four children. Hugh owns investments in his own name worth $1 million. Wendy owns investments in her own name worth $1 million. Assume that Hugh dies first.

If Hugh leaves all of his property outright to Wendy, his taxable estate will be zero ($0) because of the marital deduction. When Wendy dies, her taxable estate will be $2 million. Her estate will pay an estate tax of $435,000 (*i.e.* $780,800 less the unified credit of $345,800).

Instead, assume that Hugh leaves all of his property in a credit-shelter trust for the benefit of Wendy. The trustee (who is not Wendy) has discretion to distribute income or principal to Wendy or for her benefit. Hugh's taxable estate will be $1 million, and the tax due will be zero ($0) because of the unified credit. § 2010. When Wendy dies, only her own property will be in her gross estate. Her taxable estate will be $1 million. Her estate will pay no estate tax because of the § 2010 unified credit.

Example D.2

Hugh and Wendy are married and have four children. Hugh owns $2 million of investments; Wendy owns no property. Assume that Hugh dies first.

If Hugh left all of his property outright to Wendy, his estate will pay no estate tax because of the marital deduction. When Wendy dies, her taxable estate will be $2 million. Her estate will pay an estate tax of $435,000 (*i.e.* $780,800 less the unified credit of $345,800).

Instead, assume that Hugh leaves an amount equal to the exemption amount, *i.e.*, $1 million, in a credit-shelter trust for the benefit of Wendy. His taxable estate would be $1 million, and the estate tax due would be zero ($0) because of the unified credit. § 2010. When Wendy dies, only her own property will be in her gross estate. Her taxable estate will be $1 million. Her estate will pay no estate tax because of the § 2010 unified credit.

Example D.3

Hugh and Wendy are married and have four children. Hugh owns $2 million of investments; Wendy owns no property. Assume that Wendy dies first. Her taxable estate will be zero ($0), and her estate will pay no tax. When Hugh dies, his taxable estate will be $2 million. His estate will pay an estate tax of $435,000 (*i.e.* $780,800 less the unified credit of $345,800).

Hugh and Wendy could have avoided this tax if Hugh had transferred $1 million to Wendy outright during her life. Then Wendy's estate and Hugh's estate would each be $1 million. When Wendy dies, she would leave her property in a credit-shelter trust for the benefit of Hugh. Her taxable estate of $1 million incur no tax because of the § 2010 unified credit. When Hugh died, only $1 million would be in his taxable estate. His estate would pay no estate tax because of the § 2010 unified credit.

If Congress enacted a portability provision like that in S.722, Hugh would not need to transfer property to Wendy during life. When Wendy died, her estate would not use any of her applicable exemption amount (*i.e.*, unified credit). Her unused exemption amount would transfer to Hugh. When he died, $2 million would be sheltered from the estate tax by the § 2010 unified credit.

2. **$3,500,000 Estate Tax Exemption Amount, $1,000,000 Gift Tax Exemption Amount, and Top Rate of 45 Percent**

This model reflects the amounts and rates in effect in 2009.

Example D.4

Hank and Wilma are married. They each have children from prior marriages. They each own $3.5 million worth of property. Assume that Wilma dies first.

If she leaves all her property outright to Hank, her estate will pay no estate tax because of the marital deduction. When Hank dies, his taxable estate will be $7 million. The estate tax will be $1,575,000 (*i.e.*, 45 percent times $3,500,000).

Instead, Wilma leaves her property in a credit-shelter trust with Friendly National Bank as trustee and gives the trustee discretion to pay the income or principal to Hank during his life, and then to distribute the accumulated income and trust property to her children at his death. The trust does not qualify for the marital deduction. Wilma's taxable estate is $3,500,000, and there will be no estate tax because of the § 2010 unified credit. When Hank dies, his taxable estate will be only $3,5000,000 because the credit-shelter trust will not be included. His estate will pay no estate tax because of the § 2010 unified credit.

Example D.5

Hank and Wilma are married. They each have children from prior marriages. Wilma owns $7 million worth of property; Hank owns no property.

If Wilma dies first, her will can create two trusts: (1) a credit-shelter trust and (2) a martial deduction trust. One-half of her property will go into each trust. Her taxable estate will be $3,500,000, but her estate will pay no estate tax because of the § 2010 unified credit. When Hank dies, his gross estate will include only the property in the marital deduction trust. His taxable estate will be $3,500,000, but his estate will pay no estate tax because of the § 2010 unified credit.

Example D.6

Hank and Wilma are married. They each have children from prior marriages. Wilma owns $7 million worth of property; Hank owns no property.

If Hank dies first, his taxable estate will be zero ($0). When Wilma dies, her taxable estate will be $7 million. The estate tax will be $1,575,000 (*i.e.*, 45 percent times $3,500,000).

If Congress enacted a portability provision like that in S.722, Wilma would not need to transfer property to Hank during life. When Hank died, his estate would not use any of his applicable exemption amount (*i.e.*, unified credit). His unused exemption amount would transfer to Wilma. When she died, the full $7 million would be sheltered from the estate tax by the § 2010 unified credit.

Example D.7

Hank and Wilma are married. They each have children from prior marriages. Wilma owns $7 million worth of property; Hank owns no property so Wilma transfers $3,500,000 to Friendly National Bank as trustee to pay all the income at least annually to Hank. If Wilma survives Hank, the trustee will pay the income to her. After the death of both Hank and Wilma, the trust property will be distributed to Wilma's children. Wilma elects to treat the trust as qualified terminable interest property under § 2523(f). As a result, the transfer into trust qualifies for the gift tax marital deduction.

Hank is treated as the transferor of the property in the trust. It will be in his gross estate at his death. § 2044. His taxable estate will be $3,500,000, but his estate will pay no estate tax because of the § 2010 unified credit. Wilma will have the benefit of the income during her life. The trust will not be in her gross estate. Regulation § 25.2523(f)–1(f)(Ex. 10). Her taxable estate, therefore, will only be $3,500,000, and her estate will pay no estate tax because of the § 2010 unified credit.

If Wilma dies first, the trust property will not be in her gross estate. Regulation § 25.2523(f)–1(f)(Ex. 11). Although she has a right to trust income following Hank's death, she is not considered the transferor. Hank is treated as the transferor because of the QTIP election. Wilma and Hank will each have a taxable estate of $3,500,000. Neither estate will pay an estate tax because of the § 2010 unified credit.

If Congress enacted a portability provision like that in S.722, Wilma would not need to transfer property to Hank during life. When Hank died, his estate would not use any of his applicable exemption amount (*i.e.*, unified credit). His unused exemption amount would transfer to Wilma. When she died, the full $7 million would be sheltered from the estate tax by the § 2010 unified credit.

3. **$5,000,000 Gift and Estate Tax Exemption Amounts and Top Rate of 35 Percent**

This model reflects one of the many proposals for permanent revision of the federal transfer taxes. It assumes that the rate schedule in § 2001(c) is replaced with a flat rate of tax of 35 percent. The §§ 2010 and 2505 unified credits would be $1,750,000.

Example D.8

Henry and Wanda are married and have no children. They own a house as joint tenants with the right of survivorship; the house has a fair market value of $500,000. Henry owns a life insurance policy on his own life with Wanda as the primary beneficiary; the face amount is $1,500,000. Henry has a pension fund worth $1,000,000 that pays him and Wanda or the survivor. Wanda has investment of $1,000,000.

Because the total combined net worth of Henry and Wanda is $4 million, there is no need for tax planning. Henry can leave all his property to Wanda, and Wanda can leave all her property to Henry. The survivor will own only $4 million. The estate of the first to die will not pay any estate tax because of the marital deduction. The estate of the survivor will not pay any estate tax because of the § 2010 unified credit.

Example D.9

Henry and Wanda are married and have no children. They own a house and investments assets as joint tenants with the right of survivorship. Their total net worth is $15 million.

There will be no estate tax when the first person dies because of the marital deduction. When the survivor dies, the taxable estate will be $15 million. There will be an estate tax of $3,500,000 (*i.e.*, 35 percent times $10 million).

Instead, assume that Henry and Wanda sever $10 million worth of the joint tenancy property and now own that property as tenants in common. Henry's will leaves his property in a credit-shelter trust for the benefit of Wanda. Her will leaves her property in a credit-shelter trust for the benefit of Henry.

Assume that Henry dies first. His taxable estate will be $5 million. There will be no estate tax because of the § 2010 unified credit and the marital deduction. When Wanda dies, her taxable estate will be $10 million. The estate tax will be $1,750,000. This estate plan saves Henry and Wanda $1,750,000 in federal estate taxes.

A portability provision, such as S.722, would produce the same tax result as severing the joint tenancies. Assume Henry dies first. Because all of the property is owned as joint tenants, it all qualifies for the marital deduction. Henry's taxable estate is zero ($0). As a result, his estate does not use any of his exemption amount. His unused exemption amount transfers to Wanda. When she dies, $10 million is sheltered from the estate tax by the § 2010 unified credit. The tax due would be $1,750,000 (*i.e.*, 35 percent times $5,000,000).

TABLE OF AUTHORITIES

CASES

RULINGS

INDEX

References are to pages.

†